THE BOOK OF ANGELS

THE BOOK OF ANGELS

THE BOOK
OF ANGELS

AN ILLUSTRATED GUIDE TO CELESTIAL BEINGS AND ANGELIC LORE

LEE FABER

ARCTURUS

ARCTURUS

This edition published in 2010 by Arcturus Publishing Limited
26/27 Bickels Yard, 151–153 Bermondsey Street,
London SE1 3HA

ISBN: 978-1-84837-578-9
AD001166EN

Created for Arcturus Publishing Limited by Omnipress Limited, Eastbourne, Sussex.

Printed in Singapore

Contents

Introduction

Whether you believe that angels are the manifestations of a supreme higher being, messengers from God himself, the spirits of highly evolved human beings or personally appointed spirit guides, belief in their existence has endured for thousands of years. This belief is as popular today as it has ever been and cuts across all religions, nationalities and creeds.

Many people believe that angels are spiritual beings that try to communicate with people, watching over us and helping us in our everyday lives. Often referred to as 'guardian angels', among their many kindnesses they are believed to look after us when we are sick, help people who are struggling with exams and protect soldiers during times of conflict.

Whatever our perception of angels might be, they make a fascinating subject to explore. In this introductory section we trace the evolution of angelic lore from its roots in ancient mythology to the present day, and look at the various ways in which angels have been represented in religion, history, art and literature.

WHAT IS AN ANGEL?

An angel, if you were to define one, is a spirit without a body who allegedly has a superior intelligence, an enormous amount of strength and is pure and holy. They are composed of an ethereal matter which allows them to transmogrify into whichever physical form best suits their immediate needs. They are spirits of such magnitude that it is difficult for the human brain to register that such beings could exist. They are countless in number and carry out their assigned tasks without the slightest hesitation.

Angels are commonly represented by a figure with enormous bird-like wings and wearing a long, diaphanous robe. They are often depicted with a wreath of light, or halo, directly above their heads, which serves as a symbol of divine wisdom. Angels do not die or age; they are immortal. They are of no specific gender although they will frequently take the form of a human, male or female, if this suits their allotted task. They are generally accepted as being the guardians of our souls and, although generally divine, they have been shown to be fallible and prone to sin, as in the case of fallen angels whose halos have slipped.

People have often asked what the difference is between a fairy, an angel and a ghost. The simple answer to this is that a fairy is an anthropomorphic creature of magic and myth. Ghosts are generally believed to be the spirits or manifestations of deceased humans, while angels are not of earthly origin and never have been.

CAN YOU SEE AN ANGEL?

Those people who have been lucky enough to see an angel will have a far deeper understanding of the content of this book. Strangely, though, these people can be reluctant to discuss their experience with others as they feel somehow it was an out-of-world encounter that was meant only for them. Those people who have been willing to share their stories usually speak of near-death experiences when they have felt the presence of an angel, or times of extreme danger when there seemed no way out and an angel has stepped in and saved them. Usually, when the victim is safe and the threat of danger has gone, then so too has their rescuer, giving the person no time to ask questions or express gratitude. Although they often disappear, angels are believed to be able to communicate, usually via thought transference.

The poets John Milton and William Blake both claimed to have been in the presence of angels. Blake, from his early years, reported having experienced visions of angels and ghostly monks, and said that he had conversed with the angel Gabriel, the Virgin Mary and various historical figures. While John Milton quoted, 'Subtle he needs must be, who could seduce Angels', when he had an out-of-world experience.

It was once believed that only very creative or highly excitable people were able to see angels, but this theory has long since been disproved. Nowadays accounts of angelic encounters are told by people from all walks of life.

People who have been lucky enough to encounter an angel often say it was difficult to make out a

ABOVE: *Mary's Lamentation for Christ*
by William Blake, 1816

This illustration appears in *Paradise Regained*, a poem by John Milton published in 1671 and illustrated by Blake in 1816. *Paradise Regained* spans four books and focuses on the temptation of Christ. The illustration shows two angels delivering the message of Christ's crucifixion to Mary.

shape and described the presence as a light rather than a personification. Others have described it as a certain kind of perfume, a type of scent that they have never encountered before. Many have reported being aware of an enormous pair of wings, while others have felt or heard the fluttering of wings against their skin. So it would appear that angels can be perceived with four of our five senses, although they even project themselves as mental holograms which we can neither touch nor feel.

Whether or not you believe in these manifestations of angels, it is worth keeping an open mind while you travel through the historical part of this book.

Archangel Gabriel
Archangel Gabriel serves as a messenger from God. Both Christian and Muslim religions believe that Gabriel foretold the birth of Jesus.

Archangel Michael
In Jewish, Islamic and Christian faith, Archangel Michael is regarded as being the commander of the Army of God. He is often pictured fighting Satan in battle.

Archangel Raphael
The name 'Raphael' is 'Rophe' in Hebrew, meaning 'doctor of medicine'. Archangel Raphael works as a healer.

Archangel Uriel
Also known as the 'Fire of God', Archangel Uriel stands at the gates of Eden with a fiery sword.

Cupid
Cupid has become a traditional symbol for Valentine's Day, but his roots are in Roman mythology. He was the son of Mars (god of war) and Venus (goddess of love). In ancient art Cupid was often depicted as a boy or baby with wings holding a bow and arrow, and the same image is used today. Lovers are often said to have been struck by Cupid's magic arrow.

Eros
Cupid has an equivalent in ancient Greek mythology, Eros. He is the god of love, lust, beauty and intercourse and considered so powerful that he was worshipped as a fertility deity. Eros is portrayed in ancient art with huge wings and appears older than the cherub Cupid.

Hermes
In Greek mythology Hermes was a messenger of the gods and a guide for lost souls in the Underworld. He had wings – unusually positioned on his sandals – that allowed him to travel between the mortal and immortal world.

Nike
Nike was known as the 'Winged Goddess of Victory' in Greek mythology and she symbolized strength, speed and triumph. The legend of Nike has been used by the shoe and sports equipment company of the same name.

Ancient Angels

Religion teaches us that angels are intermediary beings that perform certain tasks and act as messengers of God. What many people perhaps do not realize is that angels also exist outside of conventional religion and have a rich heritage in pagan cultures. It is difficult to strip the mantle of religion from angels and look at them as something other than theological beings, but objectivity insists that we do so.

In the early stages of mankind, the belief in spirits was universal. Primitive man did not believe that there were good and evil spirits, but that a spirit had special powers called *manna*, with which it could do either good or bad. However, with the emergence of Christianity and other major religions, belief in these kinds of spirits was condemned and they became known only as 'demons'.

The earliest archaeological evidence of angels dates back to King Stela of Ur-Nammus in Egypt (2250BC), where they are depicted flying over his head while he kneels at prayer. Belief in angels is found in the history of all the great early civilizations – Sumerian, Babylonian, Egyptian, Roman and Greek – as well as three key religions – Judaism, Christianity and Islam.

Primitive tribal cultures also had some influence over the conception of angels. They commonly held the belief that angel spirits watched over them, although these were usually in the form of animals or birds. It is possible that there might be a shamanistic connection with angels that pre-dates even the ancient Sumerians. Shamanism existed in most parts of Central Asia until Islam took over. Archaeologists are still learning about this ancient culture from recent digs, but one thing that is coming to the fore is an obsession with winged creatures. They believed that these spirits allowed the shaman to mediate between the human world and some higher state. Shamans put themselves into trances which allows them to 'fly' into the spirit world, so this is possibly where the concept of angels is rooted.

SUMERIAN CULTURE
Sumerian society is one of the oldest cultures that has left us any clear evidence of a belief in angels. This evidence comes in the form of stone carvings, either as three-

dimensional statues or relief carvings of a winged, human motif. The religion of the Sumerians was complex and embraced a wide variety of gods and spirits, but of particular interest was their belief in 'messengers of the gods', who were angelic in form and ran errands between gods and humans. Just like belief in guardian angels today, the Sumerians believed that each individual had a 'ghost' of some kind, which remained a constant companion throughout their life. Altars dedicated exclusively to these guardian angels have been excavated from ancient Sumerian houses and temples. Wall paintings in temples also depicted human forms with wings.

The Sumerians were conquered by the Semitic tribes around 1900BC, and their polytheistic beliefs were adopted by the Semites, in particular the notion of angels caught their attention. These Semitic people formulated a hierarchy for angels, an idea which was carried forward into Zoroastrianism and monotheistic Judaism. It was these notions that probably set the scene for the development of Egyptian theology as well.

BABYLONIA

Sumerian domination of the Middle East came to an end around 2000BC and Assyrian and Babylonian cultures took over. Many examples of winged figures have been uncovered from this period. Out of the Babylonian period came the story of Harut and Marut, which has been translated into many different forms. In brief, the angels were disgusted at the debauched behaviour of humans on Earth. God informed the angels that he felt they would also have sinned were they in the same position as the humans, and to see if He was right, they elected two angels, Harut and Marut, to visit Earth in human form. They were commanded to avoid wine, idolatry, fornication and murder but they eventually succumbed to all these human lusts, becoming sinners themselves. Consequently, God punished them for their transgressions.

ABOVE: *Blessing Genius*
*c.721–705*BC

The ancient Assyrian site of Khorsabad, Iraq (Dur-Sharrukin in antiquity) was excavated between 1843 and 1854. The above relief carving was discovered in the inner passage of one of the city gates, with a duplicate carving directly opposite. In front of the winged men were a pair of winged bulls with human heads guarding the gate. These winged figures were known as *genii* and the carvings represented a faith in the powers of these beings. The purpose of a genius was, like a guardian angel, to protect an area, building or human. The Blessing Genius had another function; to bless people. Above, the genius holds a pine cone full of water in his right hand which passers-by would shake and so be blessed by the liquid.

The Blessing Genius has two pairs of wings emerging from his back and there are rings and bracelets on his arms and forearms. He is an excellent example of an ancient protective winged deity which perhaps formed the basis for the concept of the guardian angel we are familiar with today.

ABOVE: *The Fall of Icarus*
by Carlo Saraceni, 1607

The ancient Greek myth of Icarus is interesting in relation to angelology because it represents a belief in the possibility of human flight, an idea which must have stemmed from a belief in winged-humans at the time. The wings in this picture were manmade and they allowed the characters to fly through the air without celestial aid, but unlike angels' wings, these wings were not perfect and had a risk of breaking, as Icarus soon found out.

In the story, Icarus and his father Daedalus are imprisoned in Crete on the order of King Minos. Daedalus was a skilled Athenian craftsman and had been ordered by the king to construct a complex labyrinth. Once it was complete, a minotaur (half-man, half-bull) was released into the labyrinth along with Theseus, the king's mortal enemy. Daedalus wanted to ensure Theseus would not perish in the gauntlet and so gave the king's daughter, Ariadne, a rope to help Theseus to safety, angering the king immensely. However, Daedalus didn't plan on staying in Crete to be punished. Earlier, he had prepared two pairs of wings made from wax and feathers for himself and his son, and as they fastened them to their backs Daedalus warned Icarus not to fly too close to the sun as the wax would melt. The pair made their escape but in the excitement of flying, Icarus forgot his father's advice and soared too close to the sun. As his wings fell away from his body Icarus flapped his arms wildly, but it was too late and he fell to his death in the Icarian sea (named after him).

ZOROASTRIANISM

Zoroastrianism was the basis of all beliefs regarding angeology. Zoroaster was a member of an ethnic group living in Persia around 650BC. Mithraism was the most prevalent religion in Persia when Zoroaster was alive. Mithras was a light-bringer god who was considered to be an angel who mediated between Heaven and Earth. However, as a result of what Zoroaster claimed were angelic communications, he started to spread monotheistic religious messages that subsequently became the religion of the Persian empire, a religion that was based totally on angels.

Zoroastrianism identified six main archangels – Vohu Mano (Good Mind) presiding over cattle; Asha Vahishta (Highest Asha), presiding over fire; Khshathra Vairya (Desirable Dominion) presiding over metals; Spenta Armaiti (Holy Devotion) presiding over the Earth; Haurvatat (Perfection or Health) presiding over water, and Ameretat (Immortality) who also presided over the Earth. Besides these main angels they believed in at least forty lesser angels which they called the Adorable Ones. Some of these angels were considered to be male, some female and each one was attributed a particular quality. Residing over the entire hierarchy was Ahura Mazda, the Supreme Being. Zoroastrians would carefully choose a patron for their protection and throughout their lives were careful to observe prayers dedicated to this angel.

On the lowest level of the Zoroastrian hierarchy were the Arda Fravash (Guardian Angels), each one appointed as a custodian for a single human being for the entirety of their life. Regardless of their position in the hierarchy, each angel was considered to be a divine gift, manifestations of the one 'Lord of Light'. They also believed that there was a Lord of Darkness, with his complementary demons (*daevas*) and evil spirits that existed in opposition to the angelic forces (*ahuras*). Our present-day conception of the Devil actually derives from the Zoroastrian belief in the *daeva*. Zoroastrians believed that without the existence of these angels, all animals and people would cease to exist. They believed their celestial patrons could fly like winged birds and they were most commonly represented by a winged disc, often with a person superimposed on the front.

ANCIENT EGYPT

As in the earlier cultures, the Egyptians tended to see their spirits in the form of an animal or bird, which was regarded as the soul, or *Ba*, of the god. For example, Horus, the god of the sky, was represented as a falcon, while Thoth, the god of the Moon, was depicted as a man with the head of an ibis. The goddesses Isis (see page 12) and Maat were nearly always represented with wings. Isis was regarded as the pinnacle of power and she manifested herself in angelic form, usually with feathered wings that were spread to enfold her worshippers. Horus, son of Isis, also reveals himself with feathered wings and a halo. Nut, the mother of Isis, is the goddess of sky and wind, and she too is represented as a woman with outstretched wings or wings that are folded around her body.

It would be fair to say that many of the Egyptian deities – and there were over one thousand – came closer to our concept of angels than gods. One example of this was the Hunmanit, who were believed to be a group of entities connected with the Sun, similar to the Christian concept of the angel choir of the seraphim. The Hunmanit were responsible for looking after the Sun, indirectly fulfilling a responsibility to look after mankind. The idea of a unique angelic species deriving directly from the influence of the Egyptians is still a matter of conjecture, but if their drawings are anything to go by, it would appear that they regarded their gods more as guardian angels than as simple idols.

ANCIENT GREECE AND ROME

Although there are no distinctly angelic beings in Greek mythology, there is the sacred phoenix which was the symbol of immortality. The word *daemon*, in the original Greek sense, meant a guardian divinity

ABOVE: *The Winged Goddess Isis*
Egyptian Third Intermediate Period, *c.*1069–664BC

The winged goddess Isis was a figure in Ancient Egyptian religious beliefs who first appeared in written records shortly after 2,500BC. Isis was the goddess of motherhood and fertility and revered throughout the Greco-Roman world. She was worshipped for her protective and maternal nature and adored for her willingness to listen to the prayers of slaves and sinners, as well as aristocrats and rulers. In the *Egyptian Book of the Dead* she is described as 'she who gives birth to heaven and earth, knows the orphan, knows the widow, seeks justice for the poor, and shelter for the weak'.

Isis is mostly depicted with large outstretched wings which were symbolic as well as powerful. She could create strong winds with her wings, and would use this energy to fan life back into the dead, although this would not be permanent and they would only be mortal for one day. Her feathers could create light, which led to one of her many nicknames – 'Light-giver of Heaven'. Sometimes Isis is thought of as a bird. Being the 'Goddess of Magic', she had the ability to transform herself into a kite, a type of bird with long wings and weak legs. She was believed to endlessly soar through the skies, sometimes circling the corpse of her husband, Osiris. The image of Isis was used on Egyptian thrones, with the wings appearing to surround and protect a Pharaoh when seated.

In art, Isis is sometimes depicted holding her infant son Horus, and parallels between these and later paintings of Mary and the infant Jesus have been drawn. Isis appears the archetypal mother figure and is regarded as a symbol of empowered femininity and strength.

or inspiring spirit. There is evidence of angel-like gods in the Greek pantheon, with Hermes pictured with wings on his heels. In ancient Greece, the goddess Nepthys was also winged; and many reliefs depicting her appear in hieroglyphics on a number of Greek tombs. Griffins, who were winged animals with human heads, have shown up in a very ancient Etruscan tomb. The griffin was a symbol of divine power and a guardian of heavenly creatures. The other mention of a winged deity in Greek mythology was the goddess Nike, who was the goddess of Victory – although her link with angels is a little tenuous. In Greek art, the sun god Helios was often depicted with a radiant circle or halo surrounding his head, giving him the impression of being a spiritual character.

The idea of human flight crops up a number of times, for instance in the myth of Icarus, who learned to fly but met his end when he flew too close to the sun (see page 10).

The same theme of winged deities can also be seen in Roman culture with the winged goddess Victoria (Victory). She was normally depicted with wings and often carried trophies from defeated enemies. Augustus had an altar erected in honour of Victoria in the senate building, Curia Julia, with a statue of the goddess standing with one foot on a globe. The old cult of Victoria was one of the last pagan cults which succumbed to Christianity.

Finally, likened to the Greek god Hermes, the Roman god Mercury is usually pictured with wings on his sandals and cap. In ancient times, messages were carried from one ruler to another or between armies by such fleet-footed heralds.

JUDAISM

The early Semitic people of the Middle East believed in a wide variety of spirits, the majority of which were connected to inanimate objects and natural phenomena. Included in these beliefs were the spirits of wind and fire, which were held as particularly significant. History shows us that these spirits appear as the basis for what later became known as the cherubim and seraphim. The influence of Zoroastrianism continued throughout the millennium before Christ, finding its way into many early pieces of Jewish literature. It wasn't really until after the Jews returned from captivity in Babylon around 450BC, that angels became an integral part of the Jewish religion. Another strong Jewish belief was taken from the Old Testament Book of Enoch which told a story of a group of fallen angels called the Watchers or Nephilim. It was these angels who strayed from the path of righteousness and caused Noah's great flood.

KABBALISM

There was a more mystical aspect to Judaism, which developed into a discipline known as the Kabbalah. Like mainstream religions, this school believed that angels were intermediaries between the physical and metaphysical worlds. The roles of specific angels are common between Christianity, Islam and Judaism, but in the Kabbalah they have a more magical edge. For example, certain angels can be invoked in magical rites to assist the invocant in their personal problems. Through the use of magic, Kabbalism finds a link to the Occult and ceremonial magic. Occultism was widely perceived to be a malevolent practice through its mysterious nature and connotations of the dark arts, however, as in Kabbalism, angels could be channelled through divination and conjurations.

'Ceremonial magic' is a term covering a broad spectrum of spiritual traditions which utilize the help of angels. In ceremonial magic, whether it be Kabbalistic or in Occultism, often tools are needed to perform rites. These would be blessed or exorcized of demons and sometimes the invocant would need to face a particular direction in order to complete the conjuration.

Ancient astrology also has links to Kabbalism and there are believed to be angels assigned to certain planets or horoscopes.

CHRISTIANITY

The oldest version of the Hebrew Bible, the Septuagint, was used by the early Christian church until about AD350, and angels are mentioned throughout. The majority of Christian cosmology can be traced first and foremost to Judaism, but over the centuries Christians have developed their own ideas about angels. The theologian Saint Thomas Aquinas even gave a series of lectures on angels in AD1259 at the University of Paris. Today angels are generally most closely associated with Christianity, despite the fact that their origins were in much earlier cultures. Angels have been paramount to the Christian faith since its inception and there are around 300 references to angels in the Bible. They are referred to in both the Old and New Testaments, for example when the Archangel Gabriel informs Mary of her forthcoming pregnancy. The concept of guardian angels or angels sent down from Heaven to watch over individuals is one that can be found throughout the Old Testament.

The Old Testament does not go into any detail regarding the hierarchy of angels, whereas in the New Testament we find that they have been grouped into seven different ranks – angels, archangels, principalities, powers, virtues, dominions and thrones. In addition to these seven, there is also a mention of cherubim and seraphim, which do appear in the Old Testament. The two most prominent archangels mentioned in the Old Testament are Michael, the warrior leader of the heavenly ghosts, and Gabriel, the heavenly messenger. While the Book of Enoch tells of seven powerful angels – Uriel, Raphael, Raguel, Michael, Saraqael, Gabriel and Remiel.

Various hierarchies of demons have also developed, for example those associated with the seven deadly sins – Lucifer (pride), Mammon (avarice), Asmodeus (lechery), Satan (anger), Beelzebub (gluttony), Leviathan (envy) and Belphegor (sloth).

ABOVE: *Angel Gabriel*
by Girolamo Bonsignori (*c*.1440–*c*.1519)

The word 'Archangel' comes from the Greek word *archaggelos* which is a combination of two words: *archo* meaning first, in this case in terms of rank, and *aggelos* meaning messenger. Archangels are the highest rank and the closest to God, which is why they are trusted with such important duties.

Archangel Gabriel serves as a messenger for God and is a very important figure in religious texts. In Christian and Muslim faiths he is believed to have foretold the births of Jesus and John the Baptist. The Archangel Gabriel frequently appears in art that depicts the Annunciation, the moment that the Virgin Mary is told she will give birth to the Saviour.

ISLAM

Around AD630 Muhammed was still alive and spreading the religion that he had founded across parts of the Middle East and Central Asia. Believing in the existence of angels is paramount to the Islamic belief and in Muslim eyes there are no fallen angels. For example, Satan is not a fallen angel, he is one of the *jinn*, or a creation by God parallel to human beings and angels. Muslims also believe that Allah created the angels from light before the creation of human beings, as stated by the prophet Muhammed, and that they are completely obedient to him. They are described in Islamic scriptures as beautiful beings with magnificent wings.

Similar to Christian beliefs, angels in Islam form cosmic hierarchies and orders in the sense that they are of different size, status and merit. The greatest of all the angels is Gabriel, and next to him are all the attendants of God's Throne. It is alleged that the prophet of Islam actually saw Gabriel in his original form.

Muslims do not actually worship angels since the have no power to do either good or evil, except by the hand of Allah, but they do hold great faith in specific angels mentioned in the Qur'an – Jibreel (Gabriel), Mika'eel (Michael), Israfeel and Malik who guards over Hell. Of these, only Michael and Gabriel are mentioned in the Christian Bible.

Muslims also believe that there are guardian angels who are responsible for protecting the believer throughout his life, whether he is asleep or awake. Other angels are responsible for recording the deeds of man, both good and bad, and these are called the 'Honorable Scribes'. Two angels, Munkar and Nakeer, are given the task of testing the faith of believers in the grave. There are also keepers of Paradise and nineteen guards of Hell whose leader is Malik. Other angels are considered to be Allah's heavenly army, who constantly stand in rows, never tiring and always worshipping their God.

ABOVE: *Muhammed and the Archangel Gabriel* by Lutfi Abdullah, 1595

This painting is from *Siyer-I Nebi*, a Turkish epic by Mustafa son of Yusuf of Erzurum, based on the work of Arab Muslim historian Vakidi. The text documents the life of the prophet Muhammed. The work was completed around 1388 and just over 200 years later it was illustrated on the order of Ottoman ruler Murad III. The calligrapher Lutfi Abdullah was hired and in 1595 the six volumes of the *Siyer-I Nebi* were finished.

The above painting portrays the Archangel Gabriel visiting Muhammed. Over a period of 23 years, the Archangel Gabriel visited the Prophet many times and during this time Allah's messages were revealed to him and the Qur'an was written. The Archangel depicted here looks very different to the Christian representation, but they both serve the same purpose, to deliver divine prophecies.

The Portal of the Virgin is located in Notre Dame Cathedral in Paris. The complex sculpture represents Mary's death, her ascension to Heaven and her coronation as Queen of the Heavens. Angels appear in the ascension scene, lifting her to Heaven, and in the coronation scene, placing a crown on her head.

c.1230
Lincoln Cathedral in the United Kingdom was first built in 1072. Over the following centuries the cathedral was damaged, first by a fire and then by an earthquake. In the 1230s an Angel Choir was built at the east end of the building, the sculptures depicting the various members of the angel hierarchy playing instruments or holding symbolic objects.

St Thomas Aquinas
Around 1242 St Thomas Aquinas decided to join the Dominican order of the Roman Catholic Church. His family were outraged that he was not following their wishes of becoming a Benedictine monk, so they held him captive in the family castle for two years. During this time they applied pressure on him to renounce his aspiration but he refused. His brothers even resorted to hiring a prostitute to seduce him, but he threatened her with a burning stick. That night he had a vision of two angels, who gave him the strength to remain celibate in order to honour his faith.

1280
Giovanni Cimabue paints *The Virgin and Child in Majesty Surrounded by Angels*

1306
Giotto di Bondone paints *The Angel Gabriel sent by God*

1333
Simone Martini paints *The Angel of the Annunciation*

Joan of Arc
Joan of Arc was 12 years old in 1424 when she first heard the voices of angels. They said she must lead the French against the English and bring the Dauphin to Reims for his coronation. In art she is often shown in battle with angels flying above her.

c.1438–45
Fra Angelico paints *The Annunciation* (see page 21)

Medieval and Renaissance Angels

MEDIEVAL ANGELS

The Middle Ages (also known as the Dark Ages and the Medieval Period) started with the Fall of Rome in AD476 and ended with the Renaissance in the 14th century. The role of angels in the Middle Ages was very important, although it is uncertain how they came to be linked to nearly every aspect of medieval life. Despite the widespread belief in angels, scholars of the Middle Ages actually devoted very little time to the subject. Those that did write on the topic believed in the existence of a celestial hierarchy.

THE CELESTIAL HIERARCHY
The celestial hierarchy is divided into three choirs and nine ranks:

FIRST CHOIR
Seraphim: These are the angels closest to God's throne. They can speak directly with God and are beings of pure light and thought who are said to resonate with the 'Fire of Love'. The Seraphim appear in their angelic form, as human beings with four heads and six wings and encircled by flames.

Cherabim: These angels are full of knowledge and have a deep insight into God's secrets. They are the custodians of love, and as the Voices of Divine Wisdom, act as advisers to the lesser choirs of angels. The Cherabim were sent to Earth with perhaps the greatest task of all – to expel man from the Garden of Eden. They act as bodyguards and usually take the form of an animal with feathered wings.

Thrones: These angels form the last choir of the first hierarchy and are also known as the Ophanim. In Jewish lore the Thrones are described as the great 'wheels' of God's chariot, with their main characteristics being submission and peace. The Thrones are also responsible for conveying God's spirit to mankind and the inferior angels.

SECOND CHOIR

Dominations (or Hashmallim): The ruling Lords of the Dominations are said to be Zadkiel, Hasmal (the fire-speaking angel) and Muriel. They rule over the lower angelic orders and act as middlemen to the upper and lower choirs. They receive orders from the Seraphim and Cherabim and it is their duty to pass this information on to mankind. Only on very rare occasions do they reveal themselves to mortals.

Virtues (also known as Malakim and Tarshishim): These are the angels of grace who are responsible for miracles, bestowing their blessings on mortals. They are often associated with heroes as they will instill courage when it is needed most. Often called 'The Brilliant' or 'Shining Ones' their ruling princes are Michael, Gabriel and Raphael. It is through the Virtues that God is able to govern the seasons, the visible heavens and the elements in general.

Powers: These are believed to be the favourite angels among mortals. They hold one of the most dangerous tasks, controlling the border between Heaven and Earth, combatting any demonic attacks. They also act as spiritual guides, assisting people who have left their human body and have lost their way in the astral plane. With guidance from the Powers, a person's soul can find its way back into the light and find the Love of God.

THIRD CHOIR

Principalities: These are the head of the final choir and preside over the third hierarchy. They guide and protect the world's nations, towns and cities and keep a close watch over the mortal world. They are also protectors of both religion and politics and last, but not least, they are given the task of managing the duties of other angels. If one of the Principalities appears to a mortal, they are

ABOVE: *The Virgin and Child in Majesty Surrounded by Angels* by Giovanni Cimabue, 1280

Angels appear on either side of Mary and Jesus in this largely symmetrical piece of art. Four of the angels have gold halos which appear like discs behind their heads, as does the infant Christ, reinforcing his status as a spiritual figure. The two characters at the top have wings but not halos and are regarded as being saints. Mary sits on a throne with a stern expression which is mirrored in the faces of those surrounding her. The angels at the bottom have white and blue wings while the second pair have white and red wings, which is unusual as traditionally wings appear white. The angels and saints hold on to the throne protectively, giving the impression that they are guarding Mary and Jesus, who is raising his hand in a blessing gesture. The frame is decorated with 26 painted medallions.

The formula of Mary and Jesus with angels in art is known as a *Maesta*, which is the Italian word for 'majesty'. Many versions of this scene have been painted, the most famous being *Maestà with Twenty Angels and Nineteen Saints* by Duccio di Buoninsegna in 1308.

generally seen to be carrying a sceptre, cross or sword and wearing a crown.

Archangels: These are probably the angels that you are most familiar with and are often described as 'special' angels. Archangels are entrusted with the more important missions to mankind, advising us on which path to take in life and protecting us in times of danger. They also act as leaders in the divine army during times of battle and protect the Catholic Church under the leadership of St Michael. They are guardians to the Pope, cardinals, bishops and rulers of state and are ruled by four major names – Michael, Gabriel, Raphael and Uriel.

Angels: This is the last order of the celestial hierarchy and the one closest to mankind. The word 'angel' itself means 'messenger', and that is exactly what they are. These celestial beings have specific functions and can be called upon in times of need, when surrendering your worry thoughts to an angel can make the problem seem less severe.

Medieval theologians believed that angels were there to fill the gap between mankind and God. In the ancient world, with so many deities to worship, such intermediaries were not necessary, but as monotheistic religion became more widespread, so did the need for the intercession of angels. Fear of death and being damned forever in Hell inspired a belief in winged spirits who could move easily between the different worlds. Angels were said to be able to move stars, spin the planets and help all living creatures on Earth. Although they were primarily there to do God's bidding, they were also present to ease man's suffering and his eventual journey into a new spiritual world.

Details on wall paintings found in 11th- and 12th-century churches often depicted the soul leaving the body, with angels carrying it up to Heaven. These same frescoes often showed demons carrying off the souls of sinners to Hell. Pope St Gregory I (better known as Gregory the Great) cites many stories of soul transportation, describing visions of a room full of angels filled with light and sweet fragrance. He describes black demons, crows or vultures with cruel faces, breathing fire. In contrast, early Protestants had little use for the concept of angels. They felt the Renaissance churches were decorated far too lavishly, with their winged, lushly adorned angels. Their idea of a model church was one of simplicity and loyalty to the one God, and not only did they sweep away the papal bureaucracy of bishops and cardinals, but the angel hierarchy as well. They believed that man could communicate with God without a winged messenger.

ANGELS IN MEDIEVAL LITERATURE

Throughout the centuries, angels have never ceased to serve as a source of inspiration to writers. As figures of the supernatural and mysterious, angels have adapted to many different interpretations – poems, books, music and so on.

The *Book of Kells* is the most famous group of lavishly illustrated, illuminated manuscripts produced from the late 6th century to the early 9th century. The manuscripts took their name from the Abbey of Kells that was its home for centuries. Every letter and every illustration of every manuscript was created by hand, with religious texts brought to life in the monasteries of medieval Europe. The *Book of Kells* itself had a sacramental, rather than an educational purpose, and it is thought it would have been left on the high altar of the church and only taken off for reading during High Mass. The exquisite and intricate detail of some of the lettering contributed to the medieval notion that the manuscript had to be the work of angels, because only angels could have created illustrations with such precise detail. For example the letters Chi and Ro, the first two letters of the word Christ in Greek, were drawn in the most ornamental calligraphic scripts, with figures of animals, angels or men peering out at the reader from behind letters, or dangling between margins of text. Today, the *Book of Kells* is on display in the Old Library in Trinity College, Dublin. It is kept in its own glass case, displayed open to exhibit one page at a time.

One of the most prolific speakers and writers on angels in the Middle Ages was the Roman Catholic priest St Thomas Aquinas (*c.*1225–74). In his masterpiece, the *Summa Theologiae (c.1265–74)*, he discusses the nature, activities and moral state of angels. He believed that angels had three primary roles attributed to them by God – to gaze on God in wonder and contemplate the mystery of the Trilogy; to implement the will of God, and to serve as messengers to God. Aquinas also believed that angels were not equal in power and intellect and so he divided them up into nine choir groups. His argument was convincing, leading people to believe that the universe needed the existence of intellectual creatures and that these creatures were created by God. Aquinas went on to say that angels were not material objects nor were they the souls of dead humans, although they could sometimes assume the human shape to fulfil a given task. His ideas form the basis of many beliefs about angels today.

Dante Alighieri (1265–1321), often just known as Dante, was a famous Italian poet. A great believer in the Ptolemaic astronomy of his time, Dante saw the Earth as stationary and central to the universe. Round this planet, rotated the Sun, the Moon and five other visible planets. Each of these planets had its own heaven and beyond that a sphere of fixed stars. The final material heaven, which he called Crystalline, was transparent and invisible and moved at infinite speed. All nine heavens were moved and controlled by the nine orders of the angels. Dante's most famous work was *La Divina Commedia* (*The Divine Comedy*) was written between 1308 and 1321. It was divided into three parts – Inferno, Purgatory and Paradise. In the Inferno, Canto III, he wrote:

Commingled are they with that caitiff choir
Of Angels, who have not rebellious been,
Nor faithful were to God, but were for self.

The heavens expelled them, not to be less fair;
Nor them the nethermore abyss receives,
For glory none the damned would have from them.

This poem is widely considered to be an epic of Italian literature, with its imaginative and allegorical vision of the Christian afterlife. Dante generally described angels as transcendent beings of light and song.

Geoffrey Chaucer (1343–1400), often called the father of English literature, wrote a series of short stories in *The Canterbury Tales*. The majority of these stories were in verse and told of a very diverse group of pilgrims who left London together on their way to the shrine of St Thomas à Becket at Canterbury Cathedral. Some of these stories contained references to angels and the Devil, but in contrast to earlier literature, these tales were only meant to amuse rather than to teach any theological lessons. This is an excerpt from *The Monk's Tale*, entitled *Lucifer*.

With Lucifer, though he was angel fair
And not a man, with him will I begin;
For though Fortune may not an angel dare,
From high degree yet fell he for his sin
Down into Hell, and he lies yet therein.
O Lucifer, brightest of angels all,
Now art thou Satan, and thou may'st not win
From misery wherein thou far did'st fall!

ANGELS IN MEDIEVAL ART

Angels featured prominently in Western medieval art, with the earliest known example in a fresco dating back to the 2nd century – a depiction of the Annunciation scene in the cemetery of Saint Priscilla in Rome. The same subject matter was depicted again a century later, still in Rome, in the cemeteries of Saint Peter and Saint Marcillus. These paintings included the Archangel Gabriel who was shown in human form, dressed in a tunic and pallium. A 4th-century painting entitled *The Good Angel* also showed an angel in human form. Strangely, none of the angels in these paintings were depicted with either halos or wings, perhaps so as not to mimic the pagan deities.

Angelic wings did not appear in Christian art until the reign of Roman Emperor Constantine, who made Christianity into a state religion. Classical winged gods such as Cupid, Hermes and Perseus, as well as the ancient winged gods of Mesopotamia, were the most likely inspiration for this type of art.

Halos also started to appear around about the time of Constantine. The halo was a symbol of character and was traditionally only painted above the heads of pagan gods or Roman emperors. When the emperors started having their portraits painted with halos, it soon became the rage, and halos could be seen adorning the head of Jesus and later the heads of angels in 5th-century Christian art.

Giovanni Cimabue (1240–1302) was born in Florence as Cenni di Pepe. Cimabue learned to paint by studying Byzantine art, but eventually developed his own style that set him apart from artists of his generation and inspired those of later years. This earned him the title of 'Father of Italian Painting'. Some of his works included frescoes in the church of St Francis of Assisi and several paintings of the Madonna. He was also commissioned to paint angels, many examples of which can be found at the Uffizi Gallery in Florence. One his most famous frescoes, *Madonna Enthroned with the Child, St Francis and Four Angels (c.1278–80)*, can be seen at the Lower Church, San Francesco, Assisi.

Duccio di Buoninsegna (*c.*1255–*c.*1318) was another influential Italian artist of his time. He, like many of his contemporaries, painted mainly religious subjects, including angels. His works included the *Madonna with Child Enthroned and Six Angels (1285)*, now in the Uffizi Gallery, and his famous masterpiece *Maestà with Twenty Angels and Nineteen Saints (1308)*, which was commissioned for Siena Cathedral in central Italy. The centre of this piece depicts the Virgin and Child surrounded by angels and saints, as the name suggests.

RENAISSANCE ANGELS

The Renaissance (meaning rebirth or intellectual and artistic revival), was the period of European history roughly spanning from the 14th to the 16th centuries. It was the transitional period between medieval and modern times, and angels played an important role in the art of this time. In fact, right from the onset of the Renaissance period, artists and sculptors were obsessed with depicting angels in their religious works.

At the very start of the Italian Renaissance, Giotto di Bondone (*c.*1277–1337), a pupil of Cimabue, began to show emotion in the faces of his subjects, including angels. His *Lamentation* (*c.*1305) in the Scrovegni chapel in Padua shows several angels mourning the death of Christ, each with a finely detailed halo.

By the end of the Renaissance, the Dutch master Rembrandt van Rijn made the etching *Abraham Entertaining the Angels (1656)*. Abraham is sitting outdoors having a conversation with what is generally regarded as the Holy Trinity. He is informed that he and his aged wife, Sarah, will shortly give birth to a child. Rembrandt managed to make his angels appear to glow with light, being the

ABOVE: *The Annunciation*
by Fra Angelico, *c.*1438–45

Fra Angelico (1395–1455) was an Italian Renaissance painter and Dominican friar. He was commissioned to paint the monastery at San Marco's convent in Florence, Italy. He enlisted the help of Dominican assistants and together they painted 43 frescoes portraying religious scenes. The above painting remains in situ, greeting visitors to the convent.

This piece of art depicts the frequently-painted scene of the Annunciation. Here, the Archangel Gabriel is revealing to Mary that she will conceive a child who will be the Son of God. Mary's body language indicates her attitude is submissive. The Archangel Gabriel has large, colourful patterned wings which seem neat compared to other feathery representations of this era. He wears large robes which crumple into folds as he kneels down before Mary. It is interesting to note that Angelico has given Mary a slight shadow, but none to the Archangel Gabriel, since disembodied spirits would not cast a shadow. Both the Archangel and Mary have golden halos here. Halos are usually reserved for spiritual figures and, as Mary is a mortal, it is worth noting that Angelico chose to paint her with one.

This painting is interesting because despite showing an important scene, it is not packed with religious iconography unlike later versions by artists such as El Greco, Murillo and Titian. This draws the attention of the viewer directly to the purpose of the painting, the delivering of the Holy message.

master of the technique known as *chiaroscuro*, the dramatic depiction of light and shade.

Other famous Renaissance painters who depicted angels include Masaccio, who was born Tommaso Cassai (1401–28). Masaccio came from Tuscany and was the first great painter of the Quattrocento period of the Italian Renaissance. During his brief life, Masaccio exerted a strong influence on other artists and, together with Brunelleschi and Donatello, was one of the founding artists of the Renaissance. All of his works were of a religious nature, with his most famous being the fresco series for the Brancacci Chapel in Florence. These paintings illustrated one of his great innovations, the use of light to define the human body and its draperies. One of the frescoes is called *The Expulsion of Adam and Eve from the Garden of Eden (1423)*, which shows an amazing play of light and shadow, giving it a natural, almost realistic quality.

Piero della Francesca (1412–92) was an Italian artist who pioneered the use of perspective in Renaissance art. He was also a master mathematician and played a significant role in spreading the influence of Euclid's geometry. Due to his mathematical background, perspective and geometry feature prominently and subtly in all of Francesca's works. He is probably best remembered for his *Legend of the True Cross (c.1466)*, which is a series of twelve frescoes painted at the Basilica of San Francesco in Arezzo. The commission was originally awarded to the Florentine painter, Bicci di Lorenzo, who unfortunately died before he completed the first panel. In 1452, Francesca was commissioned to complete the work. The theme of the frescoes was inspired by a collection of saints' legends published in the 13th century. Francesca chose not to respect the chronological order of the original literature, but he did manage to attain a symmetry between the scenes. The 10th panel is entitled the *Annunciation*, and depicts Mary receiving the angel's message that she had been chosen to give birth to the Saviour. The frescoes are painted on three levels – the top level represents the scenes in the open air, the centre shows the court scenes and on the lower level are the battle scenes.

'Angel art can only manifest when three elements are present: transcendence, ideomotor effect and autonomous automatism. These three elements are aspects of each other.' These are the words of the great artist and master of invention, Leonardo da Vinci (1452–1519). While still a young man, da Vinci went to the workshop of the Italian Renaissance painter Andrea del Verrocchio. Verrocchio was working on a painting now called *Tobias and the Angel (c.1470–80)*, and it is alleged that Leonardo actually painted an angel on this canvas, which he executed in such a manner that his angel was far superior to any of the figures painted by Verrocchio. This, according to contemporary art historian Georgio Vasari, was the reason that Verrocchio never touched colours again.

No discussion about angels in art would be complete without mentioning at least one painting by Leonardo da Vinci. In the *Annunciation (c.1472–75)* the angel is holding a Madonna lily, which is supposed to symbolize purity. It has been suggested that Leonardo actually copied the angel's wings from a bird in flight.

In 1483, Leonardo was contracted by a Milanese confraternity to deliver an altarpiece which would decorate the chapel of the Immacolata at the Church of San Francesco Grande in Milan, a painting that would become known as the *Madonna of the Rocks*. Mary is shown with the infants St. John and Christ, with an angel, dressed in a rich red and green robe, completing the group. Local painters Evangelista De Predis and his brother Ambrogio were assigned the task of gilding the altarpiece and completing the two side panels, which showed angels singing and playing musical instruments – *An Angel in Green with a Vielle (1506)* and *An Angel in Red with a Lute (c.1490–9)*.

Albrecht Dürer (1471–1528) could perhaps be described as the odd man out in Renaissance art, as

ABOVE: *The Expulsion from Paradise*
by Albrecht Dürer, 1510

Albrecht Dürer (1471–1528) was one of the most important artists of the Renaissance. He is remembered for producing many great works using watercolours, but is best-known for his engravings and woodcuts. His *Apocalypse* woodcut series was published in 1498, earning him notoriety across Europe. The woodcuts represent fifteen scenes from the Book of Revelation, demonstrating Dürer's interest in illustrating key moments in the Bible.

The above picture is a woodcut which was created in 1510. Following Adam and Eve's decision to eat the forbidden fruit from the Tree of Knowledge, God orders an angel to expel them from Eden. The angel appears forceful in this picture, using a large sword to drive them out. The Tree of Knowledge stands between the angel and Adam and Eve, with the forbidden fruit still in view.

he was generally regarded as an engraver, not a painter. His vast body of work included altarpieces and religious works, numerous portraits and self-portraits and many copper engravings. He is famous for producing the *Sudarium of St Veronica Supported by Two Angels (1513)*. According to Christian legend, this sudarium (a Latin word, literally meaning 'sweat cloth') was a cloth used by St Veronica to wipe the face of Christ as he was carrying the cross to Calvary, and on which his features were miraculously impressed. The most striking feature of Dürer's print is the similarity of the frontal gaze of Christ to a self portrait in 1500 in which the artist paints himself as a Christ-like figure.

Raphael, born Raffaello Sanzio (1483–1520), was an Italian painter and architect of the Renaissance. Together with Michelangelo and Leonardo da Vinci, he formed the trinity of the great masters of this period. He gained the respect and patronage of Pope Julius II and spent the last twelve years of his life in Rome. Among his prolific works were projects for the pontiff, including a cycle of frescoes for a suite in the Pope's personal living quarters. Raphael's first recorded commission was the painting of *The Baronci Altarpiece* (1500-01) or the chapel in the church of Sant'Agostino in Città du Castello, near Urbino. Unfortunately the altarpiece was seriously damaged during an earthquake in 1789 and among the few fragments surviving today are two angels, one in Italy and one in the Louvre in Paris.

Tiziano Vecellio (1488/90–1576) better known simply as Titian, was the leader of the 16th-century Venetian school of the Italian High/Late Renaissance. Titian contributed to all the major areas of Renaissance art, painting altarpieces, portraits, mythological scenes, pastoral landscapes and, of course, angels. *The Assumption of the Virgin (1516–18)*, *The Rape of Europa* (1559–62) and *St John The Evangelist on Patmos (1544)* are just three examples of his depictions of angels. The latter, which hangs in the National Gallery of Art in Washington DC, shows the moment when Saint John was inspired by God to write the *Book of Revelation*. Titian's *Polytych of the Resurrection, Angel Gabriel* (1520–22) shows the angel rushing in the top left corner, with his garments streaming behind him. He spreads out his greeting on a banderole which he is holding out to Mary, shown on the opposite panel. By creating the impression that the square panel is almost too small to contain the magnificent figure of the angel, Titian has intensified the sense of tension and dynamics in this painting.

Michelangelo Buonarroti (1475–1564) was one of the greatest artists of all time, a man whose name has become synonymous with the word 'masterpiece'. As an artist, Michelangelo was outstanding, the creator of works of sublime beauty, and yet he was caught between the conflicting powers of the Medici family in Florence and the Papacy in Rome, causing him problems throughout his life. Michelangelo's first love was sculpture and among his early works the *Pièta* was a fine example of how he could transform a cold slab of marble into a brilliant evocation of human form. In 1508, Pope Julius II persuaded Michelangelo to paint the ceiling of the Vatican's Sistine Chapel. The art world, including the famous Raphael, were convinced that the young sculptor, who had never before attempted to paint a fresco, would inevitably fail. At first the young sculptor refused, protesting that he was not a painter, but the pope finally managed to convince him. It was arduous work, which involved Michelangelo having to paint while lying on his back on top of a scaffold that raised him to within inches of the ceiling. Michelangelo not only overcame these obstacles but, after only four years, had produced a masterpiece. The vast artwork depicts scenes from the Old Testament such as the story of Genesis, Adam and Eve's expulsion from Paradise and the infamous image of God giving Adam life. One important scene includes three angels sitting at a table, having prepared it for the celebration of the Eucharist. In Michelangelo's sonnet *On the Painting of the Sistine Chapel*, he

ABOVE: *The Sistine Madonna*
by Raphael, 1513

The above painting depicts the Virgin Mary holding baby Jesus in her arms. To the left is St Sixtus and to the right, St Barbara. This painting has been the focus of a lot of speculation over the centuries, with critics trying to decipher the facial expressions of Mary and Jesus, and work out who St Sixtus is pointing at. The picture is framed by two heavy curtains, lending a theatrical quality to the piece. The background is formed of a montage of babies' faces; their eyes are black and lifeless, below this are white clouds which Mary seems to have landed on.

There are two cherubs, also known as *putti*, in this picture who unusually appear at the bottom, leaning on the lower frame of the composition. This is an interesting representation of cherubs as here they seem somewhat bored and impatient, while still being the model of childlike innocence. These cherubs are now iconic as they have been replicated so many times in popular culture.

describes all the discomforts involved in painting a ceiling, how much he hated the place and the fact that he despaired of being a painter at all.

…My beard turns up to heaven; my nape falls in
Fixed on my spine: my breast-bone visibly
Grows like a harp: a rich embroidery
Bedews my face from brush-drips, thick and thin.

My loins into my paunch like levers grind:
My buttock like a crupper bears my weight;
My feet unguided wander to and fro…

Michelangelo Merisi da Caravaggio (1571–1610) was an Italian artist who worked in Rome, Naples, Malta and Sicily during the Renaissance. He was the first great representative of the Baroque school of painting and, although considered one of the greatest painters in European history, was rebellious and dangerous and handled his success atrociously. After his apprenticeship, Caravaggio caused scandal in Rome, not just because of his volatile character but because of his controversial methods of painting. His aim was to make paintings that told the truth and he was critically condemned for being a naturalist. Even with all these adverse reactions to his work, Caravaggio was still commissioned to produce an enormous number of paintings, many of which were rejected by patrons on the grounds of indecorum or theological incorrectness. In 1602, the painting *St Matthew and the Angel* was completed for the Contarelli Chapel within the church of San Luigi dei Francesi in Rome. It was intended to replace an altarpiece sculpture by the Flemish artist Jacob Cobært, who had struggled with it for decades to no avail. When his statue – without angel – was finally unveiled, the Contarelli did not want it, so they commissioned a painting on the subject by Caravaggio. Caravaggio's painting showed the angel and Saint Matthew in remarkably realistic, three-dimensional detail, poring over the scriptures. However, this painting was also rejected by the

ABOVE: *Rest During the Flight into Egypt*
by Michelangelo Merisi da Caravaggio, 1597

The flight into Egypt is a biblical event in the Gospel of Matthew (2:13–23). When Joseph is visited by an angel of the Lord he is told, 'take the child and his mother, and escape to Egypt. Stay there until I tell you; for Herod is going to search for the child to kill him', and so they immediately flee.

The above picture is based on a popular apocryphal legend of the trio resting during the journey. They stop in a wooded area and sit beneath a tree. The positioning of the adolescent angel divides the painting in two. On the left is Joseph, looking old and tired. His facial expression makes him appear worried and there is a childlike aspect to the position of his crossed feet. He holds up a sheet of music to the angel, who has his back to the viewer. The angel is wearing a white

robe which is loosely tied to his body and from his back protrude grey and black wings. He stands in a way that has been interpreted as the shape of a musical symbol and is playing a vioin. On the right side of the painting is Mary holding the sleeping baby Jesus. The angel appears to be luminous against the darker colours of the rest of the painting and almost draws attention away from the holy family. Being in the foreground and having his back to the viewer creates a barrier and gives the impression he is being protective of Mary, Joseph and Jesus.

The flight into Egypt became a popular scene for painters. Artists such as Murillo, Rembrandt and Gerard David painted their own interpretation of this story with the size and role of angels changing.

priests. They said that Saint Matthew, who was depicted with his legs crossed and his feet rudely exposed to the public, lacked decorum and did not have the appearance of a saint. Caravaggio's patron purchased the painting for his own private collection, and eventually ended up in the Kaiser Friedrich Museum in Berlin. However, the painting was destroyed towards the end of the Second World War and it is now only remembered from its original monochrome photographs.

ANGELS IN RENAISSANCE LITERATURE

The Renaissance period also produced some notable literature concerning both angels and devils. The French humanist François Rabelais (c.1483–1553) was the greatest French writer of this time and perhaps one of the most influential authors in history. Rabelais' novels contained many references to angels, devils and demonology; some of a satirical nature and some comical. His classic story of *Gargantua and Pantagruel* is a masterpiece, bringing all the exuberance and invention of the 16th century to our present day. This comic narrative, which took two decades to complete, can be traced back to medieval folklore and theatre. Pantagruel borrows his name from a diminutive theatrical demon who liked to torment drunkards by filling their throats with salt. In Book III, chapter 14, Rabelais writes:

I remember that the Cabalists and Massoretes, interpreters of the Holy Writ, in explaining how one can make sure of the genuineness of an angelic apparition – for often Satan's angels take the form of angels of light – say that the difference between the two lies in this: that when the good and consoling angel appears to man, he alarms him at first, but comforts him in the end and leaves him happy and contented; whereas the wicked and corrupting angel rejoices a man at the beginning, but in the end leaves him troubled, angry and perplexed.

Torquato Tasso (1544–95) was the greatest Italian poet of the late Renaissance and is best remembered for his masterpiece *La Gerusalemme Liberata* (Jerusalem Delivered), first published in 1581. It is an epic tale which recounts the capture of Jerusalem by the crusaders in 1099, with many references to angels. For example in the first book Tasso writes:

O heavenly Muse, that not with fading bays
Deckest thy brow by the Heliconian spring,
But sittest crowned with stars' immortal rays
In Heaven, where legions of bright angels sing;
Inspire life in my wit, my thoughts upraise,
My verse ennoble, and forgive the thing,
If fictions light I mix with truth divine,
And fill these lines with other praise than thine.

Jerusalem Delivered greatly influenced the writings of later authors such as Spenser and Milton, but after finishing the masterpiece the poet started to suffer from mental problems. For much of his career Tasso resided at the court of the Duke of Ferrera, seven years of which were spent in confinement for his apparent insanity in the hospital of Santa Anna. During this period he wrote a number of philosophical and moral dialogues, but never fully regained his sanity. Unfortunately, Tasso died just a few days before he was due to be crowned as the king of poets by the Pope.

LEFT: *Portrait of Torquato Tasso* by Alessandro Allori, *c.*1585

City of Angels

Los Angeles and Bangkok are both known as 'The City of Angels' in local translations of their names.

The Angel Islington

In 1465 a French coin named 'Angel' was introduced to England by Edward IV. The Angel coin became so iconic that English pubs began to be named after it. The historic Angel pub in Islington, dating back to 1638, is an early example. The Angel underground station opened in 1901, and was named after the Inn.

Wings

While awaiting the arrival of his daughter in hospital, ex-Beatle Paul McCartney had a vision. His wife Linda was giving birth to Stella when there were dramatic complications. Paul began to pray and the image of angels wings came to his mind. Mother and baby survived and consequently he named his band 'Wings'.

Angels

UK singer Robbie Williams struck gold with his 1997 hit single *Angels*. It sold over two million copies worldwide, won numerous awards and allegedly only took 25 minutes to write.

Oprah Winfrey

Oprah's Angel Network is a non-profit organization set up by Oprah Winfrey. It was established in 1997 to inspire and encourage people to help those in need.

Angel and Devil Food Cake

Angel Food Cake is a light and airy cake that became popular in the USA in late 19th century. It is said to be the 'food of the angels'. A rich and chocolatey counterpart named Devil Food Cake was developed in the early 20th century.

LA Angels

Los Angeles Angels of Anaheim are a professional baseball team based in Anaheim, California. The team was founded in 1966 and their nicknames include The Halos, The Wings and The Seraphs. The current logo is a large red 'A' with a halo at the top.

Angels in the Modern World

Angels do not seem to care what century it is, and they are notable for their manifestation in the modern world. In Britain, there was a great revival of interest shown in angels in the Victorian era. In fact, there was a real craze for them and many unknown artists were commissioned by lithography companies to make illustrations of guardian angels protecting small children. The marketplace was flooded with printed calendars, cheap wall prints and postcards, all depicting the same theme. Because of the high infant mortality rate in the 19th century, children were highly cherished and the idea that they were protected by an invisible spirit or angel was very popular among Victorians; they were often believed to have several guardian angels.

Gradually the focus shifted from pure religious devotion into something more fanciful, typified by today's images of Cupid on Valentine's Day cards and angels on Christmas cards. It seems that angels never fail to fascinate and, regardless of faith, people seem prepared to collect trinkets in whatever form they can – little Russian icons, earrings, thimbles, dinner plates, books, postcards – just to name a few. Angels are seen as soothing, protective creatures who can offer release from our modern world of stress.

From the time of the Industrial Revolution, angel encounters were more widely acknowledged because it was easier to spread the word. Furthermore, the authenticity of such sightings seemed more credible because many well-known figures claimed to have experienced them. For example, the English poet and painter William Blake claimed to have seen angels when he was eight years old. He said he saw an entire flock of angels up a tree, with bright wings that 'bespangled every bough like stars'. Blake's obsession with angels was illustrated in his poem *The Angel*, which goes into detail about how these visionary experiences affected his life.

The German poet Rainer Maria Rilke (1875–1926) was frequently visited by angels. He saw his own particular angel as strong, still, radiant and a divider 'between the Here and There'.

A modern Irish writer, Lorna Byrne, is also convinced that angels have had a profound effect on her life and says that they taught her everything she knows. In fact her book *Angels in My Hair* has been so convincing that it has been bought by the American publishers of *The Da Vinci Code*, and today is on the list of best-sellers.

It would appear that even agnostics are prepared to believe that angels can play a role in keeping them safe from the demands of the modern world. Even through their evolution, angels have managed to remain sexless, beautiful and beyond desire. People want to believe, and survivors of near-death experiences frequently mention shining figures with outstretched wings who wait at the end of a dark tunnel to greet them. Perhaps we all need to envisage some kind of heavenly being to ease the thought of death and make some sense of life. It is not surprising, therefore, that the world's largest angel sculpture – *Angel of the North* – is only a few years old and, rather than being placed in or near a Church, it stands overlooking the city of Gateshead in the north of England (see page 31).

Modern science has made the world a more receptive place for angels – the Internet is crowded with testimonies from people who have had 'visits'. A lot of these stories are not just poignant but also plausible, and many people wish they too could share the experience.

ANGELS IN LITERATURE, MUSIC AND ART

From John Milton's (1608–74) *Paradise Lost*, angels have had a large part to play in literature of the modern age. *Paradise Lost* is an epic work which includes many references to angels, Satan and the constant battles between Heaven and Earth. More recently, angels have also been used to understand human relationships. The popular belief that the

ABOVE: *El Angel de la Independencia*
Mexico City

El Angel, officially known as *El Angel de la Independencia*, is a victory column that stands 36 metres tall in Mexico City. The landmark looks down the 12-kilometre-long boulevard Paseo de la Reforma. The statue was built in 1902 on the order of president Porfirio Diaz, created to commemorate the centennial of the beginning of Mexico's War of Independence.

At the top of the victory column stands *El Angel*, made of bronze and coated in gold since 2006. She was sculpted by French/Italian sculptor Enrique Alciati who used the Greek legend of the winged goddess Nike as his inspiration. The angel holds a crown in her right hand and a broken chain in her left, which symbolizes freedom. *El Angel* has become a cherished landmark to the people of Mexico City and is used as a meeting place for celebrations and political rallies. In 1929 an eternal flame was installed at the base of the column to honour those that perished in the War of Independence.

ideal Victorian wife was to be akin to an 'Angel in the House' was taken up by the poet Coventry Patmore in his poem of the same name, *The Angel in the House*. Although the poem received little attention when it was first published (1854), it became increasingly popular during the latter part of the 19th and early 20th century. In fact the poem had such an effect that the liberated Virginia Woolf wrote a response to the idea of a repressed ideal woman, in *Killing the Angel in the House* in 1931.

Many authors have written stories about angels – some allegories, some serious, some funny and others utterly bizarre. Just a few examples are: *The Angel of the Odd* by Edgar Allan Poe; *The Angel of the Bridge* by John William Cheever; *A Very Old Man with Enormous Wings* by Gabriel Garcia Marquez and *Lady Merion's Angel* by Jane Yolen.

Angels have long been written about in song and references to them can be traced back to early hymns and carols. Nowadays they are mentioned in all music genres, from classical to rock and rap music to lullabies. George Friederic Handel composed the aria *Waft Her, Angels Thro' The Skies* which comes from the Oratorio *Jephtha* in 1751. Perhaps more recognizable is *Hark the Herald Angels Sing*, composed by Felix Mendelsohn in 1840, which is heard each and every Christmas. More recently, artists as diverse as Madonna, Jimi Hendrix, Frank Sinatra, Fleetwood Mac, U2 and the Beach Boys, to name but a few, have all found inspiration in our celestial helpers. Perhaps the most popular song recorded in modern times was *Angels*, sung by Robbie Williams, which became a worldwide hit single when it was released at Christmas 1997.

The world of film is equally enchanted by our spiritual messengers – some perennial favourites being: *Here Comes Mr Jordan* (1941); *It's a Wonderful Life* (1946); *The Angel Who Pawned Her Harp* (1954); *Heaven Can Wait* (1978); *Wings of Desire* (1987); *Angels in America* (1993); *The Prophecy* (1995); *Michael* (1996); *City of Angels* (1998) and *Dogma* (1999).

Television has also featured programmes about angels. *Touched by an Angel* was an American fantasy drama that ran from 1994–2003. Each episode would follow a person or group that had a big problem to resolve or decision to make. Angels would then step in with advice directly from God. *Saving Grace* is an American crime series that began in 2007. It focuses on police detective Grace Hanadarko who runs someone over while drunk. She cries out for help from God and suddenly an angel appears. A British TV show called *Angels* started in 2009, hosted by Gloria Hunniford, a television personality with a known belief in angels. In this series she speaks to people who have encountered angels and discovers how they have changed their lives.

Artists from the modern era whose work frequently contained examples of angels include Camille Corot (1796–1875); Edouard Manet (1832–83); Paul Gauguin (1848–1903); Paul Klee (1879–1940); Marc Chagall (1887–1985); André Masson (1896–1987); Salvador Dalí (1904–89) and Howard David Johnson (1954–).

The list of songs, books, films and paintings could go on and on, but just the ones mentioned are an indication of just how the modern world is still influenced by every aspect of angels and their adversaries. Even if Christmas is the only time when angels come to the forefront in your household, there are still many people who would like to prove you wrong and tell you that they do exist in our everyday lives. The following quote by George Eliot seems to say it all:

The golden moments in the stream of life
rush past us and we see nothing but sand;
the angels come to visit us,
and we only know them when they are gone.

ABOVE: *Angel of the North*
by Antony Gormley, 1998

The *Angel of the North* is a contemporary structure that has become one of the United Kingdom's most famous and recognizable landmarks. It stands at an impressive 20 metres (66 feet) high and 54 metres (178 feet) wide, is made from Corten steel and weighs 200 tonnes. The *Angel* is seen by an estimated 90,000 drivers every day as it is situated adjacent to the A1 motorway.

The wings are angled at 3.5 degrees which according to the designer, Antony Gormley, was a deliberate move to create a 'sense of embrace', implying the *Angel* is meant to communicate comfort or protection. Out of all the potential symbols or icons that could have been used, it is interesting that an angel was selected. Gormley doesn't attribute this decision to his religious orientation, but rather because angels represent 'hope'.

Gormley feels the people of the north-east of England needed hope in a time he calls, 'the gap between the industrial and the information ages.' The *Angel* is situated at the site of a former colliery. This location was chosen to serve as a reminder of the huge coal-mining industry in Gateshead and to pay homage to the workers that mined beneath the surface for over 300 years.

While symbolizing hope for the future, the *Angel* also represents Gormley's hope that people will keep imagining angels; that this ancient icon should not be forgotten as the world advances further into the technological age.

Guardian Angels

Guardian angels are thought to be spirits assigned to us to protect us from harm and guide us through life. To some people, angels are a thing of fiction or fantasy, but to those that have had an encounter of the celestial kind, they are very real indeed. They can appear in many forms; as visions, smells, or voices. They can enter our subconscious and influence our thoughts. They can bring us messages from departed loved ones. They can guide us away from danger and into safety and watch over us when we are being tested. The modern perception of an angel is a human figure with wings, but they did not start off like this. Belief in guardian angels dates back to ancient civilizations, and their interpretation was very different to ours today.

The ancient Egyptians believed that every person had their own individual guardian and that in order to cement this divine partnership you would have to consciously accept your angel, much in the same way that Christians ask to receive the holy spirit. The Sumerians believed each person had a 'ghost' which accompanied them throughout their entire life, an idea that was preserved for posterity in the form of carvings. Evidence that guardian angels were recognized and worshipped in Babylon and Assyria has also survived, one example being a monument of a guardian angel that once guarded the entrance to an Assyrian palace is on display at the British Museum.

The existence of guardian angels may not be central to the doctrine of mainstream religions but they are certainly still popular and celebrated. In the Old Testament, Jesus says of his children, 'See that you do not look down on one of these little ones. For I tell you that their angels in heaven always see the face of my Father in heaven.' (Matthew 18:10) Because of this passage it is generally believed that all children have a guardian angel. There is a question over whether only 'believers', those with faith, can receive the help of a guardian angel. If we do not believe in God, how can we be aware of his messengers? Do you have to believe it to see it, or see it to believe it? There is some debate over whether there is a guardian angel for a family, a couple, or perhaps even a country. In the Old Testament, the Archangel Michael is assigned to Israel, but it isn't confirmed in scripture if there is an angel for every individual person. Despite these questions, guardian angels are still worshipped and revered. In Catholic Schools students are taught to pray to their guardian angel, and in some schools the pupils leave a section of their desk clear for angels to rest on. On 2 October the Catholic Feast of Archangels takes place, honouring the Holy Guardian angel. In Rabbinical teachings there are guardian angels assigned to each person and city, even, to each blade of grass. In Islam, angels appear throughout the Qur'an. For example, Gabriel was the angel that gave the prophet Muhammed the holy book. It also states, 'He sends forth guardians who watch over you and carry away your souls without fail when death overtakes you.'

Guardian angels are also common in Eastern religions. In Buddhism there is a belief in protectors from Heaven that are sent down to look after the living. Winged angels are prevalent in Buddhist art, and are shown lifting Buddha to heaven when he died. Similarly, in Hinduism there is an Atman, which is a guardian angel. In both these religions the angel, or Atman, is not just a protective entity, but a spiritual force that assists and guides the individual in attaining enlightenment and becoming one with the universe.

Perhaps popular culture has shaped and moulded the ancient representation of a guardian angel to make them aesthetically pleasing; in Western culture they are never depicted with the head of a lion or body of a bird, but usually shown as a beautiful human with wings. This image is easier for us to relate to and feel protected by, and importantly, it is easier for us to believe. In contemporary times guardian angels are often reported making an appearance during disasters or war. But sometimes they appear just to let you know they are there. Many people believe that finding a feather at their feet is a symbol that an angel is nearby. There is a theory that they can influence our moods and thoughts; for example when we get strong feelings about decisions, when our intuition is telling us something, this is our guardian angel, urging us to reconsider. Guardian angels don't only appear in

ABOVE: *An angel guards New York*
21st century

On 11 September 2001 a series of co-ordinated terrorist attacks were launched against the United States. Nineteen al-Qaeda terrorists boarded four commercial passenger jet airliners and hijacked them mid-air. One plane hit the Pentagon in Virginia, just outside Washington D.C and one crash-landed in a field in Shanksville, rural Pennsylvania. The remaining two airliners were then crashed into the World Trade Center in New York, causing unprecedented damage. It is miraculous that anyone survived the atrocities, and some have since claimed it was down to otherworldly helpers.

There were many reports in the media about guardian angels helping trapped workers out of the collapsing Twin Towers. Some claimed to have been led by a hand through thick smoke and dust to arrive outside, only to find their helper had disappeared. Some reported having strong urges to help others escape, then realizing that their original way out was actually seconds away from destruction. Since 9/11, amateur videos have appeared online of the attacks on the Twin Towers. Various individuals have examined these and claimed that angelic faces can be seen forming in the billowing smoke.

times of war, when thousands of people are at risk, they work miracles everyday to individuals in need.

Author Joan Wester Anderson relates a compelling story concerning her son Tim.

In 1983, on Christmas Eve, Tim was travelling back from college in Connecticut to his mother's Chicago home, accompanied by two friends. The weather was freezing and conditions were difficult for travelling. Tim dropped one of his companions off in Indiana and continued on his journey with his friend Jim. They were driving down an isolated, rural road when the car broke down, shuddering to a halt. The radio was broadcasting warnings against venturing outside in the icy conditions. The two young men looked at each other in horror as they realized the gravity of their situation – all around them was darkness, with not a house or car in sight. They were trying to stay calm and ward off the cold, when all of a sudden they saw headlights flashing in their rear view mirror. Someone knocked on the window and called: 'Need to be pulled?' It was a tow truck driver, who hitched their car up so they could get back to their friend's home.

When they got there Tim rushed inside to ask for some money to repay their rescuer for his kindness. But when he emerged the truck and its driver had disappeared into the night, and the only set of tyre marks in the snow were those belonging to Tim's car.

Without the tow truck, the young men would almost certainly have frozen to death in their car. Tim and his mother Joan believe to this day that the mysterious rescuer was a guardian angel, who heard the friends' prayers for help on that icy Christmas Eve. Joan relates this story among other angel encounters in her book *Where Angels Walk*.

The belief in guardian angels seems to be shared amongst the rich and famous too. Celebrities such as Cameron Diaz, Megan Fox and Angelina Jolie place a lot of faith in their spirit guides. David Beckham has a tattoo of a guardian angel with its arms outstretched on his back, symbolizing his angel's omnipresence. He later had a pair of large wings added to complete the image. Socialite Nicole Richie has angel wings tattooed on her shoulder blades, positioned where her wings would be, if she was an angel.

Hollywood star Sharon Stone wrote a book about guardian angels entitled *Someone to Hold*. Stone co-wrote the book with friend Mimi Craven in 2005. Stone has a personal belief in guardian angels, she firmly believes in their ability to help people through their light energy. The foreword includes a poem called *Angels* by an anonymous author.

> *There are those who believe*
> *So the Story is told,*
> *That at birth you receive*
> *Your own Angel to hold.*
> *You come into this world*
> *On a wing and a prayer*
> *And throughout your lifetime*
> *She will always be there.*
> *A guardian angel*
> *Who will guide what you do,*
> *Her pure essence is love,*
> *Sent to watch over you*

The perception of guardian angels has changed so dramatically over the centuries, now they seem to be seen as quite romantic characters, and not necessarily religious. Some people believe their guardian angel is in fact a dead relative. They come back as a protective ghost, watching over their grieving loved one, and providing comfort in times of despair.

Whether you believe in divine intervention or are more scientifically-minded, there is no denying that accounts from people that have experienced their guardian angel are extremely compelling.

ABOVE: Guardian Angels, New York City

The Guardian Angels organization was established on 13 February 1979 in New York City. The organization was founded by American anti-crime activist Curtis Sliwa as a response to the escalating levels of crime on the New York subway system. In the beginning the Guardian Angels were met with opposition from the local government and hostility from New York's residents, but over time their good deeds started becoming recognized. The Guardian Angels were trained in first aid, CPR, conflict resolution, communication, basic martial arts and law, and were able to make citizen arrests.

In 1981 a chapter of the Guardian Angels opened in Los Angeles and by the mid-1980s there were six more chapters with over 250 members. Soon Chicago, San Francisco, Boston, Dallas and Washington D.C joined the alliance and opened chapters. The United Kingdom's

Guardian Angels began patrolling in 1989, followed by Japan in 1996 and South Africa in 2004. Today, there are 13 chapters in 140 cities worldwide, proving the Guardian Angel's slogan, 'we dare to care' has global resonance.

Curtis Sliwa used the concept of a guardian angel to establish his organization. The Guardian Angels appear non-confrontational in their uniform red berets and red jackets. Their logo (see above) incorporates an eye inside a shield which has wings, representing a watchful and protective all-seeing eye in flight. Sliwa used the idea of a guardian angel to give the organization's identity a trustworthy and approachable edge.

While some people believe in spiritual guardian angels, these patrolmen are urban guardian angels, mere mortals with the patience and heart of an ancient deity.

Hell's Angels

Hell's Angels Motorcycle Club (HAMC) originated in California in 1948. The name comes from a habit during both World Wars to give squadrons death-defying names. Authorities believe the Hell's Angels are an organized crime syndicate, but they claim to merely be motorcycle enthusiasts. Today the HAMC has chapters worldwide with over 3,600 members.

Angels and Demons

Dogma is a 1999 film by director Kevin Smith that caused great controversy as it appeared to satirize Catholic belief. It follows a range of religious figures from angels to demons as they exist on Earth. Central to the story are two fallen angels, Loki and Bartleby who through a loophole in Catholic Dogma discover a way to get back into Heaven.

Computer Angels

Sacred 2: Fallen Angel is the second computer game in the fantasy *Sacred* series. The game takes place on Ancaria, a land originally under control of the Seraphim, the ancient choir of angels.

Pop Angels

Frankie Valli and the Four Seasons released a single in 1976 called *Fallen Angel*. The chorus of the song is, 'Fallen angel, I'll forgive you anything, you can't help the things you do'.

TV Angels

Fallen Angel was a 2007 British television show based on the *Roth Trilogy* by Andrew Taylor. The main character is Rosie Byfield, the daughter of a clergyman who grows up to be a psychopathic killer. The trilogy moves backwards in time, revealing Rosie's troubled past.

Dark Angel

DC Comics villain Dark Angel is a wandering spirit that inhabits the body of Baroness Paula Von Gunther during World War II. She has numerous skills including the ability to teleport herself anywhere and can control the minds of others. In the comic book world she is famous for fighting Wonder Woman.

Fallen Angels

In the Christian faith, a 'fallen angel' is a spiritual being that has been banished or exiled from Heaven. The purpose of an angel is to serve God and act as amessenger to his people and, although they are inherently good, like humans angels have the will to think freely and are therefore fallible. If they disobeyed God, the consequences were serious.

Lucifer is thought to have been the first fallen angel. In Heaven he was God's most perfect piece of work; being a Seraphim he was the highest ranking angel, and Lucifer was fully aware how special he was. He was a narcissist, taking immense pride in his own perfection, his immortality and his closeness to God. Lucifer, however, desired to be God, not just one of his servants. Eventually, his ego grew so great that he believed himself to be above the Lord and so tempted Eve in the Garden of Eden, performing his first sin. This act was the first instance in the Bible of an angel disobeying God and falling from grace. Following his banishment Lucifer entered his new domain, Hell, and became known as Satan, from the Hebrew word for 'adversary'. Here, it is assumed, Satan lost his 'angel' status and became a demon. According to Christian mythology one third of Heaven's angels fell with him and became his demonic disciples. Naturally, Satan wasn't happy to have been banished; he desired to rule the entire universe, and in the Book of Revelations it is written that a great war raged in Heaven. Satan led the revolt against God. He took on the form of a dragon with ten heads and with his posse of fallen angels he fought against Archangel Michael and his angels, to claim the Kingdom of Heaven as their own. In the end, good triumphed over evil and the great dragon was cast out; the Archangel Michael won the war and the Kingdom of Heaven was saved.

In the first and second books of Enoch and Jubilees in the biblical Apocrypha, a group known as the 'Watchers' are introduced. The Watchers, also known as 'Grigori', were angels that were sent to Earth to watch over the people. However, they soon began to lust over the women of Earth and between themselves agreed to disobey God and satisfy their urges instead. This rebellion angered God, and they were excommunicated, becoming 'fallen angels', and were never allowed to return to Heaven again. The Watchers began fathering half-human and half-angel children with their mortal wives, this hybrid offspring were named the 'Nephilim'. These 'children' were not ordinary children, they were giants, sometimes as tall as 30 feet and extremely savage by nature. According to the Book of Enoch (a section attributed to Enoch, the great-grandfather of Noah), there were 200 Watchers but only the leaders of this army are named. Each Watcher leader had a skill or special knowledge and began imparting their celestial wisdom on to the Nephilim. Azazel taught them how to make swords, shields and knives; Chazaqiel educated them on meteorology; Penemue introduced them to writing using ink and paper. The other leaders taught them the darker arts of enchantment, sorcery, astrology and divination. With their superior strength and otherworldly knowledge the Nephilim were becoming a force to be reckoned with, killing cattle and even turning to cannibalistic measures for sustenance. God had enough of the fallen angels and their barbaric children and devised a plan to flood the Earth and wipe them out. He sent Uriel to warn Noah to protect the human race from the Great Flood. However, the Book of Genesis recounts that the Nephilim survived the Great Flood and the Watchers also remained, chained to this realm until Judgement Day.

In contemporary times, our main exposure to fallen angels is through films, art, computer games and music. Their origin in religion isn't always referenced in these mediums, and often the image and idea of fallen angels is used to appeal to certain youth cultures. The fallen angel is widely celebrated in Gothic culture where characters such as vampires, ghosts and other creatures from the underworld are revered. A fallen angel represents rebellion against the established order, which is something that many young people are drawn to.

In modern art a fallen angel can be represented smoking or drinking, both habits that contrast with our idea of the pure and good angels that remained in Heaven.

ABOVE: *The Fall of the Rebel Angels*
by Gustave Doré, 1870

Gustave Doré was an accomplished artist, engraver and illustrator. One of his most famous works were the illustrations he did for John Milton's epic poem *Paradise Lost*, almost 200 years after its publication. The poem fills a staggering twelve books and the above picture is from Book One. *Paradise Lost* tells the Christian story of how Satan tempted Adam and Eve in the Garden of Eden, leading to their expulsion. The Fall of Man is a strong theme in Book One, telling how the first humans turned against God. Some Christians believe that Adam and Eve's disobedience had a catastrophic effect on humankind, and this is reflected in the first few lines of *Paradise Lost*:

Of Man's first disobedience, and the fruit
Of that forbidden tree whose mortal taste
Brought death into the World, and all our woe,
With loss of Eden, till one greater Man
Restore us, and regain the blissful seat

Adam and Eve's original sin proved that humans, as well as angels, can be fallible through the use of free will. In the picture above there are tens of angels falling from Heaven down to Hell, having been banished for disobeying God.

A-Z

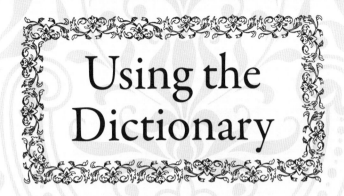

Using the Dictionary

All entries are listed alphabetically.

Alternative spellings appear in brackets next to relevant entries.

Cross-references are indicated by the abbreviation *qv* (*quod vide*).

The following phraseology occurs throughout the dictionary section:

Altitude and Chora: These are spiritual planes of existence where various angels exist and rule.

Conjuring the reed: A magical ritual in which a marsh-reed is stripped of leaves and made into knife, for use in animal sacrifice.

Conjuring the sword: In grimoire, the sword holds mysterious powers. Mortals can summon it by calling on specific angels.

Consecrating the salt: In ceremonial magic, salt represents the Earth and is blessed before use in rituals.

Exorcism of the bat, salt, water and wax: Rituals in Occultism performed to drive demons out before use in sacred ceremonies. Salt and water can also be used to cleanse and purify.

Grimoire: Books of the grimoire genre began to appear in Europe in the Middle Ages. These textbooks of magic would instruct the reader on spells and invocations.

Heavenly halls: In Judaism there are seven heavenly halls within the seven heavens. *The Hekhalot Books* focus on the visions had by mystics following extensive prayer and meditation. These visions revealed divine palaces and the seven heavenly halls.

Invoking angels: The summoning of angels by charms or incantation. Some angels can only be invoked at set times of the day, for specific reasons, or when the invocant is facing a certain direction.

Kamea: A Hebrew charm used for protection and to assist in invocation. Kameas are usually found with the name of an angel inscribed on them.

Master of the Art: In magic, the Master of the Art is the main person carrying out the conjuration or spell. According to texts such as *The Greater Key of Solomon*, this person will need to write out how to perform the desired magic spell and then bathe in water which has first been exorcised, before they can begin.

Planetary angels: In ancient astrology and occultism, each planet has a ruling angel. Depending on the belief system, planets may be assigned different angels.

Quinaries of the degrees of the zodiac: In Judaism and ancient astrology there are six quinaries (sets of five) degrees within each zodiacal sign. Each quinary has a ruling angel.

Seven Heavens: In Christianity, Judaism and Islam the universe is organised into seven heavens. In these religions the seven heavens are stacked on top of each other in a straight line, hovering above Earth. The closest to Earth is the First Heaven, and the furthest away is the Seventh Heaven.

The Four Winds: In the Book of Revelation angels stand at the four corners of the Earth holding back winds of destruction, protecting the Earth from devastation.

Tutelary angels: These are protective angels, like guardian angels. They appear in Christianity, Catholicism, Zoroastrianism, Judaism, Islam and in ancient philosophical traditions.

A'albiel: An angel serving under Michael (*qv*).

Aariel: *See* **Ariel**.

Aba: An angel who controls sexuality in humans.

Ababaloy: An angel invoked in Kabbalistic rites, mentioned in the *Grimorium Verum* (*qv*).

Abachta (Abagtha): One of the seven angels of confusion (*qv*).

Abaddon: Often mistaken for Satan (*qv*), Abaddon is the destructor or destroyer, the 'Destroying Angel of the Apocalypse', 'angel of the bottomless pit' and chief of the demons of the underworld hierarchy. It is the name the Jews gave to the Greek god, Apollyon, an angel of wrath, called upon by Moses (*qv*) in the name of God to bring the rains that devastated Egypt. In the Book of Revelation he is the angel (as Apollion), or star, of the bottomless abyss who chains Satan there for 1,000 years, although some sources ascribe this to Michael (*qv*). He is sometimes known as the dark angel who oversees the death of evil people. Other sources describe Abaddon as a place and not a spirit or demon – one of numerous prisons in Heaven that hold destructive angels. In *The Thanksgiving Hymns*, discovered among the Dead Sea Scrolls, 'the Sheol (Hell) of Abaddon' is mentioned and 'the torrents of Belial [that] burst into Abaddon'.

Abadon: A name for the underworld, according to *The Zohar* (*qv*).

Abagtha: *See* **Abachta**.

Abalidoth: An angel concerned, like Aba (*qv*), with human sexuality.

Abalim or Aralim: Another name for the order of angels known as Thrones (*qv*).

Aban: Ancient Persian angel of the month of October who also rules the tenth day of October. It is said that he sends a guardian angel to a child on his or her tenth birthday as well as ten months before eventual death.

Abariel: According to *The Greater Key of Solomon* (*qv*), Abariel's name is inscribed on the second pentacle of the moon.

Abasdarhon: Supreme ruling angel of the fifth hour of the night and of the fifth child in a family, mentioned in *The Lesser Key of Solomon* (*qv*).

Abathur Muzania: The Mandaean angel of the North Star who also oversees the scales in which the souls of the newly dead are weighed, a duty also ascribed to Nakir (*qv*) and Monker (*qv*).

Abay: An angel of the order of Dominations (*qv*) whose name is invoked in Kabbalistic rites.

Abbadona: A fallen angel and former member of the Seraphim (*qv*) who before his fall, was the close companion of Abdiel (*qv*). One source describes him as being not wholehearted in his attitude towards the rebellion and he is consequently known as 'the penitent angel'. According to Catholic doctrine, however, an angel who sins is 'fixed eternally in evil', no longer capable of having anything other than evil thoughts.

Abbaton: One of the many names meaning death, Abbaton is a guardian spirit at the gates of Hell. Also a holy angel used in magic rituals to control demons, mentioned in *The Greater Key of Solomon* (*qv*).

Abdals: Seventy mysterious spirits, according to Islam, whose names are known only to God and who ensure the continuous existence of the world. They are not immortal but, on the death of one, another is secretly appointed by God. Forty of them live in Syria.

Abdia: An angel whose name is inscribed on the outer circle of Solomon's pentagram in *The Lesser Key of Solomon* (*qv*).

Abdiel: In *The Book of the Angel Raziel* (*qv*), Abdiel is an angel of the celestial hierarchies. Milton describes him in *Paradise Lost* as the 'flaming seraph' who, on the first day of fighting in Heaven, defeats the rebel angels Ariel (*qv*), Arioc (*qv*) and Ramiel (*qv*). The Bible features Abdiel not as an angel but as a human.

Abdizriel: An angel of the mansions of the moon (*qv*).

Abedumabal: An angel invoked in magical prayer, noted in the *Grimorium Verum* (*qv*).

Abel: An angel who judges souls newly arrived in Heaven, one of 12 Powers (*qv*) allocated this task. According to the Testament of Abraham, Abel is the first of the 12 that the soul will encounter after Enoch, the heavenly scribe, has opened the book containing the soul's record. Also an angel of the Fourth Heaven ruling on Lord's Day (Sunday).

Abelech: An angel invoked to subdue infernal spirits during black magic rituals, documented in *The Lesser Key of Solomon* (*qv*).

Abezi-Thibod: Together with Rahab (*qv*), this angel is one of the damned princes who ruled Egypt. He fought Moses (*qv*) there, applying pressure to Pharaoh. When God closed the Red Sea Abezi-Thibod was drowned with Pharaoh's army and as a result he became a demon of that sea. He is the son of Beelzebub (*qv*).

Abheiel: An angel of the mansions of the moon (*qv*).

Abiou: *See* **Eiael**.

Abiressia: One of the 12 Powers (*qv*).

Ablati: According to *The Book of Ceremonial Magic* (*qv*), Ablati is invoked in the summoning of Uriel (*qv*). His was one of four names – along with Josata (*qv*), Agla (*qv*) and Calia (*qv*) – uttered by God to Moses on Mount Sinai.

Aboezra: Invoked in the benediction of the salt as laid out in the *Grimorium Verum* (*qv*).

Abracadabra: One of the most ancient words in magic said to derive from 'ha brachah dabarah' Hebrew for 'speak the blessing'. It is one of the three holy names used in conjuring the sword. Inscribed on a parchment and worn in an amulet or charm around the neck it is claimed to ward off illness and disease. Used as an invocation, 'Abracadabra' is chanted, each time reducing it by one letter until there is only the final 'A'.

Abragateh: Spirit or angel invoked in Solomonic prayer by the Master of the Art.

Abramus: *See* **Abrimas**.

Abrasiel: An angel of the seventh hour of the day, under Barginiel (*qv*), mentioned in *The Book of Ceremonial Magic* (*qv*).

Abraxas: Known before his fall as 'Abraxiel', he governed the winds alongside Ariel (*qv*). To the Gnostics, he was the Supreme Unknown, his name the same as God's. He was also an angel of the Aeons (*qv*). To the Persians he was the source of the 365 emanations, and is identified with the 365 days of the year. The word 'Abracadabra' is derived from his name and invokes Ariel's power over the healing of sickness and fever. Some sources describe him as a mediator between God and the animate creatures of Earth. He is said to be waiting, doing nothing until the arrival of the next messiah, at which point he will reappear.

Abrid: An angel of the summer equinox who in the Jewish tradition is a 'Menumim' or ministering angel, invoked to ward off evil. He is most powerful when invoked during the time of the summer equinox.

Abriel: A former member of the order of Dominations (*qv*), used in Kabbalistic ritual.

Abrimas (Abramus): An angel who is invoked at the close of the Jewish Sabbath.

Abru-El: In Islam, a manifestation of Jibril (*qv*).

Abrunael: An angel of the mansions of the moon (*qv*).

Absinthium: The Latin word for Wormwood (*qv*).

Abuhaza: An angel who rules Monday, under Arcan (*qv*), ruler of the angels of the air (*qv*) on Monday. He also assists Raphael (*qv*) and Ariel (*qv*) in the creation of warm winds.

Abuionij: An angel who serves in the Second Heaven, mentioned in *The Sixth and Seventh Books of Moses* (*qv*).

Abuiori: Resident in either the Second or Third Heaven, an angel of Wednesday invoked from the North.

Abuliel: According to Jewish Occult lore, an inconsequential angel involved in the transmission of prayers, acting as an assistant to one of the supreme angels of prayer – Akatriel (*qv*), Metatron (*qv*), Michael (*qv*), Raphael (*qv*), Sandalphon (*qv*) or Sizouse (*qv*).

Abuzohar: An angel of the moon (*qv*), serving on Monday, who in Gabriel's (*qv*) absence replaces him as the moon's 'voice'. He can also be invoked in magic rituals.

Accusing Angel: In the Book of Job, he appears as the adversary to Satan. Also known as Sammael (*qv*) or Mastema (*qv*).

Achaiah: In the Kabbalah, one of eight Seraphim (*qv*). Also the angel of patience who also holds dominion over the secrets of nature.

Achamoth: In Gnosticism, a daughter of the aeon (*qv*) Sophia (*qv*) and mother of the evil god, Iadalbaoth (*qv*).

Achartiel and Achathriel: Two names inscribed on kameas that are used to ward off the evil eye.

Achazriel: An angelic usher in the celestial court.

Acheliah: An angel of the Venus sphere whose name is inscribed on its first pentacle.

Achides: An angel of the Venus sphere whose name is inscribed on its third pentacle, mentioned in *The Greater Key of Solomon* (*qv*).

Achsah: An angel of benevolence invoked by the Master of the Art in Solomonic conjurings, documented in *The Greater Key of Solomon* (*qv*).

Achusaton: One of the 15 angels of the throne (*qv*) listed in *The Sixth and Seventh Books of Moses* (*qv*). He governs parts of Africa.

Aciel: One of seven planetary subrulers serving under the angel Raphael (*qv*), according to the *Testament of Solomon* (*qv*).

Aclahaye: An angel of luck and gambling and one of the genii of the fourth hour, documented in *The Nuctemeron* (*qv*).

Acrabiel: An angel who governs one of the Zodiac signs, according to Cornelius Agrippa (*qv*).

Acrimonymachamarei: The *Pistis Sophia* (*qv*) describes him as first among three 'standing high in the Gnostic hierarchy of deities; master of the heavenly firmaments.' He can be invoked in magic rites.

Adabiel: One of the seven archangels listed in Thomas Heywood's *The Hierarchy of the Blessèd Angels* (*qv*). One of the few angels under Zadkiel (*qv*) who governs Jupiter in his absence. He is sometimes paired with the Nergal (*qv*), king of Hades.

Adad: Divinity of thunder and 'lord of foresight' in Assyro-Babylonian mythology.

Adadiyah: One of the numerous names for the angel Metatron (*qv*).

Adam: *See* opposite.

Adatiel: A spirit of elemental air invoked in magic rituals.

Adeo: In *The Sixth and Seventh Books of Moses* (*qv*), one of the angels of the Dominations (*qv*), invoked during magic rituals.

Adernahael: An angel given a magic formula by God to create an Ethiopian amulet to cure colic and stomach problems. He gives protection and independence, honesty and strong will and is of the first Choir of Angels. He is an angel of November and is ruler of the sun sign, Sagittarius.

Adhaijijon: An angel of the seal invoked in rituals, according to *The Sixth and Seventh Books of Moses* (*qv*).

Adhar: One of the many names for the angel Metatron (*qv*).

Adiel: An angel of the Seventh Heaven.

Adir: One of the many names of God. His name is used in conjuring by progressive shortening as it is chanted.

Adirael: A servant of Beelzebub (*qv*), Lucifer's (*qv*) most loyal minister, and the only angel created by him before his fall. He fell with both of them, the third angel to be thrown into Hell.

Adiram: An angel invoked to consecrate the salt, referred to in the *Grimorium Verum* (*qv*).

Adiriah: An angel of the Seventh Heaven.

Adiriel: An angel of the Fifth Heaven, mentioned in *The Zohar* (*qv*).

Adiririon: A guard stationed at one of the halls or palaces of the First Heaven, he is a Power (*qv*) and a Dominion (*qv*) who is the angelic chief of

ABOVE: *Adam*, by Lucas Cranach the Elder, 1528

Adam: Believed to be the first man created by God in Christianity, Islam and Judaism. Known as 'the bright angel' in the book *The Life of Adam and Eve* and a 'second angel' in *2 Enoch* (see *The Book of Enoch*). Adam is described as spanning 'the Earth to the firmament' when he was created, according to the Bereshith Rabba Hebrew version of the Old Testament. According to The Talmud, Adam was originally androgynous, the exact image of God. *The Life of Adam and Eve* tells that Adam was whisked to Heaven by Michael (*qv*) in a fiery chariot. Another story has him being brought out of Hell by Jesus and taken to Heaven with the other 'saints in chains'. This book also recounts how he was buried by the archangels Uriel (*qv*), Gabriel (*qv*), Raphael (*qv*) and Michael (*qv*). In *The Kabbalah Unveiled*, S. L. MacGregor Mathers writes that the ten sephiroth (*qv*) constitute the archetypal man, Adam Kadmon.

'the might of God'. He is invoked as an amulet against the evil eye and is associated with Adiriel (*qv*). His name is also a name for God. In *The Book of the Angel Raziel* (*qv*), he is described as a 'trusty healing-God, in whose hands are the Heavenly and earthly households'.

Adityas: A group of seven celestial deities or angels of the Vedic pantheon:

> Varuna (leader)
> Mithra
> Savitar
> Bhaga
> Indri
> Daksha
> Surya.

Adjuchas: An angel of the rocks and one of the genii of the 11th hour, mentioned in *The Nuctemeron* (*qv*).

Admael: Living in the Second Heaven, one of the seven archangels holding dominion over Earth.

Adnachiel (Advachiel): A regent of the Seraphim (*qv*) who holds dominion over the zodiac sign Sagittarius and the month of November, watching all who are born in that month. One of two ruling angels of the choir of angels, the other being Phalec (*qv*). Another angel said to have been given an amulet by God that cures stomach ailments.

Adnai: An angel of the Venus sphere whose name is inscribed on its pentacle. He is invoked during love rituals, according to *The Greater Key of Solomon* (*qv*).

Adnarel: According to the writings of Enoch, one of the angelic rulers of the seasons, particularly winter.

Adoil: A divine creature of light and a primordial essence summoned by God from the invisible depths and commanded to burst asunder. Everything in the world that is visible is derived from Adoil.

Adonael: An angel invoked to exorcise the demons of illness, Bobel and Metathiax. Listed in the *Testament of Solomon* as one of the seven archangels (*qv*).

Adonaeth: An angel invoked to exorcise the demon Ichthion who causes paralysis.

Adonai: The Phoenicians considered Adonai to be one of the seven angels of the Divine Presence who created the universe. He is invoked to conjure wax and to exorcise fire. Gnostics believe him to be one of seven Elohim (*qv*) created by Iadalbaoth (*qv*) in his own image. Adonai is another name for God and in the Old Testament is written 'When I have mercy on the world, I am Adonai'.

Adonaios: According to Gnosticism, he is one of the seven archons (*qv*) of the Hebdomad, rulers of the seven Heavens and one of the 12 Powers (*qv*) created by Iadalbaoth (*qv*).

Adoniel: According to *The Lesser Key of Solomon* (*qv*), Adoniel is an angel of Jupiter used in magic rituals and a regent of midnight. His name is inscribed on the fourth pentacle of the planet Jupiter with the name of the angel, Bariel (*qv*).

Adossia: A fictional angel created by G.I. Gurdjieff.

Adoth: A Cherub (*qv*) or Seraph (*qv*) used in conjuring rites in *The Sixth and Seventh Books of Moses* (*qv*).

Adoyahel: Listed in *The Sixth and Seventh Books of Moses* as one of the 15 ruling princes of the order of Thrones (*qv*).

Adrael: An angel of the First Heaven.

Adrai: An angel invoked when conjuring ink and colours, mentioned in *The Greater Key of Solomon* (*qv*).

Adrammelechk: A fallen angel formerly of the order of Thrones (*qv*). He is the eighth of the ten archdemons, Great Minister and Chancellor of the Order of the Fly (Grand Cross), an order that Beelzebub (*qv*) is said to have founded. When conjured up during black magic rituals he appears in the form of a mule, a peacock or a horse. In Kings II he is said to be a god of the Sexpartite colony in Samaria to whom children were sacrificed. In Milton's *Paradise Lost* he is a fallen angel defeated in combat by Uriel (*qv*) and Raphael (*qv*). In *Der Messias* ('The Messiah') by

18th-century German poet, Friedrich Gottlieb Klopstock, he is the enemy of God described as 'greater in malice, guile, ambition and mischief than Satan, a fiend more curst, a deeper hypocrite.'

Adrapen: A chief angel of the ninth hour of the night who serves under Nacoriel (*qv*).

Adriel: Ruling angel of the mansions of the moon (*qv*) and an angel of death (*qv*) and final judgement. *The Hierarchy of the Blessèd Angels* (*qv*) by Thomas Heywood, says that he will 'in the last days slay all the souls then living.' Also one of the angelic guards of the gates of the South Wind.

Adrigon: One of the many names for the angel Metatron (*qv*).

Advachiel: *See* **Adnachiel**.

Aebel: With Shetel (*qv*) and Anush (*qv*) one of the three ministering angels appointed by God to serve Adam (*qv*).

Aeglun: A genius of lightning and one of the genii of the 11th hour, documented in *The Nuctemeron* (*qv*).

Aehaiah: One of the 72 angels bearing the name of God Shemhamphorae.

Aeon: The aeon, equated with archons (*qv*), is a celestial power of high order, a term that designates the first created being or beings. There have been 365 aeons since Creation, the most important being – apart from Abraxas (*qv*) – Sophia (*qv*), the female personification of wisdom, and Dynamis (*qv*), the male personification of power. The aeons were listed amongst the ten angelic orders before the 6th century, personalized by the 3rd-century Christian writer and saint, Hippolytus, as Bythios, Mixis, Ageratos, Henosis, Autophyes, Hedone, Akinetos, Nongenes and Macaria.

Aetherial Powers: Milton describes the angels thus in *Paradise Regained*.

Af: An angel of the Seventh Heaven who is 500 parasangs – 1,500 miles – tall, made from chains of black and red fire. One of the angels of destruction (*qv*), he is a prince of wrath and rules over the death of humans. He is said to have swallowed Moses (*qv*) up to the 'circumcised member' but was forced to spit him out when Moses' wife Zipporah circumcised her son Gresham to appease God's anger with her husband after he forgot to perform the rite.

Af Bri: An angel who exercises control over rain and looks after the people of Israel.

Afafiel: A guardian of the Seventh Heaven.

Affafniel: Prince of the 16 faces and a wrathful angel of God's divine anger. He has four constantly changing faces on each side of his head. Noted in *The Book of the Angel Raziel* (*qv*).

Afkiel: A guardian of the Fifth Heaven.

Afriel: Possibly Raphael (*qv*) in disguise, an angel of force or power who was able to prevent the female destroyer of children, Obizuth (*qv*), from killing young people. Afriel is thought to grant youth, vigour and vitality.

Afsi-Khof: An angelic governor of the month of Av (July-August).

Aftiel: The angel of twilight.

Agad: In Kabbalism, Agad is an angel of the order of Powers (*qv*).

Agaf: A Jewish angel of destruction invoked in rites at the end of the Sabbath.

Agalmaturod: A 'most holy angel of God' according to *The Greater Key of Solomon* (*qv*).

Agares (Agreas): A fallen angel who was once of the order of Virtues (*qv*). Served by 31 legions of infernal spirits, when invoked, he appears as an old man astride a crocodile, carrying a goshawk. He has the ability to teach languages and the power to cause earthquakes. He is said to have been one of the 72 spirits shut up by Solomon in a brass vessel that was cast into a deep lake or possibly banished to Lower Egypt.

Agason: Invoked in Solomonic ritual as 'thy Most Holy Name Agason', mentioned in the *Grimorium Verum* (*qv*).

Agathodaemon: 'The seven-vowelled serpent [Seraph], the Christ.' He comes from the

Egyptian serpent Agathodaimon, the good spirit, as opposed to Kakadaimon, the evil one. He is a guardian angel or genius comparable with the Greek god, Hermes (*qv*).

Agbas: An angel guarding the Fourth Heaven.

Agiel: One of the angels whose name is inscribed on the first pentacle of Mercury. Paracelsus (*qv*), describes him in his doctrine of talismans as the presiding angel of the planet Saturn, working together with Zazel (*qv*).

Agkagdiel: A guardian of the Seventh Heaven.

Agla: A name that is a combination of the first letters of the words of the Hebrew saying 'atha gadol leolam Adonai' meaning 'Thou art forever mighty, Lord'. He is a Kabbalistic angel of the seal invoked in conjuring the reed and is also invoked in Monday conjurations addressed to Lucifer (*qv*). Agla is a powerful magic word used in exorcizing demons and was also the name of God used by Joseph when he was set free from his brothers.

Agmatia: An angel of unknown origin who appears in *Jewish Gnosticism, Merkabah Mysticism and Talmudic Tradition* by German Jewish historian and philosopher, Gershom Scholem.

Agrat bat Mahlat (Iggereth bath Mahalath): An angel of prostitution (*qv*). One of the three wives of Sammael (*qv*), the others being Lilith (*qv*) and Naamah (*qv*).

Agreas: *See* **Agares**.

Agrippa, Cornelius: A German alchemist, magician, Occult writer and astrologer from the early 16th century.

Agromiel: An angel guarding the Sixth Heaven.

Aha: An angel of the order of Dominations (*qv*), invoked during Kabbalistic ritual as a spirit of fire, according to *The Sixth and Seventh Books of Moses* (*qv*).

Ahabiel: An angel invoked when creating love charms.

Ahadiel: An angelic law enforcer.

Ahadiss: A ruling angel of the Hebrew month of Cheshvan (October-November).

Ahaha: An angel of the seal (*qv*), according to *The Sixth and Seventh Books of Moses* (*qv*).

Ahaij: An angel of the sphere of Mercury, recorded in *The Sixth and Seventh Books of Moses* (*qv*).

Ahamniel: A chief angel-prince appointed to the Sword by God, noted in *The Sword of Moses* (*qv*). Ahamniel is tasked with presiding over law and order in Heaven and on Earth.

Ahaniel: One of the 70 amulet angels (*qv*).

Ahariel: Ruler of Monday and assistant to Gabriel (*qv*).

Ahassior: Ruler of the month of Tevet (December–January in the Hebrew calendar).

Ahaviel: The name of an angel inscribed on a kamea in Hebrew lore.

Ahiah: Son of the fallen angel Semyaza (*qv*).

Ahiel: An assistant to Qafsiel (*qv*), a regent of Saturday who is a childbirth amulet angel (*qv*).

Ahjma'il: An Islamic guardian angel invoked during exorcisms.

Ahriman (Ariman): Persian prince of evil, equivalent to Satan (*qv*), feared as the destroyer of the world. He is partnered with and recognized as being as powerful as the Asuras (*qv*) but it is predicted that he will be overcome by the great Persian 'omniscient lord of Heaven and Earth.'

Ahzariel: The name of an angel inscribed on a kamea, in Hebrew lore.

Aiavel: One of the 72 zodiac angels.

Aiel: An angelic ruler of Sunday, residing in the Fourth Heaven, mentioned in *The Lesser Key of Solomon* (*qv*).

Ailoaios: Gnostic ruler of the Second Gate 'leading to the aeon of the archons'.

Aishim: *See* **Ishim**.

Aisthesis: In Gnosticism an angel of wisdom emanating from the divine will.

Akae: Mentioned in *The Book of Enoch* (*qv*) as 'the ineffable name of God, the knowledge of which gives man the power of acting almost like one of the superior beings.' In *1 Enoch*, the angel Kasbeel (*qv*), chief of oaths, places this oath Akae in Michael's (*qv*) hand. The power of this oath enables the sea and the Earth to be created.

Akatriel (Yehadriel): A supreme prince regent of the Seventh Heaven and one of the great crown judgement princes placed over all angels. He is often paired with God himself and is equated with the Old Testament term 'angel of the Lord'. According to the Kabbalah, Akatriel is the name of the godhead that appears on God's Throne of Glory. Metatron (*qv*) appears in his place in an 8th-century apocalyptic text.

Aker: One of the nine regents – Angels at the World's End (*qv*) – who will pass judgement at the end of the world.

Akrasiel: His name is almost certainly another form of Ariel (*qv*) or Galizur (*qv*). He is the angel of proclamation, guardian of the last gate in Heaven and is a Herald of the Lord. He revealed the divine mysteries to Adam (*qv*) and he was delegated to announce that Moses' (*qv*) prayer was not to be allowed to ascend to Heaven. It was decided he was to die despite pleading to live longer.

Akriel: The angel of barrenness who is also the inspiration for intellectual achievement, memory and knowledge, appealed to in order to avoid looking stupid. He is invoked when reciting verses from Deuteronomy.

Akteriel: An angel asked by Sandalphon (*qv*) to tell him how Sammael (*qv*), a prince of evil, and his hosts could be vanquished. The venture failed, even with the help of Sandalphon's twin brother Metatron (*qv*). It proved that even the greatest of angels could not overcome evil.

Akzariel: The name of an angel inscribed on a kamea, in Hebrew lore.

Alad: A name given to Nergal, lord of the dead.

Al Ussa: A female angel in Arab mythology whose idol was destroyed on the orders of Mohammed.

Aladiah: One of the 72 angels that carry the name of God Shemhamphorae.

Alaliyah: One of the many names of the angel Metatron (*qv*).

Alamaqanael: An angel who guards the gates of the West Wind.**Alat**: An angel of the Seventh Heaven.

Alazaion: 'A most holy angel of God', according to *The Greater Key of Solomon* (*qv*). Alazaion can be invoked in the conjuring of the reed, as mentioned in *The Book of Ceremonial Magic* (*qv*).

Albim: An angel who guards the gates of the West Wind.

Albion's Angel: *See* page 48.

Albrot: One of the three holy names used in the conjuring of the sword, as mentioned in the *Grimorium Verum* (*qv*).

Alcin: An angel who guards the gates of the West Wind.

Alfatha: An angel who rules the North. Gabriel (*qv*) and Chairoum (*qv*) also exercise dominion over the North, according to various sources.

Alimiel: One of five angels of the first altitude. He is also said to be one of seven angels guarding the curtain that hangs in front of God's throne.

Alimon: Described in *The Sixth and Seventh Books of Moses* (*qv*) as a great angelic prince who, when invoked, protects from gunshot wounds and sharp instruments. His assistants are the angels Reivtip and Taftian (*qv*).

Almiras: 'The master and chief of invisibility'. To contact him the invocant must possess the magic ring of King Gyges of Lydia, a ring found by Gyges while he was a shepherd that allowed him to murder the king, win the heart of the queen and become king.

Almon: An angel who guards the Fourth Heaven.

Alphariza: An angel of the Second Heaven and an intelligence of the second altitude with Armon (*qv*), Genon (*qv*), Geron (*qv*) and Gereimon (*qv*).

Alphun: Described in *The Nuctemeron* (*qv*) as the angel of doves and a ruler of the eighth hour of the day.

Alpiel: An angel or demon ruling over fruit trees in Hebrew mysticism.

Altarib: An angel ruler of winter who can be invoked in magical rites.

ABOVE: *Visions of the Daughters of Albion*
by William Blake, 1793

Albion's Angel: An angel that appears in the painting by English artist, visionary and writer William Blake, entitled *Breach in the City – In the Morning After Battle*, used as the frontispiece for Blake's book *Visions of the Daughters of Albion*, Albion being an ancient name for England.

Al-Zabamiya: A term in the Koran used to denote the 19 angelic guards of Hell.

Amabael: One of the two angels who exercise dominion over winter, the other being Altarib (*qv*).

Amabiel: An angel of human sexuality, ruler of the planet Mars and angel of the air on a Tuesday.

Amalek: Mentioned in *The Zohar* (*qv*), as a spirit identified with Sammael (*qv*) as 'the evil serpent, twin soul of the poison god.'

Amaliel: A angel of chastisement.

Amamael: An angelic guard of the Third Heaven.

Amarlia: Described in *The Sixth and Seventh Books of Moses* (*qv*) as an angel who emerged from Sodom to heal painful boils.

Amaros: *See* **Armaros**.

Amarzyom: One of the 15 Throne angels listed in *The Sixth and Seventh Books of Moses* (*qv*).

Amatiel: One of the four angels of spring. He can be appealed to for hope, re-birth and new beginnings.

Amatliel An angelic guard of the Third Heaven.

Amator: A Kabbalistic 'holy angelic name' to be used in conjuration after proper investiture.

Amazaroc: *See* **Amezyarak**.

Ambassadors: A term used to describe angels, e.g. 'the ambassadors of peace'.

Ambriel: A prince of the order of Thrones (*qv*) and ruling angel of the month of May and of Gemini; chief officer of the 12th hour of the night. His name is inscribed on a kamea that is used to ward off evil. Cited in *The Sixth and Seventh Book of Moses* (*qv*) as a spirit invoked under the seventh seal of the planet Mars, he is said to inspire clear communication.

Amerartat: The Zoroastrian angel of immortality and in early Persian lore one of six or seven archangels (Amesha Spentas [*qv*]). Some suggest that the Mohammed Marut, a fallen angel in the Koran, derives from Ameratat.

Amertati: An angel of death in Islamic lore. Also known as Mordad.

Amesha Spentas: Zoroastrian archangels, usually six in number, who rule over the planets and in Zoroastrianism are the first six emanations of the non-created Creator, through whom all subsequent creation was accomplished. They stand before God's throne and execute his orders and are sometimes identified with the Spirit of the Tree of Life. Their highest position of Occult significance is as the Svarah, beings that cannot be perceived by the senses. Their evil counterparts are the great demons or divas headed by Anra Mainya (Ahriman). The Amesha Spentas are:

Ameretat (immortality)
Aamaiti (holy harmony)
Asha (righteousness)
Haurvatat (salvation)
Kshathra Vairya (rulership)
Vohumanah (good thought).

Amezyarak (Amazaroc, Semyaza): One of 200 angels who came down from Heaven to marry female mortals. He also instructed conjurors and root cutters.

Amhiel: An angel's name inscribed on a kamea.

Amicar: Another name for God, a name that is invoked in prayer at Vesting.

Amides: Another angel whose name is invoked during prayer at Vesting.

Amilfaton: An angelic guard of the Seventh Heaven.

Amisiel: Described in *The Lesser Key of Solomon* (*qv*) as an angel of the fifth hour, under Sazquiel (*qv*).

Amisiyah: One of the many names of the angel Metatron (*qv*).

Amisor: A great angel invoked in Solomonic rites, especially during fumigation, mentioned in *Grimorium Verum* (*qv*).

Amitiel: An angel of truth (*qv*) used as a charm to ward off evil. Amongst other angels possessing such a power are Michael (*qv*) and Gabriel (*qv*). According to rabbinic writings, the angels of truth and peace were burned for opposing the creation of man.

Ammiel: An angel of the fourth hour of the day,

serving under Vachmiel (*qv*), also serving under Mendrion (*qv*) as an angel of the seventh hour of the night.

Amnixel: One of the angels governing the mansions of the moon (*qv*).

Amnodiel: One of the angels governing the mansions of the moon (*qv*) and, as a fallen angel, an extra in the list of the seven Electors of Hell.

Amoias: A mysterious Gnostic being to whom the mysteries of Creation were revealed, according to the apocryphal Gnostic text, the *Paraphrase of Shem*.

Ampharool: An angel described by Solomon as the 'king of the genii of flying'. He governs instant travel and will appear when summoned by name.

Amra'il: A guardian angel invoked during exorcisms, according to Islamic lore.

Amriel: *See* **Ambriel**.

Amshashpands: *See* **Amesha Spentas**.

Amtiel: An angel guarding the Third Heaven.

Amudiel: An angel listed as an extra in the list of the seven Electors of Hell.

Amuhael X: An angel invoked during conjuration, mentioned in *The Sword of Moses* (*qv*).

Amulet angels: In the Kabbalistic text, *Book of the Angel Raziel*, these angels can be invoked during childbirth to protect mother and baby against evil and injury.

Amulets and Talismans: An early 20th-century book by E.A. Wallace Budge on the ancient use of amulets in various mystical practices and cultures.

Amwak'il: A guardian angel invoked during exorcisms, according to Islamic lore.

Amy: A fallen angel, formerly of the order of Angels (*qv*) and the order of Powers (*qv*) who became a 'great president' in the underworld. He instructs in the secrets of astrology and the liberal arts. He has the ambition of returning to the seventh throne in 1,200 years. An angel of success, commerce and prosperity who protects those who own or want to start their own business.

Anabiel: A Kabbalistic angel invoked to cure stupidity.

Anabona: The name of an angel 'by which God formed man and the whole universe', according to *The Greater Key of Solomon* (*qv*). His name was heard by Moses (*qv*) when he received the Ten Commandments on Mount Sinai.

Anabotas: An angel invoked in Kabbalistic ritual.

Anachiel: In *The Greater Key of Solomon* (*qv*), one of the four angels inscribed in Hebrew on the third pentacle of the planet Saturn. Presiding angel of the planet Saturn.

Anael (Hamiel, Haniel): As angel of the planet Venus he presides over love and human sexuality. One of the seven archangels of creation and a regent of the order of Principalities (*qv*), he also presides over the Second Heaven, receiving the prayers that come from the First Heaven. He governs all the kings and kingdoms of Earth, is regent of the moon, holds dominion over the air and supervises the Friday angels.

Anafiel (Aniyel): Chief of the eight crown judgement angels of the Merkabah or Divine Chariot, keeper of the keys of the pearly gates, chief soul-bearer and prince of water. Designated to punish the angel Metatron (*qv*) by flogging him with 60 lashes of fire. In *3 Enoch* (See *The Book of Enoch*) it is written that he bore Enoch to Heaven where Enoch became Metatron.

Anahel: A prince of the Third Heaven, but serving in the Fourth. One of the angels guarding the gates of the West Wind.

Anahita (Anaitis): Female angel of the highest rank in Zoroastrianism. She is responsible for fruitfulness and fertility.

Anai: An angel invoked to command demons, according to *The Greater Key of Solomon* (*qv*).

Anaireton (Amereton): An angel invoked in rites involving the exorcism of the salt, mentioned in *The Book of Ceremonial Magic* (*qv*).

Anaitis: *See* **Anahita**.

Anak: The singular version of 'Anakim' (*qv*).

Anakim: The issue of fallen angels and mortal women – giants born so tall that their necks were said to reach the sun. In Genesis they are called Nephilim (*qv*).

Ananchel or Ananehel: An angel sent by God in order to make the Persian King Ahauerus find Esther attractive.

Anane: A fallen angel, according to *1 Enoch* (See *The Book of Enoch*).

Ananel: An angel viewed as both good and evil. In his evil form he is said to have descended from Heaven to Mount Hermon to introduce sin to mankind.

Ananiel: One of the angels guarding the gates of the South Wind.

Anaphaxeton: An angel invoked in magic rituals. When pronounced on Judgement Day, his name will summon the entire universe to the bar of justice. Also invoked in the blessing of water, mentioned in *The Book of Ceremonial Magic* (*qv*).

Anapion: Listed in *The Lesser Key of Solomon* (*qv*) as serving under Mendrion (*qv*), an angel of the seventh hour of the night.

Anas: *See* **Sihail**.

Anataniel: An angel prince of the hosts of X.

Anauel: Guardian angel for bankers and those engaged in commerce etc.

Anayz: An angel of Monday residing in the First Heaven and invoked from the South.

Anazachia: An angel whose name is one of four inscribed on the third pentacle of the planet Saturn, the others being Omeleil (*qv*), Anachiel (*qv*) and Arauchia (*qv*).

Anazimur: One of the seven angels of the thrones (*qv*) who resides in the First Heaven. These angels 'execute the commands of the potentates', according to *The Book of the Angel Raziel* (*qv*).

Ancient of Days: A term with a number of applications. In the Kabbalah, it is used in connection with Kether, First of the Sephiroth (*qv*) as well as with Macroposopos who is 'God as He is in himself.' It also denotes 'the holy ones of the highest'. In The Divine Names, Dionysius defines it as 'both the Eternity and the Time of all things prior to days and eternity and time'. It has also been used in connection with Israel.

Ancor: In *The Greater Key of Solomon* (*qv*), Ancor is an angel who is invoked in conjuring the reed. Also a name of God used in prayers at the vestment.

Andas: An angelic assistant to Varcan (*qv*), a king ruling the angels of the air on Sunday.

Aneb: An angel who rules an hour with the attribute 'Dieu Clement'.

Anepaton: Described as 'a high, holy angel of God' whose name is used in invocations. It is the name that Aaron uses to conjure up God.

Anereton: An angel summoned in Solomonic rituals, noted in *Grimorium Verum* (*qv*).

Anfial One of the 64 angel wardens of the celestial halls (*qv*).

Angel Bearing the Mystical Name of God Shemhamphorae: There are 72 of these angels: Aehaiah, Aladiah, Aniel, Annauel, Ariel, Asaliah, Cahthel, Calliel, Chavakiah, Damabiah, Daniel, Eiael, Elemiah, Haaiah, Haamiah, Habuiah, Hahahel, Hahaziah, Hahia, Hahuiah, Haiaiel, Hakamiah, Hanael, Harahel, Hariel, Iahhel, Iehuiah, Ieiaiel, Ieiazel, Ieilael, Ielahiah, Ieliel, Ihiazel, Iibamiah, Imamiah, Lauiah, Lecabel, Lehahiah, Lelahel, Leuuiah, Leviah, Mahasiah, Mebahel, Mebahiah, Mehekiel, Melahel, Meniel, Michael, Mihael, Mitzrael, Monadel, Nanael, Nelchael, Nemamiah, Nithael, Nilaihan, Numiah, Omael, Pahaliah, Poiel, Rehael, Reiiel, Rochel, Sealiah, Seehiah, Sitael, Terather, Umabel, Vasariah, Vehuel, Vehuiah, Vevaliah.

Angel (Order of): The order of the Angels is the last of the nine in the celestial hierarchy. Phalec (*qv*) and Adnachiel (*qv*) are the ruling princes.

Angel of the Ark of the Covenant: The Cherubim (*qv*), Zarall (*qv*) and Jael (*qv*). Sandolphon (*qv*) has been described as 'the left-hand Cherub of the Ark'.

Angel of Abortion: *See* **Kasdaye**.

Angel of Adversity: *See* **Mastema**.

Angel of Agriculture: *See* **Risnuch**.

Angels of the Air: These are angels with dominion over the air, according to Jewish mysticism and Occult lore.

Angel of Albion: *See* **Albion's Angel**.

Angel of the Altitude: The chief angel princes of the altitudes (otherwise known as 'chora') are:

First Altitude:

Alimiel (*qv*), Barakiel (*qv*), Gabriel (*qv*), Helison (*qv*), Lebes (*qv*).

They carry in their hands a banner or flag on which is a red cross, they wear a crown of rose flowers and speak in a low voice.

Second Altitude:

Alphiriza (*qv*), Armon (*qv*), Genon (*qv*), Geron (*qv*), Gereimon (*qv*).

They appear in the form of a child wearing satin garments, wear a crown of red gilliflowers and have reddish faces.

Third Altitude:

Eliphaniasai (*qv*), Elomnia (*qv*), Gedobonai (*qv*), Gelomiros (*qv*), Taranava (*qv*).

They appear in the form of a child or small woman, wearing clothes of green or silver and a crown of bay leaves. They leave behind them a sweetly scented perfume.

Fourth Altitude:

Barakiel*, Capitiel (*qv*), Deliel (*qv*), Gebiel (*qv*), Gediel (*qv*).

They appear in the form of small men or boys, wearing black and dark-green and in their hands they hold a bird 'which is naked'.

* Chief of both the First and Fourth Altitudes. The Altitudes can only be invoked at the proper hour of the day and month of the year.

Angel of Anger: During his visit to Paradise, Moses (*qv*) meets the angels of anger and wrath in the Seventh Heaven. He describes them as composed 'wholly of fire.'

Angel of Annihilation: Harbonah (*qv*) or Hasmed (*qv*) fulfills this role in the story of Esther and Ahaseurus. *See* **Ananchel**.

Angel of Announcements: *See* **Sirushi**.

Angel of Annunciation: Gabriel (*qv*), who has been painted many times by the great masters in his role of making the annunciation to Mary.

Angel of the Apocalypse: Orifiel but also Anael (*qv*), Zachariel (*qv*), Raphael (*qv*), Sammael (*qv*), Michael (*qv*) and Gabriel (*qv*). Cornelius Agrippa (*qv*) writes that each angel is permitted to reign for 354 years.

Angel of April: *See* **Asmodel**.

Angel of Aquarius: Ausiel (*qv*) in ceremonial magic.

Angel of Aquatic Animals: *See* **Manakel**.

Angel of Aries: *See* **Machidiel**.

Angel of Ascension: Described in the Acts of the Apostles as 'two men which stood by in white apparel' during the ascension of Jesus (*qv*) to Heaven. Many sources claim that there were two angels present, but they are never named.

Angel of Aspiration and Dreams: Gabriel (*qv*), in Occult lore.

Angel of August: *See* **Hamaliel**.

Angel of Autumn: Two angels guard autumn – Guabarel (*qv*) and Tarquam (*qv*).

Angel of the Balances: *See* **Soqed Hozi, Dokiel, Michael, Zehanpuryu'h**.

Angel of Barrenness: *See* **Akriel**.

Angel of Benevolence: *See* **Zadkiel, Hasdiel, Achsah**.

Angel Over Birds: *See* **Arael**.

Angel of the Bottomless Pit: *See* **Abaddon**.

Angel of Calculations: *See* **Butator**.

Angel of Chance (gambling): *See* **Barakiel, Rubiel** and **Uriel**.

Angel of Chaos: Michael (*qv*). However, when chaos is associated with darkness and darkness is associated with death, Satan (*qv*) fills the role.

Angel of the Chaste Hands: *See* **Ouestucati**.

Angel of Childbirth: There are 70 amulet angels invoked at childbirth as listed in *The Book of the Angel Raziel* (*qv*):   * Repeated names

1.Michael, 2.Gabriel, 3.Raphael, 4.Nuriel, 5.Kiddumiel, 6.Malkiel*, 7.Tzadkiel, 8.Padiel, 9.Zumiel, 10.Chafriel, 11.Zuriel, 12.Ranuel, 13.Yofiel, 14.Sturi(el?), 15.Gazriel, 16.Udriel, 17.Lahariel, 18.Chaskiel, 19.Rachmiah, 20.Katzhiel, 21.Schachniel, 22.Karkiel, 23.Ahiel, 24.Chaniel*, 25.Lahal, 26.Malchiel* 27.Shebniel, 28.Rachsiel, 29.Rumiel, 30.Kadmiel, 31.Kadal, 32.Chachmiel, 33.Ramal, 34.Katchiel, 35.Aniel, 36.Azriel, 37.Chachmal, 38.Machnia*, 39.Kaniel, 40.Griel or Grial, 41.Tzartak, 42.Ofiel, 43.Rachmiel, 44.Sensenya, 45.Udrgazyia, 46.Rsassiel, 47.Ramiel, 48.Sniel, 49.Tahariel, 50.Yezriel 51.Neria(h), 52.Samchia* (Samchiel), 53.Ygal, 54.Tsirya, 55.Rigal, 56.Tsuria, 57.Psisya, 58.Oriel, 59.Samchia*, 60.Machnia*, 61.Kenunit, 62.Yeruel, 63.Tatrusia, 64.Chaniel*, 65.Zechriel, 66.Variel, 67.Diniel, 68.Gdiel or Gediel, 69.Briel, 70.Ahaniel.

Angel of Cold: Unnamed angels, mentioned in the New Testament apocryphon, the *Revelation of John*.

Angel of the Colonies: Characters in William Blake's *Visions of the Daughters of Albion*.

Angel of Conception: *See* **Lailah**.

Angel of Confusion: The seven angels of confusion were sent to the court of Ahasueros by God to end this king's pleasure in the reign of Queen Esther. They are said to have participated in the downfall of the Tower of Babel. The angels are:

Abachta (*qv*), Harbonah (*qv*), Bigtha (*qv*), Carcas (*qv*), Biztha (*qv*), Mehuman (*qv*), Zethar (*qv*).

Angel of Corruption: In Talmudic lore, God assigned 70 guardian angels to rule the 70 nations of the Earth. They were corrupted by national bias and became angels of corruption. Only Michael (*qv*), guardian angel of Israel, was not corrupted.

Angel of the Covenant: Ascribed variously to Metatron (*qv*), Phadiel (*qv*), Michael (*qv*), Elijah

(*qv*), Mastema (*qv*) and even God himself.

Angel of Dawn: A title ascribed to the dragon in Revelations that is itself a metaphor for Lucifer (*qv*) or Satan (*qv*).

Angel of Death: Amongst the many angels of death are listed:

Adriel, Apollion, Azrael, Gabriel (in his role as guardian of Hades), Hemah, Kafziel, Kezef, Leviathan, Malach ha-Mavet, Mashhit, Metatron, Sammael, Yehudiah, Yetzer Hara.

Falasha writing names the angel of death as Suriel and Christian theologians name Michael (*qv*) because he is the angel who leads Christian souls into 'the eternal light'. Azrael is the Islamic angel of death and Mot is the Babylonian version. 19th-century Hebrew scholar, Samuel Schonblum, lists six angels of death:

Gabriel who presides over the lives of the young, Kafziel who presides over kings, Meshabber who presides over animals, Mashhit who presides over children, Af who presides over men, Hemah who presides over domestic animals.

The angel of death is not necessarily an evil or fallen angel, remaining in the service of God.

Angel of December: *See* **Haniel** and **Nadiel**. To the ancient Persians, Dai was the angel of the month of December.

Angel of the Deep: *See* **Tamiel** and **Rampel**.

Angel of Deliverance: Pedael (*qv*), to Jewish mystics.

Angel of the Deserts: An unnamed angel who participated in the first Sabbath.

Angel of Destruction: Uriel (*qv*), Harbonah (*qv*), Azriel (*qv*), Simkiel (*qv*), Za'afiel (*qv*), Af (*qv*), Kolazonta (*qv*), Hemah (*qv*) and Kemuel (*qv*), leader of the group, according to the Revelation of Moses, although the apocryphal Old Testament book *3 Enoch* (See *The Book of Enoch*) names the leader as Simkiel. In *3 Enoch* the angels of destruction equate to the angels of punishment and these may also be equated with vengeance, wrath, death and ire. They have also been compared to the Avestan devas from Zoroastrian scripture. According to the 19th-century Jewish-British scholar, Moses Gaster, there were 4,000 angels of destruction while Jewish legend claims 90,000 in Hell alone. They are said to have helped Egyptian magicians in the time of the Pharaoh. It is disputed amongst rabbinic scholars whether the angels of destruction work for God or the Devil but it is said that even when they are doing the devil's work they are performing it with the permission of God.

Angel of the Disk of the Sun: Chur, according to ancient Persian lore.

Angel of Divination: *See* **Eistibus**.

Angel of the Divine Presence (Angel of the Face): A term used by William Blake as a subtitle for his engraving 'The Laocoön'.

Angel of Dominations or Dominions: Zacharael (*qv*), prince of this particular order in the celestial hierarchy which is placed first in the second triad of the nine choirs.

Angel of Doves: *See* **Alphun**.

Angel of the Dust: *See* **Suphlatus**.

Angel of Earthquakes: *See* **Rashiel**.

Angel of the East: *See* **Michael, Gauriil, Ishliha** and **Gazardiel**.

Angel of Edom: Edom was another name for Rome but the angel of Edom was Satan (*qv*). In his dream, Jacob saw the angel of Edom on the ladder between Earth and Heaven.

Angel of Evil Deeds: An unnamed angel.

Angel of Fall (Autumn): Torquaret.

Angel of Fascination: *See* **Tablibik**.

Angel of Fasts: *See* **Sangariah**.

Angel of Fear: *See* **Morael** and **Yrouel**.

Angel of February: *See* **Barakiel**.

Angel of Fertility: *See* **Samandiriel** and **Yushamin**.

Angel of the Fifth Heaven: *See* **Sammael**.

Angel of Fire: *See* **Nathanael, Arel, Atuniel, Jehoel, Ardarel, Gabriel, Seraph** and **Uriel**.

Angel of the First Heaven: *See* **Gabriel, Pazriel, Sabrael** and **Sidriel**.

Angel of the Footstool: In Arabic legend, Kurzi is the angel of the footstool. He offers new arrivals in Heaven a pillar of light as a support during their interrogation by the divine judge.

Angel of Force: *See* **Afriel**.

Angel of Forests: *See* **Zuphlas**.

Angel of Forgetfulness: *See* **Poteh** and **Purah**.

Angel of the Four Winds:
    Uriel – the South
    Michael – the East
    Raphael – the West
    Gabriel – the North.

Angel of the Fourth Heaven: *See* **Michael, Shamshiel** and **Shahakiel**.

Angel of Friendship: *See* **Mihr**.

Angel of Fury: There are many angels in this role but Ksoppghiel (*qv*) is their leader.

Angel of the Future: Teiaiel (*qv*) and Ieiaiel (*qv*).

Angel of the Garden of Eden: *See* opposite.

Angel of Gemini: Ambriel (*qv*) and, in ceremonial magic rituals, Giel (*qv*). Another source lists Sagras (*qv*) and Saraiel (*qv*) as angels of Gemini.

Angel of Gethsemane: Chamuel (*qv*) is said to have been the angel who gave Jesus strength in Gethsemane, assuring him of resurrection. Other sources name Gabriel (*qv*) in this role.

Angel of Glory: The angels of glory, as a group, equate to the angels of sanctification (*qv*) and the angels of presence (*qv*).

Angel of Grace: *See* **Ananchel**.

Angel of the Great (or Mighty) Counsel: The Messiah; the Holy Ghost; the Head of Days.

Angel of Greece: *See* **Javan**.

Angel of Hades Uriel (*qv*) in his capacity as angel of the newly dead; Raphael (*qv*) as supervisor of departed souls.

Angel of Hail and Hailstorms: *See* **Baradiel**. Also mentioned in this context are Nuriel (*qv*) and Yurkami (*qv*).

Angel of Healing: Raphael (*qv*), but sometimes Sariel (*qv*) and Assiel (*qv*).

Angel of Health: Mumiah (*qv*) and sometimes Raphael (*qv*).

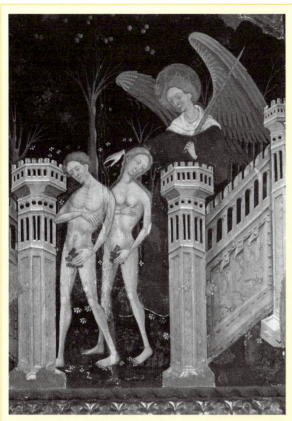

ABOVE: *Adam and Eve banished from Paradise*
Catalan School, *c.*14th century

Angel of the Garden of Eden: Metatron (*qv*) and Messiah (*qv*) – both Cherubim (*qv*) – are usually associated with the Garden of Eden. As a guardian of the Tree of Life, Raphael (*qv*) is also associated with this position. According to one source, Jophiel (*qv*) stands guard at the gates of the Garden of Eden with the flaming sword.

Angel of Heavenly Baptism: *See* **Seldac** (*qv*).

Angel of Hell: Hell has seven ruling angels under the leadership of Dumah. They are usually listed as: Dumah (*qv*), Kushiel (*qv*), Lahatiel (*qv*), Shaftiel (*qv*), Maccathiel (*qv*), Chutriel (*qv*), Pasiel (*qv*).

Angel of His Presence: Normally applied to the Tekamah – the female manifestation of God in man. Rabbinic lore lists 12 angels of this order, including Michael (*qv*), Gabriel (*qv*), Uriel (*qv*) and Zagzagael.

Angel of Hoarfrost: An unnamed angel who appears in *1 Enoch* (See *The Book of Enoch*).

Angel of the Holy Spirit: Gabriel (*qv*).

Angel of Horror: The Cherubim (*qv*) who surround the Throne of Glory, striking fear and terror into the hearts of all who behold them.

Angel of Hostility: Role usually ascribed to Mastema (*qv*).

Angel of the Hours of the Day and Night/Angel of the Days of the Week (*See* **Angel of the Seven Days of the Week**): In various faiths and traditions, certain angels are assigned specific hours of each day and night to watch over; some angels even have multiple 'shifts'. Besides the angels listed in the following tables, there are numerous other angels that can be invoked at certain days and times, to assist in magic spells and conjurations.

MONDAY			
HOURS OF THE DAY		HOURS OF THE NIGHT	
1. Gabriel	7. Raphael	1. Anael	7. Michael
2. Cassiel	8. Gabriel	2. Raphael	8. Anael
3. Sachiel	9. Cassiel	3. Gabriel	9. Raphael
4. Sammael	10. Sachiel	4. Cassiel	10. Gabriel
5. Michael	11. Sammael	5. Sachiel	11. Cassiel
6. Anael	12. Michael	6. Sammael	12. Sachiel

TUESDAY			
HOURS OF THE DAY		HOURS OF THE NIGHT	
1. Sammael	7. Sachiel	1. Cassiel	7. Gabriel
2. Michael	8. Sammael	2. Sachiel	8. Cassiel
3. Anael	9. Michael	3. Sammael	9. Sachiel
4. Raphael	10. Anael	4. Michael	10. Sammael
5. Gabriel	11. Raphael	5. Anael	11. Michael
6. Cassiel	12. Gabriel	6. Raphael	12. Anael

WEDNESDAY

Hours of the Day		Hours of the Night	
1. Raphael	7. Anael	1. Michael	7. Sammael
2. Gabriel	8. Raphael	2. Anael	8. Michael
3. Cassiel	9. Gabriel	3. Raphael	9. Anael
4. Sachiel	10. Cassiel	4. Gabriel	10. Raphael
5. Sammael	11. Sachiel	5. Cassiel	11. Gabriel
6. Michael	12. Sammael	6. Sachiel	12. Cassiel

THURSDAY

Hours of the Day		Hours of the Night	
1. Sachiel	7. Cassiel	1. Gabriel	7. Raphael
2. Samael	8. Sachiel	2. Cassiel	8. Gabriel
3. Michael	9. Sammael	3. Sachiel	9. Cassiel
4. Anael	10. Michael	4. Sammael	10. Sachiel
5. Raphael	11. Anael	5. Michael	11. Sammael
6. Gabriel	12. Raphael	6. Anael	12. Michael

FRIDAY

Hours of the Day		Hours of the Night	
1. Anael	7. Michael	1. Sammael	7. Sachiel
2. Raphael	8. Anael	2. Michael	8. Sammael
3. Gabriel	9. Raphael	3. Anael	9. Michael
4. Cassiel	10. Gabriel	4. Raphael	10. Anael
5. Sachiel	11. Cassiel	5. Gabriel	11. Raphael
6. Sammael	12. Sachiel	6. Cassiel	12. Gabriel

SATURDAY

Hours of the Day		Hours of the Night	
1. Cassiel	7. Gabriel	1. Raphael	7. Anael
2. Sachiel	8. Cassiel	2. Gabriel	8. Raphael
3. Sammael	9. Sachiel	3. Cassiel	9. Gabriel
4. Michael	10. Sammael	4. Sachiel	10. Cassiel
5. Anael	11. Michael	5. Sammael	11. Sachiel
6. Raphael	12. Anael	6. Michael	12. Sammael

SUNDAY

Hours of the Day		Hours of the Night	
1. Michael	7. Sammael	1. Sachael	7. Cassiel
2. Anael	8. Michael	2. Samiel	8. Sachiel
3. Raphael	9. Anael	3. Michael	9. Sammael
4. Gabriel	10. Raphael	4. Anael	10. Michael
5. Cassiel	11. Gabriel	5. Raphael	11. Anael
6. Sachiel	12. Cassiel	6. Gabriel	12. Raphael

Angel of Humanity: *See* **Eve**.

Angel of Hurricanes: *See* **Za'afiel**.

Angel of (or over) Immorality: Zethar (*qv*), an angel of confusion (*qv*).

Angel of Insolence: Rahab (*qv*) whose other roles encompass being angel or demon of the primordial waters and, sometimes, angel of death.

Angel of Insomnia: Michael (*qv*). He caused the sleepiness of Ahasuerus who had ordered the murder of every Jew in Persia.

Angel of Inventions: *See* **Liwet**.

Angel of Israel: *See* **Michael**.

Angel of January: *See* **Gabriel**.

Angel of Joy: *See* **Raphael**, **Gabriel**.

Angel of Judgement: *See* **Gabriel** and **Phalgus**.

Angel of July: *See* **Verchiel**.

Angel of June: *See* **Muriel**.

Angel of June-July: *See* **Imrief**.

Angel of (the planet) Jupiter: *See* **Zacharael**, **Zadkiel**, **Sachiel**, **Adabiel**, **Barchiel**.

Angel of Justice: *See* **Tsadkiel**, and **Azza**.

Angel of Knowledge: *See* **Raphael**.

Angel of the Last Judgement: *See* **Michael**, **Gabriel**, and **Abel**.

Angel (of the sign) of Leo: Ol, in ceremonial magic rituals. Sagham (*qv*) and Seratiel are governing spirits.

Angel of Libra (of the sign): Jael (*qv*). In *The Magus* (*qv*), Zuriel (*qv*) is named as the angel of liberty. The governing spirits are Grasgarben (*qv*) and Hadakiel (*qv*).

Angel of Life: Unnamed angel that features, along

with the similarly unnamed angel of death in Henry Wadsworth Longfellow's poem *The Two Angels*.

Angel of Light: Amongst those named as angels of light are Gabriel (*qv*), Jesus (*qv*) and Satan (*qv*), the latter, however, only in disguise. According to Jewish lore, the supernatural brightness of Isaac (*qv*) at birth makes him a candidate for this role.

Angel of Lightning: Barakiel (*qv*) – also angel of February and one of the seven archangels – or Uriel. *The Secret Lore of Magic* by Sirdar Ikbal Ali Shah postulates that the angel of lightning is the only power that can defeat the demon Envy.

Angel of the Light of Day: *See* **Shamshiel**.

Angel of Longevity: *See* **Seeheiah**, **Mumiah**, **Rehael**.

Angel of the Lord: Usually Michael (*qv*), Metatron (*qv*), Malachi (*qv*), Gabriel (*qv*), Akatriel (*qv*), Yehadriel (*qv*), Homadiel (*qv*), Phinehas (*qv*) amongst others. Used in the Old Testament it can most often be taken to mean God.

ABOVE: *Love and the Maiden*
by John Roddam Spencer Stanhope, 1877

Angel of Love: Theliel (*qv*), Rahmiel (*qv*), Raphael (*qv*), Donquel (*qv*) and others. The Kabbalah also describes the Roman goddess Venus as the angel of love. Talmudic, Zoroastrian and Mandean sources offer Liwet (*qv*) and Anael (*qv*) as angels of love. To the ancient Persians, Mihr (*qv*) oversaw love and friendship.

Angel of the Lord of Hosts: In Heaven it is Michael (*qv*), on Earth, it is the High Priest.

Angel of Love: *See* page 57.

Angel of Lust: Unnamed angel, although Pharzuph (*qv*) is named as 'the Hellespontian god of lust' by 4th-century Christian apologist, Arnobius of Sicca in his work, *Adversus Nationes*.

Angel of Luxury: Unnamed, but mentioned by 2nd-century Christian theologian, Origen, who claims that anyone who 'falls away from Michael (*qv*) is put into subjection to the angel of luxury, then to the angel of punishment.'

Angel of Mankind: *See* **Metatron**.

Angel of the Mansions of the Moon: Ancient astrologers not only worked with the 12 zodiac signs, but also with the 28 mansions of the moon. The mansions are the latitudes the moon passes as it completes its monthly journey around the Earth.

28 MANSIONS AND 28 ANGELS OF THE MOON

1. Geniel	15. Ataliel
2. Enediel	16. Azeruel
3. Anixiel	17. Adriel
4. Azariel	18. Egibiel
5. Gabriel	19. Amutiel
6. Dirachiel	20. Kyriel
7. Scheliel	21. Bethuael
8. Amnodiel	22. Geliel
9. Barbiel	23. Requiel
10. Ardefiel	24. Abrunael
11. Neciel	25. Aziel
12. Abdizriel	26. Tagriel
13. Jazeriel	27. Atheniel
14. Ergedial	28. Amnixiel

Angel of (the Planet) Mars: Uriel (*qv*), Sammael (*qv*). Khurdad in ancient Persian lore.

Angel of March: Machidiel (*qv*) and others. Farvardin (*qv*), who also governed the 19th day of each month, is known as angel of March in ancient Persian lore.

Angel of May: *See* **Ambriel** and **Afsi-Khof**.

Angel of Memory: *See* **Zachriel**, **Zadkiel**, **Mupiel**.

Angel of (the Planet) Mercury: Variously given as Tiriel (*qv*), Raphael (*qv*), Hasdiel (*qv*), Michael (*qv*) and Zadkiel (*qv*).

Angel of Mercy: Rahmiel (*qv*), Gabriel (*qv*), Michael (*qv*), Zehanpuryu (*qv*) and Zadkiel (*qv*).

Angel of Mighty Counsel: Another name for Christ, found in the Septuagint, a Greek version of the Hebrew Bible translated between the 3rd and 1st centuries BC in Alexandria.

Angel of Migration: Nadiel (*qv*). He is also the governing angel of the Hebrew month Kislev (November–December).

Angel of Mohammed: A 70,000-headed angel seen by Mohammed when he was transported to Heaven, each head singing praises to God.

Angel of Monday: Gabriel (*qv*), Arcan (*qv*), Missabu (*qv*), Abuhaza (*qv*) amongst others.

Angel of Mons: Angels on horseback reported to have appeared at the First World War Battle of Mons, helping the British to defeat the Germans.

Angel of the Twelve Months: There is an angel for each month of the year:

ANGEL OF THE TWELVE MONTHS

JANUARY: Gabriel	JULY: Verchiel
FEBRUARY: Barakiel	AUGUST: Hamaliel
MARCH: Machidiel	SEPTEMBER: Uriel
APRIL: Asmodel	OCTOBER: Barbiel
MAY: Ambriel	NOVEMBER: Adnachiel
JUNE: Muriel	DECEMBER: Haniel

ANGEL OF THE TWELVE MONTHS

IN ANCIENT PERSIAN LORE

JANUARY: Barman	JULY: Murdad
FEBRUARY: Isfandarmand	AUGUST: Sharivari
MARCH: Farvardin	SEPTEMBER: Mihr
APRIL: Ardibehist	OCTOBER: Aban
MAY: Khurdad	NOVEMBER: Azar
JUNE: Tir	DECEMBER: Dai

Angel of the Moon: Variously Yahriel (*qv*), Iachadiel (*qv*), Elimiel (*qv*), Gabriel (*qv*), Tsaphiel (*qv*), Zachariel, Iaqwiel (*qv*) and others.

Angel of Morals: Mehabiah who also assists mortals who want to have children.

Angel of Mountains: *See* **Rampel**.

Angel of the Muses: Uriel (*qv*), Israfel, Radueriel, Vretil (Pravuil). One source reports that the Novensiles – nine Etruscan gods – constituted the muses.

Angel of Music: *See* **Israfel**.

Angel of the Mutations of the Moon: *See* **Mah**.

Angel of Mysteries: Raziel (*qv*) and Gabriel (*qv*).

Angel of Night: *See* **Leliel**, **Metatron**, **Lailah**.

Angel of the Noonday Winds: *See* **Nariel**.

Angel of the North: *See* **Oertha**, **Alfatha**, **Uriel Chairoum**.

Angel of the North Wind: *See* **Chairoum**.

Angel of Nourishment: *See* **Isda**.

Angel of November: *See* **Adnachiel**. Azar (*qv*) was the ancient Persian angel for November.

Angel of Oblivion: *See* **Purah**.

Angel of October: *See* **Barbiel** (*qv*). Ancient Persians ascribed this role to Aban.

Angel of Omnipotence: There are eight angels are in this class, according to *The Sixth and Seventh Books of Moses* (*qv*):
Atuesuel, Ebuhuel, Elubatel, Tubatlu, Bualu, Tulatu, Labusi, Ublisi.

Angel of Oracles: *See* **Phaldor**.

Angel of Paradise: Representing Paradise in both its earthly and heavenly forms – Shamshiel (*qv*),

Michael (*qv*), Zephon (*qv*), Zotiel (*qv*), Johiel (*qv*), Gabriel (*qv*) and others. Mandaean lore names him as Rusvon (*qv*) and the ancient Persians as Sirushi (*qv*).

Angel of Patience: *See* **Achaiah**.

Angel of Peace: The angel of peace opposed the Creation, leading God to burn him along with those who served him. Along with the angel of truth, however, he was later brought back to life. Traditionally, there were seven angels of peace who visit every Jewish home at the start of the Sabbath. To the Gnostics, Melchisedec (*qv*) is angel of peace.

Angel of Persia: *See* **Dubbiel**.

Angel of Pisces: *See* **Pasiel**.

Angel of Plants: *See* **Sachluph**.

Angel of Poetry: *See* **Radueriel**.

Angel of (the Order of) Powers: Zacharael (*qv*), according to the Kabbalah. The *Testament of Abraham* names Michael (*qv*) as the angel of Powers (*qv*).

Angel of Prayer: There are six angels who are named in this role – Akatriel (*qv*), Gabriel (*qv*), Metatron (*qv*), Raphael (*qv*) and Sizouze (*qv*). It has been suggested, however, that Michael (*qv*) should be added, as there are seven archangels who convey the prayers of the saints to God.

Angel of Precipices: *See* **Zarobi**.

Angel of the Presence or **Angel of the Face**: Ten are listed:

Michael	Jehoel
Metatron	Zagzagael
Suriel	Uriel
Sandalphon	Yefefiah
Phanuel	Akatriel

They are equated with the angels of sanctification and the angels of glory (*qv*). It is an unnamed angel of the presence (*qv*) who tells Moses the story of the Creation. The patriarch

Judah claims to have been blessed by an unnamed angel of the presence.

Angel of Pride: *See* **Rahab** and **Satan**.

Angel of Priesthoods and Sacrifices: *See* **Sachiel-Meleck**.

Angel of Principalities: An order known also as Princedoms. Listed first in the third triad of the celestial hierarchy, the ruling angels include Haniel (*qv*), Nisroc (*qv*), Cerviel (*qv*) and Raguel (*qv*). The angels of Principalities (*qv*) are 'protectors of religion' and preside over good spirits.

Angel of Proclamation: Gabriel (*qv*), the angel of annunciation, but also Akrasiel (*qv*).

Angel of Progress: Mercury (*qv*), in the Kabbalah. Raphael (*qv*) is sometimes also given this title.

Angel of Prostitution: Lilith (*qv*), Naamah (*qv*) and Agrat bat Mahlat (*qv*), these angels are also named as wives of Sammael (*qv*).

Angel of Punishment: These seven angels are ruled by the archangels who are in turn answerable to the angels of death, according to The *Testament of Solomon* (*qv*):

> Kushiel ('rigid one of God')
> Lahatiel ('flaming one of God')
> Shoftiel ('judge of God')
> Makatiel ('plague of God')
> Hutriel ('rod of God')
> Pusiel ('fire of God')
> Rogziel ('wrath of God')

Amaliel (*qv*) is also sometimes considered an angel of punishment. The *Pistis Sophia* (*qv*) names Ariel (*qv*) as the angel in charge of punishment in Hell; Coptic Gnosticism names Asmodel (*qv*); the *Midrash Tehillim* (*qv*) lists five angels of punishment and five archangels of punishment:

Af – angel of anger
Kezef – angel of wrath
Hemah – angel of fury
Hasmed – angel of annihilation
Mashit – angel of destruction
Kezef – archangel of destruction

Af – archangel over the death of mortals
Hemah – archangel over the death of domestic animals
Masshit – archangel over the death of children
Meshabber – archangel over the death of animals

Angel of Purity: *See* **Taharial**.

Angel of Rain: *See* **Matarel**, **Riddia** and **Zalbesael**. The ancient Persians described Dara (*qv*) as angel of rain.

Angel of Repentance: Variously Michael (*qv*), Raphael (*qv*), Suriel (*qv*), Phanuel (*qv*).

Angel of Resurrection: This unnamed angel was responsible for rolling the stone away from the entrance to Jesus' tomb. Matthew (*qv*) calls him the angel of the Lord.

Angel of Revelation: *See* **Gabriel**.

Angel of Righteousness: *See* **Michael**.

Angel of the River Jordan: Silmai (*qv*) and Nidbai (*qv*).

Angel of Rivers: Trsiel (*qv*), according to *The Sword of Moses* (*qv*); Dara (*qv*) to the ancient Persians.

Angel of Rome: *See* **Sammael**.

Angel of Running Streams: *See* **Nahaliel**.

Angel of Sagittarius: *See* **Ayil**. The two governing spirits are Vhnori (*qv*) and Saritaiel (*qv*). According to *The Hierarchy of the Blessèd Angels* (*qv*) Adnachiel (*qv*) occupies this role.

Angel of Salvation: *See* **Haurvatat**. Uriel (*qv*) is also named in this position.

Angel of Sanctification: Amongst the main contenders for this role are Phanuel (*qv*), Suriel (*qv*), Metatron (*qv*), and Michael (*qv*). Like the angels of the presence (*qv*) with whom they are equated, they were created already circumcized.

Angel of Saturn: Variously named as Orifiel (*qv*), Kafziel (*qv*), Michael (*qv*), Orifel (*qv*), Mael (*qv*), Zaphiel (*qv*), Schebtaiel (*qv*). Several sources name him as Zapkiel. Henry Wadsworth Longfellow in *The Golden Legend* names Anachiel (*qv*) in this role.

Angel of Scandal: Zahun (*qv*) who is also one of the angels of the first hour.

Angel of Science: *See* **Raphael**.

Angel of Scorpio: *See* **Riehol** and **Saissaiel**.

Angel of the Sea: *See* opposite.

Angel of the Seal: In *The Sixth and Seventh Books of Moses* (*qv*), certain angels are assigned to seals – magical drawings which have instructions with them. Specific angels can be summoned to do the bidding of the invocant when called upon, by using the seal and following the instructions.

Angel of the Second Heaven: Raphael (*qv*) and Zacharael (*qv*).

Angel of September: Uriel (*qv*) or Zuriel (*qv*). The Hebrew month of Tishri (September-October) is governed by Pahadron (*qv*). To the ancient Persians the angel of September was Mihr (*qv*).

Angel of the Seven Heavens:

ANGEL OF THE SEVEN HEAVENS

FIRST HEAVEN (Shamain or Shamayim) – Gabriel

SECOND HEAVEN (Raquie or Raqia) – Zacharael and Raphael

THIRD HEAVEN (Sagun or Shehaqim) – Anahel and three sarim or subordinate princes, Jagniel, Rabacyel and Dalquiel)

FOURTH HEAVEN (Machonon or Machen) – Michael

FIFTH HEAVEN (Mathey or Machon) – Sandalphon or Sammael

SIXTH HEAVEN (Zebul) – Zachiel, assisted by Zebul by day and Sabath by night)

SEVENTH HEAVEN (Araboth) – Cassiel

Angel of the Seven Planets:

ANGELIC GOVERNORS OF THE SEVEN PLANETS

ACCORDING TO FRANCIS BARRETT IN *THE MAGUS*

THE SUN: Raphael and Michael	SATURN: Zaphiel and Orifiel
VENUS: Aniel or Haniel	JUPITER: Zadkiel
MERCURY: Michael	MARS: Camael
THE MOON: Gabriel	

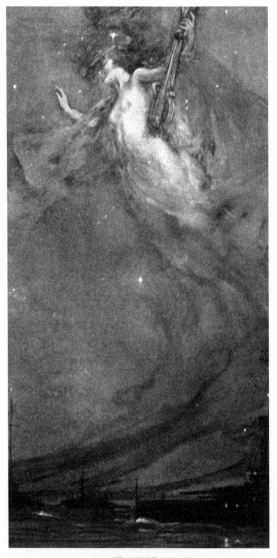

ABOVE: *The Middle Watch*, by Arthur David McCormic (1860–1943)

Angel of the Sea: Rahab (*qv*), according to the Talmud and Scripture. Rahab suffered destruction twice – for refusing to divide the upper and lower waters at Creation and for attempting to save from drowning the Egyptian soldiers pursuing the Hebrews across the Red Sea.

ANGELIC GOVERNORS OF THE SEVEN PLANETS

ACCORDING TO ISAAC AL-BARCELONI

THE SUN: Raphael	SATURN: Kafziel
VENUS: Aniel	JUPITER: Zadkiel
MERCURY: Michael	MARS: Sammael
THE MOON: Gabriel	

ACCORDING TO HENRY WADSWORTH LONGFELLOW IN 'THE GOLDEN LEGEND'

THE SUN: Raphael	SATURN: Orifel
VENUS: Anael	JUPITER: Zobiachel
MERCURY: Michael	MARS: Uriel
THE MOON: Gabriel	

The spirits, messengers and intelligences of the seven* planets are:

SUN
Spirits – Gabriel, Vionatraba, Corat
Messengers – Burchat, Suceratos, Capabile
Intelligences – Haludiel, Machasiel, Chassiel

MOON
Spirits – Gabriel, Madios
Messengers – Anael, Pabael, Ustael
Intelligences – Uriel, Naromiel, Abuori

SATURN
Spirits – Sammael, Bachiel, Astel
Messengers – Sachiel, Zoniel, Hubaril
Intelligences – Mael, Orael, Valnum

JUPITER
Spirits – Setchiel, Chedusitaniel, Corael
Messengers – Turel, Coniel, Babel
Intelligences – Kadiel, Maltiel, Huphatriel, Estael

VENUS
Spirits – Thamael, Tenariel, Arragon
Messengers – Peniel, Penael
Intelligences – Penat, Thiel, Rael, Teriapel

MERCURY
Spirits – Mathlai, Tarmiel, Baraborat
Messengers – Raphael, Ramel, Doremiel
Intelligences – Aiediat, Mediat, Sugmonos, Sallales

The Secret Grimoire of Turiel omits the Spirits,

Messengers and Intelligences for the planet Mars. The presiding spirits of the planets are:

    JUPITER – Sachiel, Castiel, Asasiel
    VENUS – Anael, Rachiel, Sachiel
    MARS – Sammael, Satael, Amabiel
    Mercury – Raphael, Uriel, Seraphiel

Angel of Showers: *See* **Zaa'fiel**.

Angel of the Sign of Cancer: Cael (*qv*). Another source says the governing spirits of this zodiac sign are Rahdar (*qv*) and Phakiel (*qv*).

Angel of the Sirocco: *See* **Sikiel**.

Angel of the Sixth Heaven: *See* **Zachiel**, **Zebul** and **Sandalphon**. The ruling prince of the Sixth Heaven is Bodiel (*qv*).

Angel of Silence: *See* **Shateiel** and **Dumah**.

Angel of the Sky: *See* **Sahaqiel**.

Angel of Sleep: An unnamed angel who brought insomnia to Ahasuerus in the story of Esther.

Angel Over Small Birds: *See* **Tubiel**.

Angel of Snow: Shalgiel (*qv*), Michael (*qv*). The apocryphal *Revelation of John* mentions angels of snow but does not name them.

Angel of Solitudes: *See* **Cassiel**.

Angel of Song: Radueriel (*qv*), choirmaster of the muses. In Islamic lore Israfel (*qv*) or Uriel (*qv*) is given the role. Rabbinic lore names Shemael (*qv*), or Metatron (*qv*) as angel of song. Metatron is also known as 'Master of Heavenly Song.'

Angel of the Sorrows of Death: *See* **Paraqlitos**.

Angel of the Souls of Men: *See* **Remiel**.

Angel of the South: *See* **Raphael**.

Angel of the Spheres: *See* **Salatheel** and **Jehudiel**.

Angels of the Spring: Amatiel (*qv*), Carcasa (*qv*), Core (*qv*) and Commissoros (*qv*) are the four angels of the spring with Spugliguel (*qv*) as the chief of the sign of spring. Milkiel (*qv*) is the ruling angel.

Angel of the Stars: *See* **Kakabel**.

Angel of Sterility: *See* **Akriel**.

Angel of the Storm: *See* **Zakkiel**, **Zaamael**.

Angel of Strength: *See* **Zeruch**.

Angel of Summer: *See* **Gargatel**, **Gaviel** and **Tariel**. Tubiel (*qv*) is the head of summer.

Angel of the Summer Equinox: Nine angels serve in this capacity, with their leader being Oranir (*qv*). They serve as amulets (protection) against the evil eye.

Angel of the Sun: A number of angels make up this order including Galgaliel (*qv*), Gazardiel (*qv*), Korshid (*qv*), Michael (*qv*), Och (*qv*), Raphael (*qv*), Uriel (*qv*), Zerachiel (*qv*) and others. The ancient Persians listed the angel of the disk of the sun as Churl.

Angel of the Sun's Rays: *See* **Schachlil**.

Angel of the Supreme Mysteries: *See* **Raziel**.

Angel of Sweet-Smelling Herbs: *See* **Arias**.

Angel Over Tame Beasts: *See* **Behemiel, Hariel**.

Angel Over Tartarus (or Hades): Uriel (*qv*) and sometimes Tataruchi (*qv*).

Angel of Taurus: *See* **Tual**.

Angel of Tears: Sandalphon (*qv*) and Cassiel (*qv*). This angel is unnamed in Islamic lore but resides in the Fourth Heaven.

Angel of Terror: Equated with the angels of quaking, they are the strongest hierarchs and surround the Throne of Glory. Pahadron (*qv*) is the main angel of terror in Jewish mysticism.

Angel of the Burning Bush: Some scholars suggest that the angel of the burning bush was not actually an angel but God himself disguised as an angel.

Angel of the Testament: John Salkeld names this angel as John the Baptist in his 17th-century work, *A Treatise on Angels*.

Angel of the Third Heaven: Rabacyel (*qv*), Dalquiel, Baradiel and Shapniel are amongst the principle rulers. Moses encountered the giant unnamed angel with 70,000 heads in the Third Heaven (Mohammed also encountered this being in Heaven). It is suggested that he is Erelim (*qv*), leader of the order of Erelim, or Raziel (*qv*).

Angel of the Throne: According to *The Book of the Angel Raziel* (*qv*), there are seven angels of the throne while Jewish lore claims that there are 70. Fifteen are listed in *The Sixth and Seventh Books of Moses* (*qv*). A number of these angels can be counted among the fallen angels residing in Hell. Thrones (*qv*) are third in the first triad of the celestial hierarchy.

Angel of Thunder: Ramiel (*qv*) and/or Uriel (*qv*) who is also the angel of fire and lightning. Assyro-Babylonian mythology ascribes the role to Adad (*qv*) and Rimmon (*qv*) is also mentioned in this capacity.

Angel of Time: Unnamed as Tarot card number 14. In *The History and Practice of Magic* Paul Christian names him as Rempha (*qv*).

Angel of the Torah: *See* **Iofiel, Zagzagel, Metatron**.

Angel of the Triplicities: Michael (*qv*) – ruler of the fiery triplicity; Raphael (*qv*) – ruler of the airy triplicity; Gabriel (*qv*) – ruler of the watery triplicity; Uriel (*qv*) – ruler of the earthy triplicity.

Angel of the Triune God: *See* **Meacheul, Lebatei** and **Ketuel**.

Angel of Truth: *See* **Amitiel, Michael** and **Gabriel**. The angel of truth was burned with the angel of peace and all their hosts, according to Jewish lore, for opposing Creation. Michael and Gabriel survived. It must, therefore have been Amitiel who was incinerated. Gabriel is the Islamic spirit of truth.

Angel of Twilight: *See* **Aftiel**.

Angel of Vegetables: *See* **Sealiah** and **Sofiel**.

Angel of Vengeance: At Creation God formed the 12 angels of vengeance amongst the first. We know the names of only six – Satanael (*qv*), Michael (*qv*), Gabriel (*qv*), Uriel (*qv*), Raphael (*qv*) and Nathanael (*qv*).

Angel of (the Planet) Venus: *See* **Anael, Hasdiel, Iurabatres, Hagiel** and **Noguel**.

Angel of Vindication: *See* **Dumah**.

Angel of Virgo: Voel (*qv*). One source says that the ruling spirits of this sign of the zodiac are Iadara (*qv*) and Schaltiel (*qv*).

Angel of (the Order of) Virtues: Among the ruling angels of this order are Ariel (*qv*), Barbiel (*qv*),

Haniel (*qv*), Peliel (*qv*) and Atuniel (*qv*).

Angel of Voyages: *See* **Susabo**.

Angel of War: *See* page 65.

Angel-Wardens of the Seven Celestial Halls:
There are 64 of these:

FIRST HEAVEN OR HALL

1. Suria	11. Huzia	19. Dahariel
2. Tutrachiel	12. Deheboryn	20. Maskiel
3. Tutrusiai	13. Adririon	21. Shoel
4. Zortek	14. Khabiel	22. Shaviel
5. Mufgar	(Head	
6. Ashrulyai	Supervisor)	
7. Sabriel	15. Tashriel	
8. Zahabriel	16. Nahuriel	
9. Tandal	17. Jekusiel	
10. Shokad	18. Tufiel	

SECOND HEAVEN OR HALL

23. Tagriel	25. Sahriel	28. Sakriel
(Chief)	26. Arfiel	29. Ragiel
24. Maspiel	27. Shariel	30. Sehibiel

THIRD HEAVEN OR HALL

31. Sheburiel	33. Shalmial	36. Hadrial
(Chief)	34. Savlial	37. Bezrial
32. Rtsutsiel	35. Harhaziel	

FOURTH HEAVEN OR HALL

38. Pachdial	41. Shchinial	44. Kfial
(Chief)	42. Shtukial	45. Anfial
39. Gvurtial	43. Arvial (or	
40. Kzuial	Avial)	

FIFTH HEAVEN OR HALL

46. Techial	49. Ganrial	53. Drial
(Chief)	50. Sefrial	54. Paltrial
47. Uzial	51. Garfial	
48. Gmial	52. Grial	

SIXTH HEAVEN OR HALL

55. Rumiel	58. Arsabrsbial	61. Machkiel
56. Katzfiel	59. Egrimiel	62. Tufriel
57. Gehegiel	60. Parziel	

SEVENTH HEAVEN OR HALL

63. Zeburial	64. Tutrebial

Angel of Water: *See* **Tharsis**. In Occult lore Michael (*qv*) and Anafiel (*qv*) appear in this role.

Angel of Water Insects: *See* **Shakziel**.

Angel of Weakness: *See* **Amaliel**.

Angel of the West: *See* **Gabriel**.

Angel of the Wheel of the Moon: *See* **Ofaniel**.

Angel of the Wheel of the Sun: *See* **Galgaliel**.

Angel of the Whirlwind: *See* **Zavael**.

Angel of the Wild Beasts: *See* **Mtniel** and **Hayyel**.

Angel of the Wilderness: The planet Saturn occupies this role, according to Jewish Kabbalah and other sources. Orifiel (*qv*) has also been named.

Angel Over Free Will: *See* **Tabris**.

Angel Over Fruit and Fruit Trees: *See* **Alpiel**, **Eirnilus**, **Ilaniel**, **Serakel** and **Sofiel**.

Angel Over Hidden Things: Sartael (*qv*) and Gethel (*qv*).

Angel Over Wild Fowl: *See* **Trgiaob**.

Angel of Winter: *See* **Amabael**, **Cetarari** and **Altarib**.

Angel of Wisdom: *See* **Zagzagel**.

Angel of the Womb: *See* **Armisael**.

Angel of Women's Paradise: These nine angels were once the wives, mothers and daughters of the Hebrew patriarchs. They resided in a separate part of one of the seven Heavens.

Angel (or Prince) of the World: *See* **Satan**.

Angel at the World's End: Nine angels will rule at the end of the world. *See* **Michael**, **Gabriel**, **Uriel**, **Raphael**, **Gabuthelon**, **Beburos**, **Zebuleon**, **Aker**, **Arpugitonos**.

Angel of Wrath: Hemah (*qv*), Af (*qv*), Mzpopiasaiel (*qv*), Ezrael (*qv*). Moses (*qv*) describes the angels of anger and wrath that he encountered during his visit to the Seventh Heaven as composed 'wholly of fire'.

Angel of the Wrath of God: Seven unnamed angels of the wrath of God are spoken of in Revelations.

Angel of Yetzirah: The angel of the Lord or God, himself. The term was used in the Old Testament to reduce the number of instances of God intervening in human affairs. It gave the appearance of his commands being carried out by angels.

Angel of the Zodiac: *See* **Twelve Spirits of the Zodiacal Cycle**.

Angerecton: An angel invoked for fumigation rites, mentioned in *Grimorium Verum* (*qv*).

Angromainyus: In Persian lore, he was God's adversary. He is the Zoroastrian equivalent of Satan (*qv*) but is not a fallen angel and is not subject to God. In the *Zend Avesta*, the main collection of sacred Zoroastrian texts, Angromainyus jumps from Heaven disguised as a snake. He then tries to fool Zoroaster (Zarathustra) into rebelling against the Persian equivalent of the supreme power, but fails.

Aniel: One of the numerous angelic guards of the gates of the West Wind. He is also one of the 72 angels bearing the name of God Shemhamphorae.

Anihi'el: One of the angel princes appointed by God to the Sword, according to *The Sword of Moses* (*qv*). Anihi'el is tasked with presiding over law and order in Heaven and on Earth.

Animastic (Animated): An order of angels called the Issim and consisting of nobles, lords and princes. Also refers to the guardian angel of Moses (*qv*).

Animated: *See* **Animastic**.

Anitor: An angel invoked in magical rites, according to *The Greater Key of Solomon* (*qv*).

Anituel: *See* **Aniquel**.

Anixiel: One of the angels governing the mansions of the moon (*qv*).

Aniyel: *See* **Anafiel**.

Anmael: A leader of the fallen angels who, like Semyaza (*qv*), comes to an arrangement with a mortal female (Istahar) in order to learn the Explicit Name (of God).

Annael: *See* **Aniel** and **Anael**.

Annauel: One of the 72 angels who have the name of God Shemhamphorae.

Annointed Cherub: The Prince of Tyre.

Anpiel: Guardian angel of birds, residing in the Sixth Heaven where he supervises 70 gates. He sanctifies the prayers of mortals with his 70 crowns before sending them to the Seventh Heaven for additional sanctification.

Ansiel: An angel who can be invoked in Jewish mysticism.

Antiel: An angel's name found on a kamea.

Anunna: Angels who, in Akkadian theology, are almost always terrestrial spirits.

ABOVE: *Stone figure of an angel half-buried in rubble following Allied bombing* by a German Photographer, 1945

Angel of War: *See* **Gadriel**.

Anush: One of three angels God appointed to serve Adam (*qv*), the others being Aebel (*qv*) and Shetel (*qv*).

Apar: Sometimes known as Aparsiel, Apar serves Sadqiel (*qv*) who rules the fifth day.

Aphiriza: *See* **Alphariza**.

Apollion: A Greek translation of the Hebrew name Abaddon which means 'the destroyer'. The angel of the bottomless pit who bound Satan for 1,000 years. In Occultism, he is an evil angel, emphasized by the fact that in his 17th-century Christian allegory, *Pilgrim's Progress*, John Bunyan made Apollo the devil.

Apostate Angel: *See* **Satan**.

Apragsin: *The Sword of Moses* (*qv*), describes Aparagsin as a divine messenger that God appointed to the Sword, he is tasked with presiding over law and order in Heaven and on Earth.

Apsu: The Babylonians considered Apsu as probably a female angel of the abyss. She is 'father' of the Babylonian gods and 'wife' of Tamat. Her son Ea finally kills her.

Apudiel: One of Cornelius Agrippa's (*qv*) Electors (*qv*) – the seven underworld planetary rulers.

Aputel: An angel mentioned in *The Greater Key of Solomon* (*qv*) used in invocation rites as well as the name worn by priests on their breasts when entering the holiest of holies. The name is supposed to have the power to revive the dead when uttered. Engraved on vessels of gold or brass it wards off evil.

Aqrab: In Islamic lore, an angel used in invocations.

Aquachai: A holy name used in rituals to control demons, documented in *The Greater Key of Solomon* (*qv*).

Arabonas: A spirit invoked in Solomonic rites by the Master of the Art.

Araboth: The Seventh Heaven. God resides here as well as the Seraphim (*qv*), Ofanim (*qv*), and the angels of love, fear, grace and dread.

Araciel: *See* **Araqiel**.

Arad: In Indo-Persian lore, an angel who is guardian over religion and science.

Araebel: An angel of the sixth hour, ruled by Samil (*qv*).

Arael: *See* Ariel.

Arafiel (Arapiel): According to *3 Enoch* (See *The Book of Enoch*), a great prince who stands before God's throne and represents 'the divine strength, majesty, and power.'

Arakiba: Fallen angel responsible for introducing sin to the Earth, according to *1 Enoch* (See *The Book of Enoch*).

Arakiel: *See* **Araqiel**.

Aralim: *See* **Erelim**.

Aramaiti (Armaiti): One of six Zoroastrian archangels (Amesha Spentas [*qv*]). He represents holy harmony.

Araphiel: A guardian of the second hall in Seventh Heaven.

Araquael: *See* **Araqiel**.

Araqiel (Araquael, Arakiel, Araciel): One of the fallen angels, according to *1 Enoch* (See *The Book of Enoch*). The angel of geography. In the 'Sibylline Oracles' – a collection of Occult utterances written in Greek and ascribed to the Sibyls (prophetesses) – he is not a fallen angel, but one of the five angels who leads souls to judgement.

Arariel: An angel in Occultism who cures stupidity and one of seven with dominion over the Earth, particularly water.

Ararita (Araritha): A name used in conjurations to command demons. Inscription on a gold plate means the invocant will not suffer a sudden death.

Araritha: *See* **Ararita**.

Arasbarasbiel: A guard of the Sixth Heaven in Judaism.

Arasek: Another name for Nisroc (*qv*), a fallen angel once of the order of Principalities (*qv*). Some sources say that he is chief of cuisine in Hell.

Arathiel: Chief angel of the first hour of the night, mentioned in *The Lesser Key of Solomon* (*qv*).

Arathron (Aratron): Chief of the angels over the planet Saturn and ruler of 49 of the 196 Olympic Provinces. Instructor of alchemy, magic and medicine, he can make people invisible and cause barren women to become fertile.

Aratron: *See* **Arathron**.

Arauchia: Name inscribed on the third pentacle of the planet Saturn, recorded in *The Greater Key of Solomon* (*qv*).

Araxiel: A fallen angel as listed by Enoch.

Arayekael: An angel prince appointed to the Sword. Arayekael is tasked with presiding over law and order in Heaven and on Earth.

Araziel: An angel who came to Earth to unite with female mortals. With Bagdal (*qv*) is a ruler of the zodiac sign, Taurus.

Arbatel: A 'revealing' angel, mentioned in *The Lesser Key of Solomon* (*qv*).

Arbiel: An angel working under Anael (*qv*), ruler of the sixth day.

Arcade: A fictional guardian angel from French writer Anatole France's novel *Revolt of the Angels*.

Arcan: Chief of the angels of the air and ruler of Monday.

Archan: An angel exercizing dominion over the moon's lower rays.

Archana: Name of an angel found inscribed on the fifth pentacle of the planet Saturn, mentioned in *The Greater Key of Solomon* (*qv*).

Archangels: *See* page 69.

Archangel of the Covenant: The Coptic text, the *Apocalypse of Paul*, describes Michael (*qv*) thus.

Archarzel: An angel invoked by the Master of the Arts in magic ritual.

Archer: A governing spirit, with Ssakmakiel (*qv*), of the zodiac sign Aquarius.

Archons (Rulers): Angels with responsibilities for nations and are identified or equated with aeons (*qv*). They are primordial planetary spirits.

Ardarel: An angel of fire in Occultism.

Ardefiel: An angel, sometimes known as Ardisiel, of the mansions of the moon (*qv*).

Ardibehist: The angel of April and an Amesha Spenta (*qv*) in ancient Persian religion. Ruler of the third day of the month.

Ardors: Term used by Milton in *Paradise Lost* to describe an order of angels of which Michael is a member.

Ardour: An angel governing the month of Tammuz (June-July).

Arehanah: An angel whose name is inscribed on the third pentacle of the planet Saturn, mentioned in *The Greater Key of Solomon* (*qv*).

Arel: An angel of fire whose name is inscribed on the seventh pentacle of the sun. He can also be invoked in ritual magic, according to *The Sword of Moses* (*qv*).

Arelim: *See* **Erelim**.

Arghiel: An angel whose name is invoked in magic ritual.

Arhum Hii (Rhum): Mandaean lore lists him as an angel of the North Star.

Ariael: *See* **Ariel**.

Arias: An angel of sweet-smelling herbs. To Occultists he is a demon – one of the 12 rulers of Hell, mentioned in *Dictionairre Infernal* (*qv*).

Ariel (Aariel, Arael, Ariael): Described in *The Hierarchy of the Blessèd Angels* (*qv*) as one of the seven princes ruling the waters and as 'Earth's great lord'. Jewish mystics called Jerusalem by the name Ariel. Cornelius Agrippa (*qv*) describes Ariel as an angel who is also sometimes a demon and a city, Ariopolis, where 'the idol is worshipped.' The Bible describes Ariel as variously a city, a man, and an altar. To Occultists Ariel is the third archon (*qv*) of the winds. He is also an angel who helps Raphael (*qv*) in curing disease. The *Pistis Sophia* (*qv*) places him in charge of punishments in Hell, while to the Gnostics, he is a ruler of the winds. Kabbalah lists him as originally coming from the order of Virtues (*qv*). In Shakespeare's *The Tempest* he is a sprite and the poet Milton makes him a rebel angel defeated by Abdiel (*qv*) on the first day of fighting in Heaven. He is also one of the 72 angels bearing the name of God Shemhamphorae

Ariman: *See* **Ahriman**.

Arioc (Ariukh, Oriockh): A guardian angel of the ancestors or children of Enoch, with the appointed task of protecting Enoch's writings. Arioc is the name given to an executioner in Genesis in the Bible.

Arioch: A spirit of vengeance; a fallen angel.

Ariukh: *See* **Oriockh**.

Arkhas: According to *2 Enoch (See The Book of Enoch)*, a primordial spirit summoned by God and divided.

Armaita (Aramaiti, Armaiti): One of the Zoroastrian Amesha Spentas (*qv*) or archangels. The spirit of truth, wisdom and goodness. She visited the Earth to help the good.

Armaros (Armers, Pharmaros, Abaros): A fallen angel as listed by Enoch.

Armas: An angel invoked in magic at the end of the Sabbath, according to Jewish mysticism.

Armasa: An angel used in Aramaic magic.

Armaziel: A Gnostic angel.

Armen: A fallen angel in *1 Enoch (See The Books of Enoch)*.

Armers: *See* **Armaros**.

Armesi: One of the angels of the tenth hour of the day, mentioned in *The Lesser Key of Solomon* (*qv*).

Armesiel: An angel of the fourth hour of the night, mentioned in *The Lesser Key of Solomon* (*qv*).

Armiel: An angel of the 11th hour of the night.

Armies: Name of a celestial order, as used by the poet Milton in *Paradise Lost*.

Armimas: An angel invoked at the end of the Sabbath, according to Jewish mysticism.

Armisael: An angel of the womb, invoked to ease childbirth in Jewish mysticism.

Armon: An angel of the second chora or altitude invoked in magic.

Arsyalalyur: An angelic messenger sent by God to Enoch and to the son of Noah to warn him of the flood.

Artafika: An archangel mentioned in Enoch lore.

Aruru: To the Sumerians a female messenger from the gods who created man from clay and was also the mother of Gilgamesh, the great Sumerian hero.

Arvial: An angel guarding the Fourth Heaven.

Arzal: One of the four angels of the East.

Asach: An angel invoked in magic ritual, according to *Grimorium Verum* (*qv*).

Asacro: An angel invoked in black magic ritual.

Asael: A fallen angel.

Asaf: *See* **Asaph**.

Asaliah: To Kabbalists an angel of the order of Virtues under Raphael's leadership. He also holds dominion over justice. *The Magus* (*qv*) lists him amongst the 72 angels bearing the mystical name of God Shemhamphorae.

Asamkis: An angel who guards the Seventh Heaven.

Asaph (Asaf, Azaf): Principal of hosts of angels who chant God's name at night. In Jewish legend, he is the angel of medicine.

Asariel: An angel of the mansions of the moon (*qv*).

Asasiah: Another of Metatron's (*qv*) many names.

Asasiel: An angel of Thursday, who shares his rule with Sachiel (*qv*) and Cassiel (*qv*). A ruling spirit of the planet Jupiter.

Asath: An angel whose name is invoked in magic rites, according to *Grimorium Verum* (*qv*).

Asbeel: A fallen angel listed by Enoch.

Ascobai: An angel invoked in exorcisms of wax, mentioned in *The Greater Key of Solomon* (*qv*).

Asderel (Asradel, Sahariel): An evil archangel who taught the course of the moon.

Asentacer: An angel equating with Lelahel (*qv*).

Asfa'el: A luninary mentioned in *Enoch 1 and 2* (See *The Book of Enoch*).

Ashael X: An angel whose name is invoked during magic ritual, noted in *The Sword of Moses* (*qv*).

Ashamdon: *See* **Shamdan**.

Asha Vahishta: An Amesha Spenta (*qv*).

Ashkanizkael: An angelic guard of the Seventh Heaven.

ABOVE: *The Archangels triumphing over Lucifer* by Marco D'Oggiono (c.1475–1530)

Archangels: Name for high-ranking angels in all traditions. In the pseudo-Dionysian celestial hierarchy, the archangels occupy eighth place in the nine orders of choirs, strangely placed second to last. They are seven in number and are thought to be the 'seven angels who stand before God,' as described in the Book of Revelation. The various lists of archangels follow:

According to 1 Enoch:
Uriel, Raphael, Raguel (Ruhiel, Ruagel, Ruahel), Michael, Zerachiel (Araqael) Gabriel, Remiel (Jeremiel, Jerahmeel).

According to 3 Enoch (Hebrew Enoch):
Mikael, Gabriel, Shatqiel, Baradiel, Shachaqiel, Baraqiel (Baradiel), Sidriel (or Pazriel).

According to the Testament of Solomon:
Makael, Gabriel, Uriel, Sabrael, Arael, Iaoth, Adonael.

According to Christian Gnostics:
Miachael, Gabreil, Raphael, Uriel (Phanuel), Barachiel, Sealtiel, Jehudiel.

According to Gregory the Great:
Michael, Gabriel, Raphael, Uriel, Simiel, Orifiel, Zachariel.

According to Pseudo-Dionysius:
Michael, Gabriel, Raphael, Uriel, Chamuel, Jophiel, Zadkiel.

In Geonic lore:
Michael, Gabriel, Raphael, Aniel, Kafziel, Samael, Zadkiel.

According to Talismanic magic:
Zaphkiel, Zadkiel, Camael, Raphael, Haniel, Michael, Gabriel.

According to The Hierarchy of the Blessèd Angels:
Raphael, Gabriel, Cahmuel, Michael, Adabiel, Haniel, Zaphiel.

According to Muslim legend, there are only four archangels:
Gabriel, Michael, Azrael, Israfel.

Ashmedai: An evil spirit sometimes identified as the serpent who seduced Eve (*qv*) in the Garden of Eden. However, he is not considered evil by other sources, characterized as a Cherub, 'prince of Sheddim' or 'the great philosopher'.

Ashmodiel: An angel ruling the zodiac sign of Taurus.

Ashraud: *The Greater Key of Solomon* (*qv*) describes him as 'a prince over all the angels and Caesars.'

Ashriel: One of the seven angels holding dominion over the Earth and the angel that seperates the soul from the body at the time of death. In Kabbalism, he can also be invoked to cure stupidity.

Ashu: *See* **Sirushi**.

Asiel: One of five angels – including Dabria (*qv*), Ecanus (*qv*), Selemiah (*qv*) and Sarea (*qv*) – appointed by God to transcribe the 204 books dictated by Ezra. 70 were to be delivered only to the wise and the remainder were to be available to all. According to the *Testament of Solomon* (*qv*), he is a demon who detects thieves and can help find hidden treasure.

Asimon: An angel referenced in *The Zohar* (*qv*).

Asimor: One of the seven princes of power. The other six angels are Kalmiya (*qv*), Boel (*qv*), Psachar (*qv*), Gabriel (*qv*), Sandalphon (*qv*) and Uzziel (*qv*).

Asiyah: *See* **Assiah**.

Asmadai: A 'potent throne' mentioned in *Paradise Lost*.

Asmodal: An angel involved in Solomonic Wax exorcisms, documented in *The Greater Key of Solomon* (*qv*).

Asmoday: A fallen angel who is said to teach mathematics and can render mortals invisible. He leads 72 legions of infernal spirits. He appears, when invoked, as a creature with the heads of a bull, a ram and a man. His name may be spelt Hasmoday – a demon of the moon.

Asmodee: *See* **Ashmedai**. According to one source, he equates with Sammael (*qv*) or Satan (*qv*).

Asmodel: The angel holding dominion over the month of April and ruler of the zodiac sign of Taurus. Once a leader of the order of Cherubim (*qv*), he is now, according to the *Pistis Sophia* (*qv*), a demon of punishment. In the Kabbalah, he is one of the ten Sephiroth (*qv*).

Asmodeus: A devil in Persian and Jewish lore, he is said to have made Noah drunk and to have slain the seven bridegrooms of the young Sarah before being defeated by Raphael (*qv*) and exiled in upper Egypt. In Hell, he controls gambling establishments and when invoked, according to one source, the invocant must be bareheaded, otherwise Asmodeus will deceive him. He is also variously known as a demon of impurity, father-in-law of the demon Bar Shalmon and the inventor of carousels, music, dancing and drama.

Asradel: *See* **Asderel**.

Asrael: An angel in an opera of the same name by Alberto Franchetti, with text written by Ferdinando Fontana and first performed in 1888. Asrael falls in love with a female angel, Nefta, but loses her before meeting her again in Heaven.

Asrafil: The Islamic angel of the last judgement.

Asriel X: Principal of the 63 angels guarding the Seven Heavens.

Asron: A guard at the gates of the East Wind.

Assad: An angel in Arabic lore, invoked in magical ritual.

Assafsissiel: An angelic guard of the Seventh Heaven.

Assarel: An angelic guard of the Fourth Heaven

Asser Criel: Name that must not be uttered and is inscribed on the breastplates of Moses (*qv*) and Aaron. The wearer of these breastplates will not be victim of a sudden death.

Assi Asisih: A messenger of the Sword.

Assiah (Asiyah): One of the lowest of the four worlds; the world where the prince of darkness resides.

Assiel: An angel of healing, mentioned in *The Book of the Angel Raziel* (*qv*).

Assimonem: Angels that can be invoked to grant invisibility and to command demons, documented in *The Greater Key of Solomon* (*qv*).

Astachoth: An angel invoked to bless water.

Astad: To the ancient Persians an angel guarding the 64th of the hundred gates of paradise who also rules the 26th day of the month.

Astagna (Astrgna): An angel who resides in the Fifth Heaven, according to *The Magus* (*qv*). He rules on Tuesday. To invoke him one must be facing West.

Astaniel: One of the principal angel-princes appointed to the Sword by God. Astaniel is tasked with presiding over law and order in Heaven and on Earth.

Astaroth (Asteroth): A fallen angel, once a Seraph (*qv*) and now a great lord in Hell.

Astarte: The principal female deity in a number of cultures – Phoenician, Carthaginian, Syrian. To the Syrians she was a moon goddess of fertility. The Greeks borrowed their goddess, Aphrodite, from Astarte. In Occult lore, she is the demon for the month of April. She is a fallen angel.

Astel: A spirit who resides on the planet Saturn.

Asteraoth: One of the seven great rulers of the planets. He defeated the demoness named Powers (*qv*) who, according to legend, was summoned by King Solomon.

Astiro: An angel equating to Mehiel (*qv*).

Astm Kunya X: One of the 14 conjuring angels and one of the unutterable names of God.

Astoreth: A fallen angel, equated with Astarte (*qv*), in *Paradise Lost*.

Astrachios: An angel invoked in blessing the water, according to *Grimorium Verum* (*qv*).

Astral Iao Sabao: An angel's name found inscribed on a kamea.

Astrgna: *See* **Astagna**.

Astrocon: One of the angels of the eighth hour of the night, under Vadriel (*qv*).

Astrompsuchos (Etrempsuchos, Strempsuchos): A guardian of one of the seven Heavens.

Astroniel: An angel of the ninth hour of the day, according to *The Lesser Key of Solomon* (*qv*).

Asuras or Ahuras: Evil angels or spirits in Hindu lore, who constantly wage war with the great deities (the suryas). Similar to the fallen angels of Christianity.

At -Taum: The angel from whom the Manichaean Mani received revelations; the equivalent of the Holy Ghost of Christian doctrine.

Ata'il: Islamic guardian angel invoked in exorcism rites.

Ataf: An evil angel invoked to help defeat an enemy. Also useful in separating a husband and wife, according to *The Sword of Moses* (*qv*).

Ataliel (Atliel): An angel presiding over one of the mansions of the moon (*qv*).

Ataphiel: An angel who supports Heaven with three fingers.

Atar: Zoroastrian angel of fire and chief of the Yazatas (*qv*), good celestial beings.

Atarculph: The French writer and philosopher, Voltaire, named Atarculph as a leader of the fallen angels. Enoch listed Atarculph as a fallen angel.

Atarniel: *See* **Atrugiel**.

Atarph: A corresponding angel for Hahaiah (*qv*), an angel of the order of Cherubim.

Atatiyah: A secret name for Metatron or Michael.

Atbah: To the Gnostics, a secret name for the dekas, the great archons.

Atbah Ah: Lord of Hosts, summoned by the angel Akatriel (*qv*).

Atel: An angel of the Fourth Heaven. Also an angel of the air ruling on the Lord's day evoked from the east.

Atembui: An angelic assistant to Mumiah (*qv*).

Aterchinis: An angel of the hour, corresponding to Teasel (*qv*).

Aterestin: In black magic Aterestin can be conjured to find hidden treasure.

Athamas: An angel invoked in the conjuration of Ink and Colours, according to *The Greater Key of Solomon* (*qv*).

Athanatos: A conjuring spirit of the planet Mercury. A name used to discover hidden treasure.

Atheniel: One of the angels guarding the mansions of the moon (*qv*).

Athoth: One of the 12 powers created by Iadalbaoth (*qv*).

Atliel: *See* **Ataliel**.

Atmon: One of Metatron's (*qv*) many names.

Atriel: *See* **Araziel**.

Atropatos: One of the angel Metatron's (*qv*) many names.

Atrugiel (Atarniel, Atrugniel): A guardian angel of the Seventh Heaven. Also one of the angel Metatron's (*qv*) many names.

Atrugniel: *See* **Atrugiel**.

Atsaftsaf: Angels who guard the Sixth Heaven.

Atsiluth: In the Kabbalah, the highest of the four worlds in the Tree of Life, the world of emanation. This is the realm where God and the highest angels reside.

Attarib: One of the four angels of winter and head of the sign of winter, mentioned in *The Magus* (*qv*) and *Dictionnaire Infernal* (*qv*).

Atuesuel: One of eight all-powerful angels of the Kabbalah. He is invoked to 'smoke out the monsters of hell', according to *The Sixth and Seventh Boooks of Moses* (*qv*).

Atufiel: An angel guarding the Sixth Heaven.

Atuniel: An angel of the order of Virtues (*qv*), as well as an angel of fire. May be compared with Nathanael (*qv*).

Aub: Name of an angel that is inscribed on the third pentacle of the moon, noted in *The Greater Key of Solomon* (*qv*).

Auel: An angel of the sun whose name is used in Kabbalistic invocations, according to *The Sixth and Seventh Boooks of Moses* (*qv*)

Aufiel: An angel over birds.

Aufniel: *See* **Ofniel**.

Auphanim: *See* **Ofanim**.

Aupiel: The angel who carried Enoch to Heaven while he was still alive. Also described as the tallest angel in Heaven.

Auriel: One of 72 angels of 72 quinaries of degrees of the zodiac who is invoked during the conjuring of the Sword.

Ausiul: An angel holding dominion over the zodiac sign of Aquarius who can be invoked in magic ritual.

Authorities: Another name for the angelic orders of Powers (*qv*) or Virtues (*qv*) or possibly a separate and distinct pre-Dionysian order of angels.

Autogenes: To the Gnostics, an aeon (*qv*) surrounded by four great angels.

Auza (Aza): A fallen angel, in Kabbalism.

Auzael: *See* **Azazel**.

Auzhaya (Avzhia): One of the many names of the angel Metatron (*qv*).

Avagbag: An angelic guard of the Sixth Heaven.

Avahel: A prince of the Third Heaven, mentioned in *The Sixth and Seventh Books of Moses* (*qv*).

Avartiel: Name of an angel inscribed on a kamea, in Hebrew lore.

Avatar: *See* page 74.

Avenging Angels: Also known as the angels of destruction, these 12 angels, whose chief resides in the Third Heaven, were the first angels created by God, according to Jewish lore.

Avial: An angel who guards one of the halls of the Seventh Heaven.

Avirzahe'e: Benevolent but fearsome angel-prince who guards the gate that leads to the Sixth Heaven.

Avitue: One of the many names for Lilith (*qv*).

Avniel: An angel-prince appointed by God to the Sword, according to *The Sword of Moses* (*qv*). Avniel is tasked with presiding over law and order in Heaven and on Earth.

Avriel: An angel who guards the Seventh Heaven.

Avtsangosh: One of the many names for the angel Metatron (*qv*).

Avzhia: *See* **Auzhaya**.

Awar: One of the sons of the angel Eblis (*qv*).

Awel: An angel invoked in Kabbalistic magic, mentioned in *The Sixth and Seventh Books of Moses* (*qv*).

Awitel: An angel invoked in Kabbalistic magic, mentioned in *The Sixth and Seventh Books of Moses* (*qv*).

Awoth: An angel invoked in Kabbalistic magic, mentioned in *The Sixth and Seventh Books of Moses* (*qv*).

Axineton: An angel whose name God pronounced to create the world, according to *The Greater Key of Solomon* (*qv*).

Ayar Ziva: *See* **Ram Khastra**.

Ayib: An angel whose name is inscribed on the fourth pentacle of the planet Venus, according to *The Greater Key of Solomon* (*qv*).

Ayscher: An angel invoked in Kabbalistic magic, referred to *The Sixth and Seventh Books of Moses* (*qv*).

Aza: *See* **Auza**.

Azael: One of the two fallen angels who co-habited with Naamah (*qv*), daughter of Lamech. Their progeny were the Sedim, Assyrian guardian angels. Azael is said to be chained in the desert and will remain thus until judgement day.

Azaf: *See* **Asaph**.

Azar (Azur): A Persian angel of November, governing the ninth day of the month.

Azaradel: A fallen angel who instructed mortals in the motions of the moon, mentioned in *1 Enoch* (See *The Book of Enoch*)

Azarel: An angel whose name is inscribed on the fifth pentacle of the moon, according to *The Greater Key of Solomon* (*qv*).

Azariah: In the apocryphal *Book of Tobit*, Raphael (*qv*) takes this name, later revealing his true identity.

Azariel: Listed by Occultists as one of the angels of the mansions of the moon (*qv*).

Azazel: *See* opposite.

Azaziel: An alternative name for the Semyaza (*qv*).

Azbugah: An angel who clothes the new arrivals in Heaven with righteousness. His name can be invoked for healing and for warding off evil.

Azdai: A Mandaean angel.

Azer: An angel of elemental fire as well as the name of the father of Zoroaster.

Azeruel: An angel of the mansions of the moon (*qv*).

Azfiel: An angel guarding the first of the seven heavenly halls.

ABOVE: *The Angel Azazel*
by John Roddam Spencer Stanhope (1829–1908)

Azazel: One of the principals amongst the 200 fallen angels. He taught men how to make swords and shields and women learned about make-up from him. In rabbinic literature he is something of a scapegoat. He is said to have refused to worship Adam (*qv*) and was consequently cast out of Heaven by God, changing his name to Eblis (*qv*).

Azibeel: A fallen angel according to Enoch's list.

Aziel: An angel of the mansions of the moon (*qv*).

Aziziel: An angel invoked in Syriac incantations.

Azkariel: *See* **Akhraziel**.

Azkeel: One of the principals among the fallen angels, according to Enoch's list.

Azliel X: An invocation angel according to *The Sword of Moses* (*qv*).

Azrael: An angel of death (*qv*), residing in the

ABOVE: *The Ten Avatars or Incarnations of Vishnu*
engraved by A. Thorn, *c.*19th century

Avatar: In the Vedic religion, a human or animal incarnation of a god. There were ten of these angelic beings, mainly associated with Vishnu, the first Avatar. The complete list is:

Vishnu (the fish Avatar), Kurmavatar (the tortoise Avatar), Barah (the bear Avatar), Narsinha (man-lion Avatar and lord of heroism, Vamana (dwarf Avatar and lord of reason, Paras u Rama (Parasuram) or Chirangivah the immortal, Ram Avatar (Rama or Ramachandra), Krisn Avatar (Krishna), Buddha (Budh avatar), Kalki Avatar.

The times of the first nine avatars have already passed – Kalki will arrive in the shape of a whitehorse with wings at the end of the four ages to destroy the Earth. The complete list is:

Vishnu (the fish Avatar), Kurmavatar (the tortoise Avatar), Barah (the bear Avatar), Narsinha (man-lion Avatar and lord of heroism, Vamana (dwarf Avatar and lord of reason, Paras u Rama (Parasuram) or Chirangivah the immortal, Ram Avatar (Rama or Ramachandra), Krisn Avatar (Krishna), Buddha (Budh avatar), Kalki Avatar.

The times of the first nine avatars have already passed – Kalki will arrive in the shape of a whitehorse with wings at the end of the four ages to destroy the Earth.

Third Heaven who is forever writing in a large book and forever erasing what he writes: what he writes is the birth of a man, what he erases is the name of the man at death. To Muslims, he is Raphael (*qv*) and has 70,000 feet and 4,000 wings while his body has as many eyes and tongues as there are men in the world. He succeeded in providing seven handfuls of Earth for the creation of Adam (*qv*) when Michael (*qv*), Gabriel (*qv*) and Israfel (*qv*) failed. As a reward, he was given the task of separating the body from the soul at death. In Jewish lore, he is evil itself. He is invoked with Michael and Gabriel in Syriac charms.

Azra'il: An Islamic guardian angel invoked in exorcism rituals.

Azriel: A powerful angel commanding 60 myriads of legions of angels, residing on the northern side of Heaven. One source describes him as an angel of destruction. His name on oriental charms can be used to protect from evil.

Azur: *See* **Azar**.

Azza (Shem-yaza): A fallen angel suspended between Earth and Heaven as punishment for enjoying carnal relations with mortal women. He is perpetually falling, one eye open, one closed so that he can see his situation and suffer even more. He is being punished for opposing the high rank given to Enoch when he was transformed from a mortal into the angel Metatron (*qv*). He is the angel said to have revealed the heavenly arcana to King Solomon, making the Jewish king the wisest man on Earth. Talmud says that he fathered the Sedim (Assyrian guardian angels) with Naamah (*qv*), daughter of Lamech.

Azzael: *See* **Azza**. Sometimes Azza and Azzael are viewed as two distinct beings, and at others they are one and the same. In *3 Enoch* (See *The Book of Enoch*), Azzael is one of three ministering angels with Uzza and Azza, residing in the Seventh Heaven. He becomes a fallen angel punished by having his nose pierced. He taught witchcraft to men, causing the sun, the moon and the stars to fall from Heaven to bring them closer as objects of worship.

Baaberith: *See* **Balberith.**

Baabiel: In the Kabbalah, an angel serving in the First Heaven.

Baal: A deity worshipped regularly throughout much of the ancient Near East, particularly by the Canaanites. The name is derived from the Semitic word meaning 'possessor' or 'lord'. Baal was eventually adopted as the chief fertility god and lord of rain, whose benevolence in supplying moisture was essential for crops. By the time of the Israelites' arrival in the land of Canaan, the worship of Baal was firmly established. Baal even came to be understood as representing the Lord of Israel.

Baal Davar: A name for Satan used by 18th-century Chasidic Jews.

Baalesbul: *See* **Beelzebub.**

Babel (Babiel): A messenger of the planet Jupiter who is also viewed as an angel of Wednesday.

Babhne'a: A powerful angel whose name is invoked to ward off evil, documented in *Amulets and Talismans* (*qv*).

Babiel: *See* **Babel.**

Bachanael: *See* **Bachanoe.**

Bachanoe (Bachanael): In Occultism, an angel of the First Heaven and a ruler of Monday.

Bachiel (Baciel): An angel of the air residing in the Fourth Heaven who is invoked from the East. Also a spirit of the planet Saturn and a guard of the gates of the West Wind.

Bachliel: An angel who is a guard at the gates of the South Wind.

Baciel: *See* **Bachiel.**

Badariel: *See* **Batarel**.

Badpatiel: Name of an angel inscribed on a kamea to protect against evil spirits.

Bae: In the *Testament of Solomon* (*qv*), an angel summoned for the exorcising of demons.

Bael: *See* page 77.

Ba-En-Kekon (Bainkhookh): An aeon (*qv*) known as 'the soul of darkness'.

Bagdal: Angel who presides with Araziel (*qv*) over the zodiac sign of Taurus, according to *Transcendental Magic* (*qv*).

ABOVE: *Tobias and the Archangel Raphael* by Francesco Botticini, *c.*1470

Bael (Bael): Equated in *The Zohar* (*qv*) with the archangel Raphael. In other sources, however, he is a prince of the eastern part of Hell commanding around 60 legions of demons. When invoked, he appears as a beast with three heads – a man, a toad and a cat.

Baglis: According to grimoire, an angel of measure and balance who may be invoked during the second hour of the day.

Bagnael: An angel of the gates of the East Wind.

Bahaliel: An angel who guards the gates of the East Wind.

Bahman: *See* **Barman**.

Bahram: *See* **Barman**.

Baijel: An angel serving in the Fifth Heaven.

Bainkhookh: *See* **Ba-En-Kekon**.

Baktamael: An angel who guards the gates of the West Wind.

Balam (Balan): A fallen angel, formerly of the Dominations (*qv*), described as having three heads (bull, ram and man) and the tail of a serpent. He rides naked on the back of a bear and commands 40 legions of demons.

Balan: *See* **Balam.**

Balay: An angel of Monday residing in the First Heaven who can only be invoked from the North.

Balberith (Baaberith, Berith, Elberith): A fallen angel, known as 'Scriptor', once a prince of the Cherubim (*qv*) who is now master of ceremonies in Hell and counter-signatory to the pacts between mortals and the devil.

Baldach: An angel invoked in magic rituals, in *The Book of Ceremonial Magic* (*qv*).

Balhiel: *See* **Baliel**.

Balidet: A Saturday angel of the air who ministers to Mammon (*qv*), principal angel of the air.

Baliel (Balhiel): A Monday angel who resides in either the First or Second Heaven and can only be invoked from the North.

Balkin: In Occultism, a beneficent angel and ruler of the northern mountains.

Ballaton: An angel whose name is used by sorcerers when drawing the pentagram of Solomon, a powerful symbol used for summoning spirits and conducting esoteric rites.

Baltazard: In Solomonic magic, Baltazard is invoked in a spell to protect oneself on long journeys.

Balthial (Balthiel): A planetary angel who has the unique ability to overcome jealousy, mentioned in *3 Enoch* (See *The Book of Enoch*).

Balthiel: *See* **Balthial.**

Banech: An angel of the seven planets invoked in magical rituals, according to *The Sixth and Seventh Books of Moses* (*qv*).

Baniel: A lesser spirit invoked in magic rituals in *The Book of Ceremonial Magic* (*qv*).

Baracata: An angel who figures in the ancient and very arcane rites of magic associated with King Solomon. Baracata may not be precisely considered an angel, but traditionally it takes a sorcerer of considerable powers to summon him.

Baraborat: In Occultism, an angel of the planet Mercury who is a Wednesday angel residing in the Second or Third Heaven and has to be invoked from the East.

Barach: An angel of the seal in *The Sixth and Seventh Books of Moses* (*qv*).

Barachiel: *See* **Barakiel**.

Baradiel: One of the princes of the Seven Heavens mentioned in *3 Enoch* (See *The Book of Enoch*). Baradiel is one of the 'seven great, beautiful, wonderful, and honoured princes.' Presiding over the Third Heaven, he is also one of the princes (or angels) who guide the progress of the world and has dominion over hail.

Barael: One of the seven Angels of the Throne (*qv*), of the First Heaven.

Barah: The Bear Avatar, one of Vedic lore's ten incarnations of the deity. *See* page 74.

Barakiel (Barachiel, Baraqiel, Barchiel, Barkiel): Ruler of the order of Seraphim (*qv*), governor of the month of February, one of the seven archangels and prince of the Second Heaven as well as of the order of Confessors (*qv*). He is a chief angel of the first and fourth altitudes. He has dominion over lightning and is ruler of Jupiter, Scorpio and Pisces. Barakiel is benevolent and grants success, fortune and luck to mortals who pray to him. He is invoked, with Uriel (*qv*) and Rubiel (*qv*) to bring gambling success.

Barakon: In Solomonic magic, Barakon is invoked in rituals.

Baraqel: A fallen angel.

Baraqiel: *See* **Barakiel**.

Baraqijal: A fallen angel who teaches astrology.

Barattiel: A powerful angel-prince said to be able to hold up the highest Heaven on three fingers, as mentioned in *3 Enoch* (See *The Book of Enoch*).

Barbatos: A fallen angel previously of the order of Virtues (*qv*). He knows the secrets of birdsong and can tell the future. He can be invoked when the sun is in the zodiac sign of Sagittarius.

Barbell: A great archon (*qv*), female consort of Cosmocrator (*qv*). In the *Texts of the Saviour*, she is named as the daughter of Sophia (*qv*), procreator of the higher angels.

Barbiel (Barbuel, Baruel): A fallen angel, once an archangel. He is a ruling angel of the order of Virtues (*qv*), of October and one of the angels of the mansions of the moon (*qv*).

Barbuel: *See* **Barbiel**.

Barchiel: *See* **Barakiel**.

Barcus: An angel of the fifth hour, according to *The Nuctemeron* (*qv*).

Baresches: In grimoire, an angel invoked in order to win a woman's heart.

Barginiel: Presiding angel of the seventh hour of the day, in *The Book of Ceremonial Magic* (*qv*).

Bariel: According to *The Greater Key of Solomon* (*qv*), Bariel is the presiding angel of the 11th hour of the day. He is also an angel of the fourth pentacle of Jupiter.

Barinian (Huristar) To the ancient Persians supreme beings.

Barkiel: *See* **Barakiel**.

Barku: *See* **Rimmon**.

Barman (Bahman, Bahram): An angel overseeing all the earthly creatures apart from man. Also leader of the angels appointed by God to rule over the days of the month. In the 17th-century religious treatise, *The Dabistan*, he is an Amesha Spenta (*qv*), 'the mightiest of the angels whom the Mohammedans call Jabriel' (Gabriel, [*qv*]). The angel of January and ruler of the second day of the month, he appears in human form, a red crown on his head.

Barpharanges (Sesenges-Barharanges): In Gnosticism, an angel in charge of baptism.

Barsabel: An angel with the Kabbalistic number 325 who guards the planet Mars.

Bartyabel: Paracelsus describes this angel as a spirit of Mars, under the angel Graphiel (*qv*), ruler of the planet.

Barzachia: An angel's name inscribed on the first pentacle of the planet Mars, in *The Greater Key of Solomon* (*qv*). Other names inscribed thus are Ithuriel (*qv*), Madimiel (*qv*) and Eschol (*qv*).

Baruch: According to the Jewish text *Apocalypse of Baruch*, the principal guardian angel of the Tree of Life. (Raphael [*qv*] is also described thus). Baruch is a name of Hebrew origin meaning 'blessèd'.

Baruel: *See* **Barbiel**.

Barya'il: An angel encountered by the sufi Abu Yazid in the Seventh Heaven, according to Islamic apocalyptic texts. He is described as 'of the tallness of the distance of 500 years'. He tries to bribe the sufi with 'a kingdom such as no tongue can describe', but the sufi rejects his offer, remaining loyal to God.

Basasael: An evil archangel, according to *1 Enoch* (See *The Book of Enoch*).

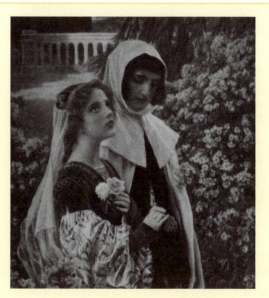

ABOVE: *Dante and Beatrice in the garden* by Cesare Saccaggi (1868–1934)

Beatrice: The poet Dante's beloved who he writes about as an angel in his work, *La Vita Nuova*.

Bashmallin (Hashmallim): An order of angels equated with the Dominations (*qv*).

Baskabas: An alternative version of Kasbak and a secret name of Metatron (*qv*).

Basus: An angelic guard of the Fourth Heaven.

Bataliel: In *The Sixth and Seventh Books of Moses* (*qv*), Bataliel is one of the angelic rulers presiding over the 12 signs of the zodiac.

Batarel (Badariel, Batariel, Metarel): In *3 Enoch* (See *The Book of Enoch*), a fallen angel who may be invoked in magic rituals.

Batariel: *See* **Batarel**.

Bathor: In White Magic, one of seven Olympian spirits, known as stewards or electors of Heaven who rules over Jupiter.

Bath Kol: In Judaism, Bath Kol is a female angel who encourages truthful communication and prophecy and can tell the future. She is revered by rabbis as the voice of God and is symbolized by a dove. She may be equated with the Holy Ghost. She is said to have appeared to Simeon ben Yohai, 2nd-century author of *The Zohar* (*qv*). Bath Kol is a name of Hebrew origin and means 'heavenly voice'.

Batsran: One of Metatron's (*qv*) many names.

Bat Zuge: A name for the evil Lilith (*qv*), according to *The Zohar* (*qv*).

Bazathiel: An angel guarding the First Heaven.

Bazazath: Archangel residing in the Second Heaven who is reputed to have put a female winged dragon named Obizuth to flight.

Baz Baziah: According to Talmudic lore, an angel invoked to cure skin problems.

Bazkiel: An angel guarding the Third Heaven.

Baztiel: An angel guarding the First Heaven.

Beal hares: Characterized as a demon in one source, but also described as 'the noblest carrier that ever did serve any man upon the Earth.' His name is not included in *Dictionnaire Infernal* (*qv*), however, and he must, therefore, be considered benign.

Bearechet: An angel of the seal in *The Sixth and Seventh Books of Moses* (*qv*).

ABOVE: *Satan and Beelzebub*
by Gustave Doré, *c.*1868

Beelzebub (Baalsebul, Belzaboul, Belzebub): Originally a god of Ekron in Assyrian lore in Philistia, in the Kabbalah he is an archdemon ruling the nine infernal hierarchies that follow the first which is presided over by Satan (*qv*) or Sammael (*qv*). He is, therefore, second only to Satan himself in Hell. He was a Cherubim (*qv*) before his fall and is also known as 'Lord of Chaos'. He is invoked at the invocant's peril. Beelzebub is a name of Hebrew origin and means 'god of flies'.

Beatiel: An angel serving in the Fourth Heaven.

Beatrice: *See* page 79.

Beburos: One of the angels mentioned in the apocryphal book the *Revelation of Esdras*. Beburos is ranked as one of the nine angels who will come and reign at the end of the world.

Bedaliel: Angel invoked to command demons in *The Greater Key of Solomon* (*qv*).

Beelzebub (Baalsebul, Belzaboul, Belzebub): *See* left.

Behemiel (Hariel, Harael): An angel presiding over tame beasts, chief of the order of Hashmallim (*qv*) which equates with the order of Cherubim (*qv*).

Behemoth: *See* page 82.

Beleth (Bilet, Bileth, Byleth): A former leader of the order of Powers (*qv*) who fell. He rides a pale horse and is announced by the sound of trumpets.

Belhar: *See* **Bernael**.

Beli: An angel guarding the gates of the North Wind.

Belial (Berial): A fallen angel, formerly of the order of Virtues (*qv*), often identified with Satan.

Beliael: An angel guarding the gates of the North Wind.

Beliar: An alternative for Belial (*qv*), appearing in Deuteronomy, Judges and I Samuel in the Bible. He is always evil and is considered to be the prince of darkness.

Belphegor: A fallen angel who is the infernal ambassador to France. He is the demon of inventions and discoveries. He was a member of the order of Principalities (*qv*) prior to his fall and appears as a young woman when invoked.

Belsal: An angel of the first hour of the night, serving Gamiel (*qv*).

Belzaboul: *See* **Beelzebub**.

Belzebub: *See* **Beelzebub**.

Benad Hasche: Female angels worshipped in the Islamic tradition. Benad Hasche translates to 'daughters of God'.

Ben Ani: A name used to command demons in *The Greater Key of Solomon* (*qv*).

Bencul: One of the nine angels listed in *The Sixth and Seventh Books of Moses* (*qv*) invoked during Kabbalistic rites in the general citation of Moses.

Bene Elohim: A group of angels who belong to the order or choir of Hashmallim (*qv*). Meaning 'sons of God,' the Bene Elohim are considered a part or division of the Hashmallim, with the duty of forever singing God's praises. As the sons of God, they are sometimes thought to be the beings mentioned in Genesis who enjoyed relations with mortal women. The progeny of this union were the giants, the Anakim (*qv*). The Bene Elohim are also thought to be the angels called the Ischim (*qv*). Bene Elohim is a name of Hebrew origin that means 'sons of God'.

Beniel: An angel invoked to command demons to make the invocant invisible according to *The Greater Key of Solomon* (*qv*).

Benign Angel: The Benign Angel was sent down to slay Moses for not circumcizing his son. His wife, Zipporah, performed the rite, saving her husband.

Ben Nez: An alternative name for the angel Rubiel (*qv*) or Ruhiel (*qv*). He holds dominion over the wind. The name can also refer to a mountain.

Beodonos: An angel summoned in the conjuring of the reed, noted in *The Greater Key of Solomon* (*qv*).

Beratiel: A ruling angel of the 12th hour of the day in *The Book of Ceremonial Magic* (*qv*).

Berekeel: An angel of the seasons in *1 Enoch* (See *The Book of Enoch*).

Berial: *See* **Belial**.

Berith: *See* **Balberith**.

Berka'el: A leading angel of three months of the year, under Melkejal (*qv*), mentioned in *The Book of Enoch* (*qv*).

Bernael: The angel of darkness in Falasha lore. An angel of evil when partnered with Beliel (*qv*).

Beshter: In Persian lore, the name for Michael (*qv*).

Bethor: One of the seven angelic beings ruling the 196 divisions of Heaven. To assist him in his work, Bethor commands some 29,000 legions of angels. His area of authority is the planet Jupiter.

Bethuael: One of the angels governing the mansions of the moon (*qv*). Bethuael is a name of Hebrew origin and means 'house or man of God'.

Bethuel: Name of an angel inscribed on a kamea.

Betuliel: One of the angels presiding over the zodiac according to *The Sixth and Seventh Books of Moses* (*qv*).

Bezaliel: An angel who guards the gates of the North Wind.

Bezrial: An angel guarding the Third Heaven.

Bhaga: In the Vedic tradition, one of seven, or possibly 12, celestial beings.

Bibiyah: Another name for the angel Metatron (*qv*).

Bifiel: An angel who guards the Sixth Heaven.

Bigtha: An angel of confusion (*qv*).

Bilet: *See* **Beleth**.

Bileth: *See* **Beleth**.

Binah ('understanding'): The third Sephira (*qv*) of the Tree of Life. Named 'the sea' in *The Book of Concealed Mystery*, part of *The Zohar* (*qv*).

Biqa: Meaning 'good person' in Amharic, the language spoken by the Amhara of North Central Ethiopia, it is the original name of the angel Kasbeel (*qv*) who fell by turning away from God the instant he was created. He was re-named Kasbeel, 'he who lies to God'.

Bird of God: Dante used this term to describe angels.

Bizbul: A secret name for Metatron (*qv*).

Biztha: An angel of confusion (*qv*).

Black Angel: Black angels are usually considered to be demons. Two are named in Islamic demonology – Monker (*qv*) and Nakir (*qv*). Another is unnamed in Mohammed al-Sudi's Treatise on *Astrology and Divination*.

Blaef: In Occult lore, a Friday angel of the air and subject to the West Wind.

Blautel: In *The Greater Key of Solomon* (*qv*), an angel invoked in magic ritual.

Blinded Angel: The term used by Pope John Paul II for the devil, Satan. He implied that the devil has chosen to blind himself to the light and beauty of God and so exists in perpetual darkness, the blackness of sin. *See* **Fallen Angels**.

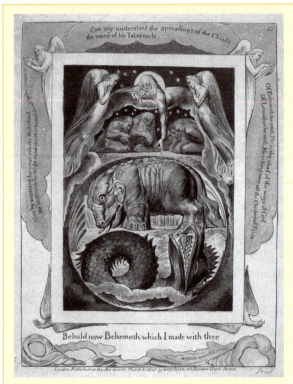

ABOVE: *Behemoth and Leviathan from the Book of Job (pl.15), by William Blake, c.1793*

Behemoth: A male monster of chaos, part whale, crocodile and hippopotamus who was created on the fifth day and who is a fallen angel who encourages gluttony. He is generally associated with Leviathan (*qv*), a monstrous female entity and paired with Rahab (*qv*), the angel of the seas (*qv*) as well as the angel of death (*qv*). To Roman Catholics, he is the principal of darkness. In Kurt Segelmann's book *The History of Magic and the Occult*, Behemoth is depicted as an elephant with bear's feet. Represented mostly as a dark figure, in the Book of Job (40:19) Behemoth is said to be 'the chief of the ways of God'. In *Dictionnaire Infernal* (*qv*), Behemoth appears in an illustration with the head of an elephant, with claw-like hands clutching his bloated stomach.

Bludon: One of the seven Electors (*qv*) of the Underworld according to Cornelius Agrippa (*qv*).

Bne Seraphim: In the Kabbalah, the angel who governs the planet Mercury. In talismanic magic, the spirit of the planet Venus.

Boamiel: An angel mentioned in the Jewish mystical work *The Book of the Angel Raziel* (*qv*), ranked as one of the six angels with authority over the four divisions of Heaven. The others are Scamijm (*qv*), Gabriel (*qv*), Adrael (*qv*), Dohel (*qv*) and Madiel (*qv*).

Bodiel: An angel of the Sixth Heaven in *3 Enoch* (See *The Book of Enoch*).

Boel: One of the seven angels of the throne (*qv*). He is believed to reside in the First Heaven, however *The Magus* (*qv*) claims Boel resides in the Seventh Heaven. He holds the four keys to the four corners of the Earth and using these keys is able to enter the Garden of Eden. He also governs the planet Saturn.

Book of Ceremonial Magic, The: This book was written in 1913 by Arthur Edward Waite, a scholar with an interest in mysticism and the Occult. Waite attempted to combine famous grimoires into one text and discuss the history and theology surrounded them.

Book of Enoch, The: This book includes five sections and is believed to have been written by Enoch, Noah's great-grandfather. The first section tells the story of the Watchers (*qv*), a group of fallen angels.

Book of the Angel Raziel, The: Kabbalistic textbook of magic from the Middle Ages. Enoch has been accused of plagiarizing it and Noah got his instructions for the construction of the Ark from it. According to *The Zohar* (*qv*), it contains secret writing that reveals the 1,500 keys to the mysteries of the world that even the angels had not been told. The book's author is unknown, but thought to be Eleazer of Worms or Isaac the Blind, both sages of medieval times. Legend has it that it was written by Raziel who gave it to Adam (*qv*), but it was seized by the other angels who jealously threw it into the sea. God then ordered Rahab (*qv*) to retrieve it and return it to Adam.

Bottomless Pit: An angel of The Abaddon (Hell), who is also known as the Angel of the Abyss, 'the destroyer' and 'king of the demonic locusts'. To St John he is not evil as he is the angel who in Revelations binds Satan for 1,000 years.

Briel: One of the 70 amulet angels (*qv*).

Brieus: The only angel who can stand up to and overcome the demon Rabdos (*qv*).

Bualu: According to *The Sixth and Seventh Books of Moses* (*qv*), one of the eight angels of omnipotence (*qv*). Amongst the others are Artuesuel (*qv*), Ebuhuel (*qv*), Tabatlu (*qv*), Tulau (*qv*), Labusi (*qv*) and Ublisi (*qv*). They have to be called three times from the four corners of the world and when the name of each is uttered three times, three blasts must be blown on a horn.

Buchuel: An angel's name inscribed on a kamea.

Buddha: *See* **Budh Avatar**.

Budh Avatar: The ninth of the ten avatars in the Vedic tradition. *See* page 74.

Buhair: One of the ten Mandaean angels or uthri that accompany the sun on its daily course.

Bull: To the Zoroastrians the source of all light. Created by Ormazd (*qv*) and destroyed by Ahriman (*qv*), Adam and Eve (*qv*) were created from his scattered seed.

Burc(h)at: In Kabbalistic lore, an angel of the air serving in the Fourth Heaven. He rules on Sunday and must be invoked from the West. A messenger of the sun.

Burkhan: An incarnate Manichean messenger of the God of Light to man. Zoroaster is described as a Burkhan.

Busasejal: A fallen angel in *1 Enoch* (See *The Book of Enoch*).

Butator: The angel of mathematical calculus who also serves in the third hour of the day. He may also be invoked in magic ritual, according to *The Nuctemeron* (*qv*).

Byleth: *See* **Beleth**.

Cabiel: An angel of the mansions of the moon (*qv*).

Cabriel (Kabriel): An angel presiding over the zodiac sign of Aquarius. One of the six guardians of the four cardinal points of Heaven in Thomas Heywood's *The Hierarchy of the Blessèd Angels* (*qv*).

Cadulech: A holy angel invoked in the conjuration of the sword, noted in the *Grimorium Verum* (*qv*).

Cael: A regent over the zodiac sign of Cancer mentioned in *The Lesser Key of Solomon* (*qv*).

Cafon: *See* **Zephon.**

Cahethel: In Jewish mysticism, a Seraphim (*qv*) who rules over agriculture and is one of 72 angels who bear the name of God Shemhamphorae. He is invoked to increase crop yield.

Cahor: An angel of deceit and of the third hour, according to *The Nuctemeron* (*qv*).

Caila: One of the angels invoked to conjure the appearance of the archangel Uriel (*qv*). It is also one of the four words that God spoke to Moses (*qv*), the others being Josata (*qv*), Agla (*qv*) and Ablati (*qv*).

Caim (Camio, Caym): A powerful fallen angel who appears in the form of a thrush, according to *Dictionnaire Infernal* (*qv*).

Caldulech (Caldurech): 'A most pure angel' invoked in Occultism.

Caldurech: See **Caldulech.**

Caliel: *See* **Calliel.**

Calizantin: A 'good angel' used in conjurations.

Calliel (Caliel): An Angel of the Throne (*qv*) serving in the Second Heaven, invoked to bring prompt help during times of adversity. One of 72 angels who bear the name of God Shemhamphorae, his corresponding angel is Tersatosoa.

Caluel (Calvel): A Wednesday angel, invoked from the South and residing in the Third Heaven.

Calvel: *See* **Caluel.**

Calzas: An angel of Tuesday residing in the Fifth Heaven who must be invoked from the East.

Camael (Kemuel): A powerful angel often confused with Samael (*qv*). His name means 'He who sees God' and he is the prince regent of the order of Powers (qv) and one of the seven archangels. He is the angel of war with 120,000 angels of destruction under him and is supreme regent of Mars and the zodiac sign of Aries. He attempted to stop God giving Moses the Torah and in Kabbalah he is identified with the fifth Sephira of the Tree of Life – Severity. In Occult lore, he is a fallen angel – Count Palatine – but this may only be because he has been confused with Samael (qv).

Camal: One of the archangels in the Kabbalah. The name Camal is of Hebrew origin and means 'to desire God'.

Camaysar: An angel of the fifth hour and an Occult angel of 'the marriage of contraries'.

Cambiel: An angel presiding over the zodiac sign of Aquarius, and also an angel of the ninth hour of the day.

Cambill: An angel of the eighth hour of the night, under Narcoriel (qv).

Cameron: An angel of the 12th hour of the day, assisting Beratiel (qv). Some sources view him as a demon ruled by Beelzebub (qv) and Astarte (qv) and he can, therefore, be used in the conjuration of these two beings.

Camio: See **Caim**.

Camuel: See **Camal**.

Caneloas: An angel invoked in magical rituals, as mentioned in *The Greater Key of Solomon* (qv).

Capabile: A messenger of the sun, in grimoire.

Capabili: An angel of the Fourth Heaven ruling on Sunday and invoked from the West.

Caphriel: Chief ruler of the seventh day (the Sabbath). In Occultism, a powerful angel invoked in the conjuration of the planet Saturn.

Capitiel: An angel of the fourth altitude.

Captain of the Host of the Lord: The man Joshua beheld with drawn sword and claimed to be the' Captain of the Host of the Lord', usually identified as Michael (qv).

Captains of Fear: See **Angels of Dread**.

Caracasa: An angel of spring along with Core (qv), Amatiel (qv) and Comissoros (qv).

Caraniel: An angel serving in the Third Heaven.

Carcas: One of the seven angels of confusion (qv).

Cardiel: An angel invoked in special magical rites.

Cardinal Virtues: *See page 90.*

Caretaking Angels: Temeluch (qv) and others. They look after the offspring of adulterous liaisons and 'children of untimely birth'.

Carmax: An angel who ministers, with Ismoli (qv) and Paffran (qv), to Samax (qv), chief of the Angels of the Air.

Carniel: Angel serving in the Third Heaven.

Carnivean (Carniveau): A fallen angel, formerly a prince of the Powers. *See* Carreau.

Carniveau: *See* **Carnivean**.

Carreau (Carnivean): A fallen angel who, with Baruch (qv), was involved in the famous possession of Sister Seaphica of Loudun.

Carsiol: An angel of the second hour, under Anneal (qv).

Casmaron: An angel of the air.

Casmir's: An angel of the 11th hour of the night, under Dardariel (qv).

Cass Cassiah: An angel invoked in order to heal skin disorders.

Cassiel: Ruler of Saturday. The angel of solitudes and tears who 'shews forth the unity of the eternal kingdom'. A ruler of the planet Saturn who is also the ruling prince of the Seventh Heaven. Cassiel is one of the Sarim (princes) of the order of Powers. Sometimes, he appears as the angel of temperance. He is said to be one of three angels of Saturday, the others being Uriel (qv) and Machatan (qv).

Castiel: In Occult lore, an angel of Thursday.

Casuojiah: An angel holding dominion over the zodiac sign of Capricorn, according to *The Lesser Key of Solomon* (qv).

Cathetel: Guardian angel of the garden who is responsible for increasing growth and yield of vegetables and fruits.

Catroije: An angel serving in the Second Heaven.

Causub: An angel of the seventh hour who can be invoked to charm snakes.

CELESTIAL HIERARCHY

ACCORDING TO ST AMBROSE
(IN APOLOGIA PROPHET DAVID, 5)

1. Seraphim
2. Cherubim
3. Dominations
4. Hashmallim
5. Principalities
6. Potentates (Powers)
7. Virtues
8. Archangels
9. Angels

ACCORDING TO ST JEROME

1. Seraphim
2. Cherubim
3. Powers
4. Dominations
(Dominions)
5. Hashmallim
6. Archangels
7. Angels

ACCORDING TO GREGORY THE GREAT (IN HOMILIA)

1. Seraphim
2. Cherubim
3. Hashmallim
4. Dominations
5. Principalities
6. Powers
7. Virtues
8. Archangels
9. Angels

ACCORDING TO PSEUDO-DIONYSIUS
(IN CELESTIAL HIERARCHY) AND ST THOMAS AQUINAS (IN SUMMA THEOLOGICA)

1. Seraphim
2. Cherubim
3. Hashmallim
4. Dominations
5. Virtues
6. Powers
7. Principalities
8. Archangels
9. Angels

ACCORDING TO CONSTITUTIONS OF THE APOSTLES
(IN CLEMENTINE LITURGY OF THE MASS)

1. Seraphim
2. Cherubim
3. Aeons
4. Hosts
5. Powers
6. Authorities
7. Principalities
8. Hashmallim
9. Archangels
10. Angels
11. Dominations

ACCORDING TO ISADORE OF SEVILLE (IN ETYMOLOGIARUM)

1. Seraphim
2. Cherubim
3. Powers
4. Principalities
5. Virtues
6. Dominations
7. Hashmallim
8. Archangels
9. Angels

CELESTIAL HIERARCHY

ACCORDING TO MOSES MAIMONIDES
(IN MISHNE TORAH)

1. Chaoth ha-Qadesh
2. Auphanim
3. Aralim (Erelim)
4. Chashmalim
5. Seraphim
6. Malachim
7. Elohim
8. Bene Elohim
9. Kerubim
10. Ishim

ACCORDING TO THE ZOHAR (EXODUS 43A)

1. Malachim
2. Erelim
3. Seraphim
4. Hayyoth
5. Ophanim
6. Hamshalim
7. Elim
8. Elohim
9. Bene Elohim
10. Ishim

ACCORDING TO MASKELET AZILUT

1. Seraphim
2. Ofanim
3. Cherubim
4. Shinanim
5. Tarshishim
6. Ishim
7. Hashmallim
8. Malakim
9. Bene Elohim
10. Arelim

ACCORDING TO JOHN OF DAMASCUS
(IN DE FIDE ORTHODOXA)

1. Seraphim
2. Cherubim
3. Hashmallim
4. Dominations
5. Powers
6. Authorities (Virtues)
7. Rulers (Principalities)
8. Archangels
9. Angels

ACCORDING TO BERITH MENUCHA

1. Arelim
2. Ishim
3. Bene Elohim
4. Malakim
5. Hashmallim
6. Tarshishim
7. Shinnanim
8. Cherubim
9. Ofanim
10. Seraphim

ACCORDING TO DANTE

1. Seraphim
2. Cherubim
3. Hashmallim
4. Dominations
5. Virtues
6. Powers
7. Archangels
8. Principalities
9. Angels

> ## CELESTIAL HIERARCHY
> ### ACCORDING TO FRANCIS BARRETT (IN *THE MAGUS*)
>
> | | |
> |---|---|
> | 1. Seraphim | 7. Principalities |
> | 2. Cherubim | 8. Archangels |
> | 3. Hashmallim | 9. Angels |
> | 4. Dominations | 10. Innocents |
> | 5. Powers | 11. Martyrs |
> | 6. Virtues | 12. Confessors |

Caym: *See* **Caim**.

Cazardia: *See* **Gazardiel**.

Cedrion: An angel invoked in the conjuring of the reed who also governs the South.

Celestial Hierarchy: *See* page 86 and above.

Cendrion: An angel invoked in Kabbalistic magic.

Cernaiul: Angel of Venus and the seventh Sephira (*qv*) of the Tree of Life in *The Sixth and Seventh Books of Moses* (*qv*).

Cerviel (Cervihel, Zeruel): One of the chiefs of the order of Principalities. He was the angel that God sent to help David slay Goliath.

Cetarari (Crarari, Ctatiriri): One of the four angels of winter.

Chabalym: An angel of either the Seraphim (*qv*) or Cherubim (*qv*) invoked in Kabbalistic magical rites.

Chabril: Serving under Farris (*qv*) as an angel of the second hour of the night.

Chachmal: One of 70 amulet angels (*qv*).

Chachmiel: *See* **Chachmal**.

Chadakiel: *See* **Hadakiel**.

Chafriel: One of 70 amulet angels (*qv*).

Chahoel: One of the 72 angels who rule the 72 quinaries of the degrees of the zodiac.

Chaigidiel: In Kabbalism, the averse Sephira (*qv*) corresponding to Chochma (wisdom) from the Tree of Life in the Briatic world.

Chairoum: The angel of the North, according to the apocryphal *Gospel of Bartholomew*.

Chaldkydri: Archangels of the flying elements of the sun, residing in the Fourth Heaven, linked to phoenixes and in between Cherubim (*qv*) and Seraphim (*qv*). They have 12 wings and at the rising of the sun they burst into song. They reside in the Fourth Heaven. To the Gnostics they are demons.

Chalkatoura: The *Gospel of Bartholomew* describes him as one of nine angels 'that run together throughout the heavenly and earthly places'.

Chamuel (Simiel): An archangel and chief of the Dominations (*qv*). He also rules the Powers (*qv*) along with Nisroc (*qv*) and others. Like Gabriel (*qv*), he is described as the angel of Gethsemane (*qv*) who reassured Jesus about resurrection.

Chamyel: Listed with 14 other angels in *The Sixth and Seventh Books of Moses* (*qv*).

Chaniel: One of the 70 amulet angels.

Chantare: *See* **Hahael**.

Charavah: *See* **Charbiel**.

Charbiel (Charavah): An angel appointed to 'draw together and dry up all the waters of the Earth.' He was the angel who dissipated the waters of the Flood.

Charby: An angel of the fifth hour, under Abasdarhon (*qv*).

Charciel (Charsiel): Angel of the Fourth Heaven who rules on the Sabbath and must be invoked from the South.

Chardiel: An angel of the second hour, under Anael (*qv*).

Chardros: An angel of the 11th hour, under Bariel (*qv*).

Chariots: The angelic hosts in the Hebrew Bible.

Chariots of God: The Ophanim (*qv*), a class of angel identified by Milton with the Cherubim (*qv*) and Seraphim (*qv*).

Charis: A great angel created by the divine will. The name Charis is of Greek origin and means 'Grace' and 'kindness'.

Charman: An angel of the 11th hour of the night, under Dardariel (*qv*).

Charmeas: An angel of the first hour of the day, under Sammael (*qv*).

Charms: An angel of the ninth hour of the day, under Vadriel (*qv*).

Charnij: An angel of the tenth hour of the day.

Charoum: An angel who presides over the North.

Charouth: The Gospel of Bartholomew describes him as one of nine angels 'that run together throughout the heavenly and earthly places'.

Charpon: A ruling angel of the first hour of the day, under Samael (*qv*).

Charsiel: *See* **Charciel**.

Charuch: Angel of the sixth hour of the day, under Samil (*qv*).

Chasan: An Angel of the Air whose name is inscribed on the seventh pentacle of the sun, in *The Greater Key of Solomon* (*qv*).

Chasdiel: A name for Metatron (*qv*) when he is being kind to the world.

Chaskiel: One of 70 amulet angels that can be summoned to help at childbirth.

Chasmal: *See* **Hashmal**.

Chasmodai: Paracelsus (*qv*) describes this angel as the spirit of the moon.

Chassiel: An angel of the sun, in grimoire.

Chastiser: The Kolazonta, the destroying angel.

Chaumel: One of the 72 angels who rule the 72 quinaries of the degrees of the zodiac.

Chavakiah: One of the 72 angels who bear the name of God Shemhamphorae.

Chaya: The singular of Hayyoth (*qv*).

Chaylim: Armies of angels ruled by Chayyliel (*qv*).

Chaylon: Either a Cherub (*qv*) or a Seraph (*qv*) mentioned in *The Sixth and Seventh Books of Moses* (*qv*) who may be used in invocations.

Chayo: An Angel of the Throne (*qv*) listed in *The Sixth and Seventh Books of Moses* (*qv*) who may be called upon in ritual magic.

Chayoh: *See* **Hayyoth**.

Chayyiel: Chief of the Holy Hayyoth (Cherubim).

Chayyliel H' (Chayyiel, Haileal, Hayyel): A great Merkabah angel, ruling prince of the Chayyoth or the Hayyoth. Enoch describes him as so great and powerful that he could swallow the Earth in one gulp. He is in charge of the celestial choirs and punishes with floggings of fire if angels sing the Holy Trisagion out of time.

Chebo: One of the 72 angels who rule the 72 quinaries of the degrees of the zodiac.

Chedustaniel (Chedusitanick): A Friday angel of the Third Heaven who must be invoked from the East. Also an angel of the planet Jupiter.

Chemos: Angel equated with Peor (*qv*) and Nisroc (*qv*). The poet Milton describes him as a fallen angel in *Paradise Lost*.

Cheratiel: Angel of the sixth hour of the night, under Zaazonash.

Cheriour: A 'terrible angel' responsible for punishment of crime and the pursuit of criminals, mentioned in *Dictionnaire Infernal* (*qv*).

Chermes: Angel of the ninth hour of the night, under Nacoriel (*qv*).

Chermiel: An angel of Friday, residing in the Third Heaven who must be invoked from the South.

Cherub (Kerub): Singular for Cherubim (*qv*), an angel of the air who as Cherub was created to be 'Guardian of the Terrestrial Paradise, with a sword of flame.'

Cherubiel (Kerubiel): Head of the order of Cherubim (*qv*). Gabriel (*qv*) is also named in this role.

Cherubim (Kerubim): *See* right.

Chesed: The fourth Sephira (*qv*). Chesed is a name of Hebrew origin and means 'kindness'.

Chesetial: A governing angel of the zodiac.

Chieftains: To Kabbalists, a term describing the 70 prince-guardians ascribed to the nations of the Earth.

Children of Heaven: The sons of the angels who fell and co-habited with mortal women.

Chirangiyah: *See* **Parasurama**.

Chismael: The ruling spirit of the planet Jupiter, according to Paracelsus (*qv*).

Chiva: *See* **Hayyoth**.

Chobaliel: In his work *Of Angels, Genii and Devils*, French philosopher Voltaire lists Chobaliel as a fallen angel.

Choch(k)ma: The second of the holy Sefiroth or divine emanations, equated with Ratziel (Raziel, *qv*). In Mathers' *The Kabbala Unveiled*, Choch(k)ma is the first of God's creations to have actually reached materialization.

ABOVE: *The Annunciation to the Shepherds*
by Nicolaes Pietersz Berchem, 1656

Cherubim (Kerubim): Assyrian or Akkadian in origin and derived from the word 'karibu' meaning 'one who prays' or 'one who intercedes'. The Assyrians depicted them as huge, winged creatures with leonine or human faces and the bodies of bulls, sphinxes or eagles and they were placed at entrances to palaces or temples to guard against evil spirits. To the early Canaanites they were not angels, but later began to be conceived as heavenly spirits. Philo, living in the first century AD believed them to be God's highest and most important Powers. They are the first angels mentioned in the Old Testament. They guarded the Tree of Life and Eden. In the Dionysian scheme of the celestial hierarchy, they rank second of the nine choirs of angels. They are guardians of the fixed stars and rulers include Ophaniel (*qv*), Rikbiel (*qv*), Cherubiel (*qv*), Raphael (*qv*), Gabriel (*qv*), Zophiel (*qv*) and Satan (*qv*), before his fall. Islam claims that the Cherubim were formed from the tears of the archangel Michael (*qv*) who was made to weep by the sins of the faithful. In art, Cherubim are always depicted as baby-like angels, the very epitome of innocence. Beloved babies and toddlers are often affectionately referred to as 'cherubs'.

LEFT: *Justice*
by Simon Vouet, *c*.1637–38

Cardinal Virtues: In some aspects of Christianity it is believed that there four Cardinal Virtues: Justice, Temperance, Prudence and Fortitude. Each Cardinal Virtue serves as a hinge on which all moral virtues depend. In the Bible the three heavenly graces (faith, hope and love) are mentioned, and sometimes the four Cardinal Virtues are grouped with these. Plato linked these figures to his idea of society in his famous work *The Republic*.

Chochmael (Hochmel): An angel of the Sephira (*qv*) who can be invoked in magic rituals.

Choesed: *See* **Hoesediel**.

Chofniel: Chief of the Bene Elohim (*qv*).

Choriel: An angel of the eighth hour of the day, under Osgaebial (*qv*).

Chorob: An angel of the tenth hour of the day, under Oriel (*qv*).

Chosniel: An angel invoked in order to obtain a good memory and an open heart.

Chrail (Chreil): A Mandaean angel.

Chreil: *See* **Chrail**.

Chromme: An angel who corresponds to Nanael (*qv*).

Chrymos: An angel of the fifth hour, under Abasdarhon (*qv*).

Chuabotheij: An angel of the seal (*qv*).

Churl (Churdad): To the ancient Persians, an angel in charge of the disk of the sun.

Chusha: Listed with 14 other angels of the throne (*qv*) in *The Sixth and Seventh Books of Moses* (*qv*).

Chushiel: A guard at the gates of the South Wind.

Chutriel: A ruling angel of Hell.

Cochabiel: Angel of the planet Mercury. According to Cornelius Agrippa (*qv*), one of seven princes 'who stand continually before God and to whom are given the spirit names of the planets.'

Cogediel: One of the angels of the mansions of the moon (*qv*).

Cohabiting Glory: A name given to Shekinah (*qv*).

Colopatiron: A spirit who opens prison gates, according to *The Nuctemeron* (*qv*), and an angel of the ninth hour.

Comadiel: An angel of the third hour of the day, under Veguaniel (*qv*).

Comary: An angel of the ninth hour, under Narcoriel (*qv*).

Comato(s): An angel invoked in the exorcism of wax.

Comforter: Another name for The Holy Ghost.

Comissoros: One of the four angels of spring.

Conamas: An angel invoked in the exorcism of wax.

Confessors: An order of the celestial hierarchy as listed in *The Hierarchy of the Blessèd Angels* (*qv*). The chief of this order is Barakiel.

Coniel: An angel of Friday, residing in the third Heaven, invoked from the West. Also noted as a messenger of the planet Jupiter.

Contemplation: A Cherub mentioned in Milton's poem, 'Il Penseroso'.

Cophi: An angel invoked in the exorcism of wax.

Corabael: A Monday angel who resides in the First Heaven and who must be invoked from the West.

Corael: Invoked along with Setchiel (*qv*) and Chedustaniel (*qv*) and can be petitioned for the satisfaction of the invocant's desire.

Corat: An angel of the air of Friday, invoked from the East and residing in the Third Heaven.

Core: One of the angels of spring, according to *The Magus* (*qv*).

Coriel: An angel of the seventh hour of the night, under Mendrion (*qv*).

Corobael: *See* **Corabael**.

Cosel: An angel of the first hour of the night, under Gamiel (*qv*), mentioned in *The Book of Ceremonial Magic* (*qv*).

Cosmagogi: The three angelic guides of the universe, according to the Chaldean cosmological scheme.

Cosmiel: An angel who travelled with the 17th-century Jesuit scientist, Athanasius Kircher on his journeys to other planets, as told in his *Oedipus Aegyptiacus*.

Cosmocrator: According to Valentinian Gnosticism, the ruler of the cosmos disguised as Diabolos, the devil. With his consort, Barbelo, he sings praises to the powers of the Light. He is, therefore, probably not entirely evil.

Covering Cherub: **William** Blake names him as 'Lucifer in his former glory', in his mythological writings.

Craoscha: *See* **Sraosha**.

Cripon: An angel invoked in magic, especially when the reed is being conjured, according to *The Greater Key of Solomon* (*qv*) and *The Lesser Key of Solomon* (*qv*).

Crocell (Crokel, Pocel, Pucel): A fallen angel once of the order of Powers (*qv*), now commanding 48 legions of demons. He expects to return to his former position in Heaven but for the moment teaches geometry and the liberal arts.

Crociel: An angel who under Barginiel (*qv*) rules the seventh hour of the day.

Crowned Seraph: The devil. He is depicted as a crowned Seraph (*qv*) in his role as tempter in Eden. Fabricius claimed that it was his crown, worn by right of his office as light-bearer, that distinguished Lucifer (*qv*) from other Seraphs.

Cruciel: An angel of the third hour of the night, under Sarquamich.

Ctarari: One of the two angels of winter, the other being Amabael (*qv*).

Cukbiel: An angel who is used in the binding spell, 'Binding the Tongue of the Ruler', in the Syrian text of invocation rituals, *The Book of Protection* edited by Herman Gollancz and in E.A. Wallis Budge's *Amulets and Talismans* (*qv*).

Cuniali: The spirit of association and one of the ruling genii of the eighth hour, mentioned in *The Nuctemeron* (*qv*).

Cupra: A member of the Novensiles (*qv*) – the nine great Etruscan deities who controlled thunderbolts.

Curaniel: A Monday angel residing in the First Heaven, who is invoked from the South.

Cureton: An angel invoked in black magic ritual.

Curson: *See* **Purson**.

Cynabal: An angel serving under Varcan (*qv*) who is king of the air on the Sabbath.

Daath: According to the Kabbalah, the hidden Sephira (*qv*) between the first and second spheres. Representing knowledge, it has sexual connotations, but these are of spiritual sexuality representing divine union and ecstasy. The word Daath is of Hebrew origin and means 'knowledge'.

Dabariel: *See* **Radueriel**.

Dabria: One of the five angelic transcribers of the Book of Ezra. The other four were Ecanus (*qv*), Sarea (*qv*), Selemiah (*qv*) and Asiel (*qv*).

Dabriel: An angelic scribe, residing in the First Heaven. A ruler of Monday who is invoked from the North.

Daden: A powerful celestial being residing in the Sixth Heaven.

Daemon (Daimon, Demon): *See* page 93.

Daeva (Deva): Malicious Zoroastrian beings created by Ahriman (*qv*). In both Hinduism and Theosophy, however, they are benign, in Theosophy making up an order of spirits that 'rules the universe under the deity.'

Daghiel: *See* **Dagiel.**

Dagiel (Daghiel, Daiel): In *The Magus* (*qv*), Dagiel is a powerful Friday angel holding dominion over fish and also an angel of the planet Venus.

Dagon: The poet Milton describes him in *Paradise Lost* as a fallen angel. The ancient Phoenicians considered him a national god, depicting him with the body of a fish.

Dagymiel: A ruling angel of the zodiac, according to Cornelius Agrippa (*qv*).

Dahak: *See* **Ahriman**, the Satan of Persia.

Dahariel (Dariel): A guard of the First Heaven of the Shinanim order. Other sources say he is a guard of the Fifth Heaven.

Dahavauron: A guard of the Third Heaven.

Dahaviel (Kahaviel): One of the First Heaven's seven angelic guards.

Dahnay: An angel who can be invoked in black magic rituals despite being cited as a 'holy angel of God'. Dahnay features in grimoires.

Dai (Dey): An angel of the order of Powers (*qv*). The ancient Persians considered him the angel of December.

ABOVE: *St. Michael Overwhelming the Demon* by Raphael, 1518

Daemon (Daimon, Demon): The ancient Greeks considered them to be benign spirits, familiars, or angels. One source suggests that Daemon stands for the 'father-mother of the universe'. The modern understanding of a 'daemon' or 'demon' is the opposite of an angel; a dark and malevolent creature, linked closely to Satan (*qv*) and the residents of Hell.

Daiel: *See* **Dagiel**.

Daimon: *See* **Daemon**.

Daksha: A Vedic deity equivalent to Judaeo-Christian angels.

Dalkiel: An angel of Hell who is equated with Rugziel (*qv*). He assists Duma (*qv*), the angel of the stillness of death. According to 13th century Spanish Kabbalist Joseph Gikatilla ben Abraham, Dalkiel works in the seventh lodge of Hell and is responsible for 'punishing ten nations.' Documented in his work *Bairata de Massachet Gehinnon*.

Dalmai(i) (Damlay): Invoked to consecrate fire.

Dalquiel: One of three princes of the Third Heaven, the other two being Jabniel (*qv*) and Rabacyel (*qv*). All rule over fire under Anahel (*qv*).

Damabiah: An angel with dominion over naval construction. One of the 72 angels bearing the name of God Shemhamphorae.

Damabiath: Angel of the order of Powers (*qv*) used in Kabbalistic magic ritual. When summoned, he appears as a beautiful being.

Damsel: A Tuesday angel, resident in the Fifth Heaven, invoked from the East.

Dameb'el: One of the 72 angels who rule the 72 quinaries of the degrees of the zodiac.

Damiel: An angel of the fifth hour, under Sequel (*qv*) or angel of the ninth hour, under Vadriel (*qv*).

Damlay: *See* **Dalmai**.

Daniel: Angel of the order of Principalities, listed as a fallen angel by Enoch. In the Underworld he holds dominion over lawyers. In *The Magus* (*qv*), however, he is described as a high holy angel. He bears the name of God Shemhamphorae, like 71 other angels. Daniel is a name of Hebrew origin meaning 'God is my judge'.

Danjal: *See* **Daniel**.

Dara: An angel of rains and rivers in ancient Persian lore.

Darbiel: An angel of the tenth hour of the day.

Dardael: *See* **Dardiel**.

Darda'il: In Arab mythology, a guardian angel invoked in magic rituals.

Dardariel: The ruling angel of the 11th hour of the night.

Dardiel: With Michael (*qv*) and Hurtapal (*qv*), an angel of Sunday.

Daresiel: An angel of the first hour of the day.

Dargitael: A guard of the Fifth Heaven.

Dariel: *See* **Dahariel**.

Dark Angel, The: A being (part angel, part man, part God) who fought with Jacob at Peniel and is recognized as either Michael (*qv*), Metatron (*qv*), Uriel (*qv*) or God himself. *The Zohar* (*qv*) names him as Samael and Talmudic scholars say he was Michael-Metatron.

Darkiel: One of the guards at the gates of the South Wind.

Darmosiel: An angel of the 12th hour of the night, under Sarindiel.

Darquiel: A Monday angel, residing in the First Heaven, invoked from the South.

Daryoel: *See* **Radueriel**.

Dasim: In Islam, one of five sons of the fallen angel, Iblis (Eblis – *qv*). They are:

Awar – demon of lubricity

Dasim – demon of discord

Sut – demon of lies

Tir – demon of fatal accidents

Zalambur – demon of mercantile dishonesty.

Daveithe: To the Gnostics, one of four great beings surrounding God.

David: An archon (*qv*) in Gnosticism.

Dealzhat: A powerful and secret name of God or a great entity invoked by Joshua to make the sun stop moving.

Degaliel: Name of an angel inscribed on the third pentacle of the planet Venus, mentioned in *The Greater Key of Solomon* (*qv*).

Degalim: One of the sub-choirs that sings the Trisagion under the leadership of the archangel, Tagas.

Deharhiel: A guard of the Fifth Heaven.

Deheborym: A guard of the First Heaven.

Deliel: An angel of the fourth chora who can be invoked in magic ritual. Named by Cornelius Agrippa (*qv*) as a governing angel of the zodiac.

Delafield: A guard of the Seventh Heaven.

Demiurge: The great archon (*qv*) in Gnosticism, equated with God and the Jews. Identified with Mithras, he is also known as the 'Architect of the Universe', suggesting that he, not God, created the world at the insistence of En Soph, the Unknowable.

Demon: *See* **Daemon**.

Demoniarch: Another name for Satan (*qv*).

Deputies: French philosopher Voltaire claimed them to be an order of angels.

Deputy Angels: In Jewish magic the deputy angels are the Menunim and they are usually viewed as evil. The 13th-century sage, Eleazar of Worms, believed them to be holy angels.

Deramiel: Angel serving in the Third Heaven.

Derdekea: A powerful female angel, referred to as the Supreme Mother, who descends to Earth to save mankind.

Destroying Angel: The angel of death.

Devatas: Angels in Vedic lore.

Devil: *See* **Satan**.

Dey: *See* **Dai**.

Dictionnaire Infernal (Infernal Dictionary): Jacques Auguste Simon Collin de Plancy wrote this book on demonology and superstition in 1818.

Didnaor: An angel mentioned in *The Book of the Angel Raziel* (*qv*).

Dina: Following Creation Dina taught mortals 70 different languages. He is a guardian angel of the law (Torah) and resides in the Seventh Heaven.

Diniel: One of the 70 amulet angels (*qv*). He is also a spellbinding angel in 'the binding of the tongue of the ruler', according to *Amulets and Talismans* (*qv*).

Dirachiel: One of the angels of the mansions of the moon (*qv*).

Dirael: A guard of the Sixth Heaven.

Divine Beasts: The holy Hayyoth (*qv*).

Divine Wisdom: The Second of the holy Sephiroth (*qv*), personified by the angel Raziel (*qv*).

Djibril (Gabriel, Jibril): In the Koran, the 'Faithful Spirit'.

Dobiel: *See* **Dubbiel**.

Dodekas: Divine Powers under the rule of Ogdoas.

Dokiel: The *Testament of Abraham* (*qv*) describes

him as 'the archangel who is like the sun, holding the balance in his hand.'

Domedon-Doxomedon: The 'aeon of aeons' (*qv*) who is under the rule of Ogdoas.

Domiel (Dumiel): A guardian angel of the sixth hall of the Seventh Heaven. Prince of majesty, fear and trembling, he is an archon (*qv*) and a ruler of the four elements.

Dominations (Dominions, Lords, Lordships): An order ranked fourth in the celestial hierarchy. Hebrew lore names them as the Hashmallim. According to Dionysius, they regulate angel duties and aspire to true lordship. The chief of the order is Pi-Zeus (*qv*) and sceptres and orbs are the emblems of authority.

Dominion: The oldest angel, according to the philosopher, Philo of Alexandria. Documented in *Thrice-Greatest Hermes*, by G. R. S. Mead.

Domos: An angel invoked in magic ritual whose name is another name for the evil eye, mentioned in *Amulets and Talismans* (*qv*).

Donachiel: An angel summoned to control demons, according to *The Greater Key of Solomon* (*qv*).

Donahan: An archangel invoked in magic ritual, mentioned in *The Sixth and Seventh Books of Moses* (*qv*).

Donel: A guard at the gates of the South Wind.

Doniel: A ruler of the zodiac, according to Kabbalah.

Donquel: A ruler of love who is invoked to win the heart of a desired woman, in *The Book of Ceremonial Magic* (*qv*).

Doremiel: A guard at the gates of the West Wind.

Dormiel: A guard at the gates of the East Wind.

Doucheil: A Mandaean angel.

Douth: One of the nine angels said to 'run together throughout the heavenly and earthly places', from the *Gospel of Bartholomew* (*qv*)

Doxomedon: A great angel mentioned in the Gnostic work *Revelations of Zostrian*.

Dracon: An angel of the sixth hour of the night, according to *The Lesser Key of Solomon* (*qv*).

Dragon: A name for Satan in the Book of Revelation.

Dramazod: An angel of the sixth hour of the night, under Zaazonash.

Dramozin: An angel of the eighth hour of the night, under Narcoriel (*qv*).

Drelmeth: An angel of the third hour of the day, under Veguaniel (*qv*).

Drial: A guard of the Fifth Heaven.

Drsmiel: A malevolent angel, summoned to separate a husband from a wife, mentioned in *The Sword of Moses* (*qv*).

Druiel: A guard at the gates of the South Wind.

Dubbiel: The guardian angel of Persia and a special accuser of Israel. Is said to have stood in for Gabriel (*qv*), officiating in Heaven for 21 days. All the angels of the nations became corrupted, apart from Michael (*qv*), angel of Israel; Dubbiel must, therefore, be regarded as an evil angel.

Duchiel: An angel invoked for controlling demons, from *The Greater Key of Solomon* (*qv*).

Duhael: A Jewish angel with a name not of Jewish origin.

Dumah or Douma: The tutelary angel of Egypt, a prince of Hell in charge of thousands of angels of destruction and 120,000 servants charged with punishing sinners. He is the angel of silence, of the stillness of death and of vindication. He is also the guardian of the 14th gate of Hell.

Dumariel: An angel of the 11th hour of the night, under Dardariel (*qv*), according to *The Lesser Key of Solomon* (*qv*).

Dumiel: *See* **Domiel**.

Dunahel: *See* **Alimiel**.

Dunamis: *See* Dynamis.

Durba'il: Islamic guardian angel invoked in exorcism ritual.

Duvdeviyah: Another of the many names of the angel Metatron (*qv*)

Dynamis (Dunamis): One of the most important of the seven aeons (*qv*), as the male personification of power.

Ea: *See* **Taurine Angel**.

Ebed: One of the numerous names for Metatron (*qv*).

Eblis: Satan (*qv*), in Islam, and to the ancient Persians. He is said to have formerly been treasurer in Heaven while another source says that his name was Azazel (*qv*) before his fall which was caused by his refusal to worship Adam (*qv*).

Ebriel: Ninth of the ten unholy Sephiroth (*qv*).

Ebuhuel: One of the eight angels of omnipotence (*qv*) listed in *The Sixth and Seventh Books of Moses* (*qv*) who may be invoked in ritual conjuration.

Ecanus (Elkanah): One of the five angels who transcribed the books dictated to them by Ezra (*qv*). Seventy were to be kept hidden while the remainder were for general use.

Efniel: A Cherubim (*qv*).

Egibiel: One of the angels of the mansions of the moon (*qv*).

Egion: A guard of the Seventh Heaven.

Egoroi: *See* **Grigori**.

Egregori: *See* **Grigori**.

Egrimiel (Egrumiel): A guard of the Sixth Heaven.

Eheres: An angel invoked in the exorcism of wax.

Eiael (Abiou): An angel holding dominion over the Occult sciences and who has the power to prolong life. One of the 72 Shemhamphorae, when he is invoked the invocant must recite the fourth verse of Psalm 36.

Eighth Heaven: Muzaloth in Hebrew and the home of the 12 signs of the zodiac, according to *2 Enoch* (See *The Book of Enoch*), although the ninth Heaven is also named as the home of the zodiac signs.

Eirnilus: An angel holding dominion over fruit and an angel of the sixth hour, according to *The Nuctemeron* (*qv*).

Eisheth Zenunim: According to *The Zohar* (*qv*), she is an angel of prostitution (*qv*) and married to Smal (*qv*).

Eistibus: An angel of divination, and an angel of the fourth hour.

El: The singular of Elohim. God or an angel. El is also an angel who had children – Shahar and Shalim – by a mortal woman.

El El: A guard at the gates of the North Wind.

Eladel: In Kabbalism, Eladel is one of the angels who rule the zodiac.

El-Adrel: In grimoire, El-Adrel is an angel invoked to bring the invocant music.

Elamiz: An angel of the 11th hour of the night, under Dadariel (*qv*), according to *The Lesser Key of Solomon* (*qv*).

Elamos: An angel invoked by the Master of the Art according to the *Grimorium Verum* (*qv*).

Elberith: *See* **Balberith**.

Elders: Twenty-four elders, dressed in white, sit on 24 Hashmallim (*qv*) around the throne of God, each with a harp and a bowl of incense representing the prayers of the saints. One source says they represent a college or choir of angels that derives from the 24 Babylonian star-gods and represent the 24 priestly orders. *2 Enoch* (See *The Book of Enoch*) describes them as being in the first of the Seven Heavens.

Elect One, The: Identified as Metatron and the Son of Man in *1 Enoch* (See *The Book of Enoch*).

Electors: The seven planetary spirits or angels of Hell are listed in the *Testament of Solomon* (*qv*) as:
Barbiel, under Zaphiel
Mephistophiel, under Zadkiel
Ganael, under Apadiel and Camael
Aciel, under Raphael
Anael, under Haniel
Ariel, under Michael
Marbuel, under Gabriel.

Eleinos: One of the aeons (*qv*).

Eleleth (Heleleth): One of four angels that surround the arch-aeon Autogenes (*qv*).

Elemiah: A guardian angel to those travelling on water, a Seraphim (*qv*) of the Tree of Life and a member of the 72 Shemhamphorae.

Elijah: *See* page 98.

Elilaios: An aeon (*qv*) who is also a resident of the Sixth Heaven.

Elim: Guardian angel of Libbeus, the Apostle, but also a term for a high order of angels. The name Elim is of Hebrew origin and means 'mighty ones'.

Elimelech: An angel of summer, associated with the angel He'el. Elimlech means 'my God is king' in Hebrew.

Elimiel: In Kabbalism, the angel of the moon.

Elion or Elyon: An assistant to Ofaniel (*qv*) in the First Heaven and also invoked in conjuring the reed. Moses summoned Elion to bring down hail on Egypt at the time of the Plagues.

Eliphaniasai: An angel of the third chora, who may be invoked in magical prayer.

Elkanah: *See* **Ecanus**.

Eloa: A great male angel who is the hero of the 18th-century German poetic epic, *The Messiah*, by Friedrich Gottlieb Klopstock. French novelist Alfred de Vigny wrote a poem entitled "Eloa" in which the eponymous angel has been formed from a tear shed by Jesus.

Eloai: An archon (*qv*).

Eloeus: In Phoenican mythology, Eloeus is one of the seven angels of the presence, the creators of the universe.

Elogium: An angel governing the Hebrew month of Elul (September).

Eloha: The singular form of Elohaym or Elohim (*qv*). Listed in *The Sixth and Seventh Books of Moses* (*qv*) as an angel of the order of Powers (*qv*).

Eloheij: An angel of the seal (*qv*), as mentioned in *The Sixth and Seventh Books of Moses* (*qv*).

Elohi: In *The Greater Key of Solomon* (*qv*), Elohi is an angel of fire whose name when invoked can dry the seas and rivers by divine command. Must be invoked by a Master of the Art. Elohi are also the fifth of the celestial hierarchies answering to the ten names of God.

Elohim: Hebrew for Jehovah, Elohim is made up of the female singular 'eloh' plus the masculine plural 'im' rendering God androgynous. The Elohim rank ninth in the celestial hierarchy.

Eloiein: One of the seven Elohim (*qv*) created by Iadalbaoth (*qv*) in his own image.

ABOVE: *Elijah in the Wilderness*
by Frederic Leighton, 1878.

Elijah (Elias in Greek): Elijah was one of the two Old Testament Hebrew patriarchs who were taken up to Heaven while they still lived, the other being Enoch. They were both taken on a chariot of fire drawn by fiery horses and Enoch became Metatron (*qv*) while Elijah may have become Sandalphon (*qv*). One story has Elijah almost defeating the angel of death in battle, stopped only by God who had other plans for that particular angel. Pirke Rabbi Eliezer says that Elijah has to stand at the crossways of Paradise and guide the pious to their appointed places. Another rabbinic source names Elijah as the Angel of the Covenant. At Jewish Passover festivals, a place is set for Elijah as 'the expected guest'.

Elomeel (Ilylumiel): A regent of the seasons in *1 Enoch* (See *The Book of Enoch*).

Elomnia (Elomina): One of the five princes of the third chora.

Elorkhaios: A mysterious Gnostic being to whom the secrets of creation were revealed.

Elspeth Zenunim: Zoroastrian angel of prostitution, a wife of Sammael (*qv*), the others being Lilith (*qv*), Naamah (*qv*) and Agrat bat Mahlah(t) (*qv*).

Elubatel: One of the eight omnipotent angels and an angel invoked during conjurations of the beast Leviathan (*qv*), over which he has control.

Emekmiyahu: One of the many names of the angel Metatron (*qv*).

Emial: An angel invoked for the exorcism of the bat.

Emmanuel: The angel who appeared in the fiery furnace beside Sidras (*qv*), Misac (*qv*) and Abednego (*qv*). He is invoked under the third seal. Emmanuel is a Hebrew name meaning 'God with us'.

Empire: Angelic order taking the place of Virtues in *A History of the Warfare of Science with Theology in Christendom* by Andrew Dickson White.

Empyrean: The abode of God and the angels. To Ptolemy, Milton and Dante it lay in the Fifth Heaven.

Enediel: One of the angels of the mansions of the moon (*qv*).

Enejie: An angel of the seal (*qv*) invoked in magical rites.

Enga: A name of God used to invoke Lucifer in Monday conjurations.

Enoch-Metatron: In Heaven Enoch was transformed into the great hierarch, Metatron, 'king over all the angels'. It is said that Enoch-Metatron is the twin brother of Sandalphon (*qv*) and that he had 365,000 eyes and 36 pairs of wings. In Islam, Enoch is Idris (*qv*) and legend also connects him with Behemoth (*qv*).

En Soph: In Kabbalism, En Soph is a name for the creator of the universe, God.

Entities: An order of angels wrapped in gold lame.

Enwo: The uthra (Mandaean angel) of science and wisdom, the equivalent of the Judaeo-Christian Raphael who is also a spirit of the seven planets.

Eoluth: A Cherub (*qv*) or Seraph (*qv*) used for Kabbalistic conjuring.

Eomiahe: Occult angel invoked in the exorcism of the bat.

Eon: *See* Aeon.

Ephemerae: A group of angels re-created every day by God to sing his praises. They fade away at the end of the singing.

Epima: Equivalent to Eiael (*qv*).

Epinoia: To the Gnostics, the first female manifestation of God.

Epititiokh: A virgin aeon (*qv*).

Eradin: In black magic, Eradin is an angel invoked in special ceremonial rites.

Erastiel: An angel serving in the fourth hall of the Fifth Heaven.

Erathaol (Erathaoth): One of the seven archons (*qv*).

Erathaoth: *See* Erathaol.

Eregbuo: Angel corresponding to Daniel (*qv*).

Erel: A name uttered in Solomonic conjuration to make demons appear, mentioned in *The Greater Key of Solomon* (*qv*).

Erelim: Hebrew for the Hashmallim (*qv*). They are formed of white fire and reside in the Third Heaven, although some place them in the Fourth or Fifth. There are 70,000 myriads of them and they provide protection for trees, grasses, grains and the fruits of the Earth. One of ten classes of angels under the rule of Michael (*qv*).

Eremiel (Hierimiel, Jeremiel, Remiel): An angel who watches over souls in the Underworld. He is equated with Ariel (*qv*).

Ergedial: One of the angels of the mansions of the moon (*qv*).

Erionas (Erione): An angel invoked during the exorcism of the wax.

Ermosiel: An angel of the second hour, under Anael (*qv*).

Ero: The angel corresponding to Haziel (*qv*).

Erotosi: Spirit of the planet Mars, invoked in talismanic magic ritual.

Ertrael: A fallen angel.

Erygion: Joshua invoked the name of this angel to achieve victory over the Moabites.

Erzla: In Occult lore, Erzla is a benign angel invoked in magic rituals.

Esabiel: An angel of the order of Powers (*qv*).

Escavor: An angel invoked in magic rituals according to the *Grimorium Verum* (*qv*).

Eshiel: *See* Eschol.

Eschol (Eshiel): An angel – along with three others – whose name is inscribed on the first pentacle of the planet Mars, the others being Ithuriel (*qv*), Madimiel (*qv*) and Barzachia (*qv*).

Eschiros: In Kabbalism, Eschiros is a planetary angel invoked in conjuring.

Eserchie/Oriston: The angel invoked by Moses when God introduced the plague of frogs to Egypt. Also invoked, according to one source, when the rivers of Egypt were turned to blood.

Eshiniel: An angel whose name is used for Syriac spellbinding charms.

Eshmadai: A demon king.

Esor: A Cherub (*qv*) or Seraph (*qv*) used in Kabbalistic conjuration.

Esphares: Name of an angel or of God used in conjuration.

Espiacent: An angel used in exorcism of wax for bringing about successful accomplishments. Psalms must be cited after these rites.

Estael: To black magicians, an intelligence of the planet Jupiter. The other three are Kadiel (*qv*), Maltiel (*qv*) and Huphatriel (*qv*).

Estes: Another of the many names of Metatron (*qv*).

Eth: A ministering angel responsible for ensuring that things happen punctually.

Ethnarchs: The 70 tutelary angels given guardianship of nations.

Etraphill: Islamic angel who will sound the trumpet on Judgment Day.

Etrempsuchos (Astrompsuchos): A guard of the Seventh Heaven.

Euchey: An angel invoked to exorcise evil spirits while using incense and fumigation.

Eudaemon: A good spirit. A Greek term for angel.

Eurabatres: *See* **Iurabatres**.

Eve: *See* opposite.

Eved: One of the many names for Metatron (*qv*).

Exael: An angel of whom Enoch says: 'tenth of the great angels that taught men how to fabricate engines of war, works in silver and gold, the uses of gems and perfume.' He resides in the Underworld.

Existon: An angel invoked in the blessing of the salt.

Extabor: An angel used in the exorcism of wax.

Exterminans: Latin for Abaddon (*qv*).

Ezeqeel: A fallen angel who taught fortune-telling.

Ezgadi: Name of an angel used in magic ritual for ensuring the safe completion of journeys.

Ezoiil: A spirit invoked in the exorcism of water.

Ezra: Heavenly scribe. Vretil (*qv*), Enoch and Dabriel (*qv*) are also given this role.

Ezrael: An angel of wrath. The name Ezrael is of Hebrew origin and means 'help of God'.

Ezriel: Name of an angel that was discovered on an Aramaic amulet found with the Dead Sea Scrolls.

ABOVE: *Adam and Eve*
by William Strang, 1899

Eve: Considered by the Hebrew Bible, Old Testament and Koran to be the first female, and second mortal, in creation. Eve is an important figure in Christianity, Judaism and Islam. She is thought to have been formed from Adam's (*qv*) rib and is responsible for bringing sin into the world by giving into temptation in the Garden of Eden. According to the *Revelation of Moses*, Eve was in the Garden of Eden praying on her knees for forgiveness of her sins when the Angel of Humanity appeared before her. "Arise, Eve, from thy repentance; for behold, Adam thy husband has gone forth from his body", said the angel, as Eve rose to her feet.

Fabriel: An angel serving in the Fourth Heaven.

Faith: One of the three theological Virtues (*qv*) often depicted in art in the form of angels by 15th-century artists.

Fakr-Ed-Din: A Yezidic archangel invoked by prayer.

Fallen Angels: The idea of the fallen angel, absent from the Old Testament, appears in the New Testament, in Revelation 12. 'And his [the dragon's, or Satan's] tail drew the third part of the stars of Heaven and did cast them to the Earth…and Satan, which deceiveth the whole world; he was cast out into the Earth and his angels were cast out with him.' The number who fell was estimated by Enoch to be 200. *1 Enoch* (See *The Book of Enoch*) names the 19 leaders, the most prominent being Semyaza (*qv*), Azazel (*qv*), Sariel (*qv*), Rumiel (*qv*), Danjal (*qv*), Turel (*qv*) and Kokabiel (*qv*). Some estimates say a tenth of all the angels fell but that in their fallen state they retained their rank. Cardinal Bishop of Tusculum maintained in 1273 that a third fell, numbering 133,306,668, leaving behind a total of 266,613,336. Some said that angels fell from each order while others say that only angels of the tenth order fell. As there are only supposed to be nine orders, it is unclear which is being referred to. The list below is drawn from Enoch's lists as well as others:

Abbadonna (formerly of the Seraphim), Adramelec, Agares (Agreas), Amezyarak (Amiziras, another version of Semyaza), Amy (formerly partly of the Powers and partly of the Angels), Anmael (identified with Semyaza), Arakiel (Araqiel), Araziel, Ariel (Formerly of Virtues), Arioc(h), Armaros (Abaros, Armers, Pharmaros), Armen, Artaqifa (Arakiba), Asbeel, Asmoday, Asmodeus (Sammael, formerly of the Seraphim), Astaroth (formerly of the Seraphim and Hashmallim), Astoreth (Astarte), Atarculph, Auza (Oza), Azaradel Azazel (formerly of the Cherubim), Azza,

Azzael (Asael), Balam (formerly of the Dominations), Baraqel (Barakel, Baraqijal), Barbatos (formerly of Virtues), Barbiel (formerly of Virtues), Batarjal, Beelzebub (formerly of the Cherubim), Beliar (Belial, formerly partly of Virtues and partly of Angels), Busasejal, Byleth (Beleth, formerly of the Powers), Balberith (formerly of the Cherubim), Caim (Caym, formerly of the Angels), Carniveau (formerly of the Powers), Carreau (formerly of the Powers), Dagon, Danjal, Ezekeel (Ezequeel), Flauros (Hauras), Gaap (formerly of the Potentates), Gadreel, Gressil (formerly of the Hashmallim), Hakael Hananel (Ananel), Harut (Persian), Iblis (Eblis, Haris, Mohammedan Satan), Ielahiah (formerly of Virtues), Iuvart (formerly of the Angels), Jeqon, Jetrel, Kasdeja, Kawkabel (Kokabel), Lau(v)iah (formerly partly of the Hashmallim and partly of the Cherubim), Leviathan (formerly of the Seraphim), Lucifer (erroneously identified as Satan), Mammon, Marchoasias (formerly of the Dominations), Marut (Persian), Mephistopheles, Meresin, Moloc(h), Mulciber, Murmur (formerly partly of the Hashmallim and partly of the Angels), Nelchael (formerly of Hashmallim), Nilaihah (formerly of Dominations), Oeillet (formerly of Dominations), Olivier (formerly of Archangels), Ouzza (Uziel), Paimon (Paymon, formerly of Dominations), Penamue, Procell (formerly of Powers), Pursan (Curson, formerly of Virtues), Raum (Raym, formerly of Hashmallim), Rimmon, Rosier (formerly of Dominations), Rumael (Ramiel, Remiel), Sammael (Satan, Asmodeus), Samsaweel, Saraknyal, Sariel, Satan, Sealiah (formerly of Virtues), Semyaza (Shemhazai, Azaziel, formerly of the Seraphim), Senciner (formerly partly of Virtues, partly of Powers), Shamshiel, Simapesiel, Sonneillon (formerly of Hashmallim), Tabaet, Thammuz, Tumael, Turael, Turel, Urakabarameel, Usiel (Uzziel, formerly of Virtues), Verrier (formerly of Principalities), Verrine (formerly of Hashmallim), Vual (Vvall, formerly of Powers), Yomyael, Zavebe, Belphegor (Baal-Peor, formerly of Principalities), Forcas (Foras).

Famiel: A Friday angel of the air (*qv*) who serves in the Third Heaven and must be invoked from the South.

Fanuel (Phanuel): One of the four angels of the divine presence.

Farohars: *See* Favashi.

Farris: A ruling angel of the second hour of the night.

Farun Faro Vakshur: The guardian angel of mankind.

Farvardin: An angel of March in ancient Persian lore, who also governed the 19th day of each month. Known as 'one of the Cherubim.'

Favashi (Farohars, Ferchers, Ferouers, Fervers): To Zoroastrians the guardian angels of believers and the prototypes of all beings. They have a duality – angels and beings with human traits and thoughts.

Feluth: *See* **Silat**.

Female Angels: In the Jewish tradition there are few female angels. In Gnostic lore there is Sophia (*qv*) who is a powerful female aeon (*qv*), archon (*qv*) or angel. There are female angels in Islamic legend who were venerated; they were often called Bead Hasche, meaning 'daughters of God'.

Ferchers: *See* **Favashi**.

Ferouers: *See* Favashi.

Fervers: *See* Favashi.

Fiery Angel: *See* **Angel of Fire**.

Fifth Heaven: Where God and the angels reside, the Empyrean, according to Ptolemy. The Grigori, giant fallen angels, crouch in the northern regions 'in silent and everlasting despair'. The prince guardian of the Fifth Heaven is Satqiel (*qv*). In Islamic legend, the Fifth Heaven is the 'seat of Aaron and the Avenging Angel'.

Fire-Speaking Angel: *See* Hashmal.

First Heaven: In Islam, the home of the stars, each with its angelic guardian. Also the abode of Adam (*qv*) and Eve (*qv*).

ABOVE: *Five Angels Playing Musical Instruments c.1487–90*

Five Angels: Who lead the souls of men to judgement, these are Arakiel (*qv*), Remiel (*qv*), Uriel (*qv*), Samiel (*qv*) and Aziel (*qv*).

Flaef: A Kabbalistic luminary concerned with human sexuality.

Flames: An order of angels, said by Voltaire in his *Work Of Angels*, *Genii, and Devils* to be 'one of the classes in Talmud and Targu'. Supreme ruler of the order is Melba, the Buddhist equivalent of the Judaeo-Christian angel Michael (*qv*).

Flaming Angel: *See* **Angel of Fire.**

Flauros: *See* **Hauras.**

Focalor (Forcalor): A fallen angel formerly of the order of the Hashmallim (*qv*) but now a great lord in Hell, commanding 30 legions of demons. His task is to sink warships and kill men. He told Solomon he hopes to return to the Seventh Heaven after 1,000 or 1,500 years. Invoked, he manifests himself as a man with a griffin's wings.

Forcalor: *See* **Focalor.**

Forcas (Foras, Forras, Fourcas): A fallen angel now a grand duke in the Underworld, commanding 29 legions of demons, according to *Dictionnaire Infernal* (*qv*). He instructs humans in rhetoric, logic and mathematics and helps to find things that have been lost. He grants the gift of invisibility when invoked.

Forces: An angelic order sometimes identified as Powers (*qv*) and sometimes as Virtues (*qv*) or Authorities (*qv*). Their specific responsibility was to govern earthly affairs.

Forerunner Angel: *See* **John the Baptist.**

Forfax (Marax, Morax): An angel found in various grimoire, Forfax is a great duke in Hell, commanding 36 legions of demons. He teaches astronomy and liberal arts and manifests in the form of a calf.

Forneus: A fallen angel formerly of the order of the Hashmallim (*qv*). A great duke in the Underworld, he commands 29 legions of demons. He teaches art, rhetoric and every language and causes men to be loved by their enemies. He manifests in the shape of a sea monster.

Fortitude: A cardinal virtue (*qv*).

Four Angels Of the East (or of the rising Sun): Urzla (*qv*), Zlar (*qv*), Larzod (*qv*) and Arzal (*qv*). Benign beings invoked so that the invocant may partake of some of the secret wisdom of the Creator.

Four Archangels: Michael (*qv*), Gabriel (*qv*), Raphael (*qv*) and Phanuel (*qv*), according to *1 Enoch* (See *The Book of Enoch*). The *Universal Standard Encyclopedia* replaces Raphael (*qv*) and Phanuel (*qv*) with Uriel (*qv*) and Suriel (*qv*). In the Islamic tradition they are Gabriel (*qv*), angel of revelation; Michael (*qv*), fighter of the battle of the faith; Azrael, angel of death and Israfel, who will sound the trumpet on judgement day.

Four Sprits of the Heaven: Angels in the shape of four horses – black, white grizzled and grey.

Fourcas: *See* **Forcas.**

Fourth Angel: *See* opposite.

Fourth Heaven: Residence of Shamshiel (*qv*), Sapiel (*qv*), Zagzagael (*qv*) and Michael (*qv*). The Talmud says the heavenly Jerusalem and the altar were there. Sandalphon (*qv*), the angel of tears (*qv*), is also said to dwell here. Mohammed (*qv*) and Enoch met in the Fourth Heaven.

Fowl of Heaven: *See* **Angels of Service**.

Fraciel: In Occultism, Fraciel is a Tuesday angel of the Fifth Heaven who must be invoked from the North.

Framoch: An angel of the seventh hour of the night, under Mandrion (*qv*), mentioned in *The Lesser Key of Solomon* (*qv*).

Fremiel: An angel of the fourth hour of the night, referred to in *The Lesser Key of Solomon* (*qv*).

Friagne: In Occultism, Friagne is a Tuesday angel serving in the Fifth Heaven, invoked from the East.

Fromezin: An angel of the second hour of the night under Farris (*qv*), according to *The Lesser Key of Solomon* (*qv*).

Fromzon: An angel of the third hour of the night, under Sarquamich (*qv*).

Fuleriel: An angel of the sixth hour of the night, under Zaazonash.

Furiel: An angel of the third hour of the day, under Veguaniel (*qv*).

Furlac: In Occult lore, Furlac is an angel of the Earth.

Furmiel: An angel of the 11th hour of the day, under Bariel (*qv*).

Fustiel: An angel of the fifth hour of the day, under Sazquiel (*qv*).

Futiniel: An angel of the fifth hour of the day, under Sazquiel (*qv*).

ABOVE: *The Fourth Angel Poured out his Bowl on the Sun* by Nicolas Bataille, *c*.1373–87

Fourth Angel: In the Book of Revelation, John tells of the seven angels of wrath (*qv*) who each sound trumpets, signalling the end of the world. The sound of the trumpet of the fourth angel destroys a third of the sun, moon and stars.

Gaap (Goap, Tap): A fallen angel formerly of the order of Powers (*qv*). Now a great prince in Hell where he is king of the South and commands 66 infernal legions.

Gabamiah: A powerful angel invoked with the use of the name of the angel Uriel (*qv*).

Gabriel: *See* page 108.

Gabuthelon: One of the nine angels who will rule at the end of the world.

Gadal: An angel invoked in magic ritual, mentioned in *The Book of Ceremonial Magic* (*qv*).

Gadamel: *See* **Hagiel**.

Gader: A guard at the fourth heavenly hall.

Gadiel An angel of the Fifth Heaven and one of the many guards at the gates of the South Wind.

Gadreel: A fallen angel reputed by some to have led Eve (*qv*) astray instead of Satan (*qv*) Gadreel taught man about weapons of war, like Azazel (*qv*).

Gadriel: Ruler of the Fifth Heaven who is in control of wars between nations. He also accompanies prayers to the Sixth Heaven, after

crowning them, according to *The Zohar* (*qv*).

Ga'ga: A guard at the seventh Heavenly Hall.

Gaghiel: A guard of the Sixth Heaven.

Galdel: A Tuesday angel residing in the Fifth Heaven who is to be invoked from the South.

Gale Raziya: One of the numerous names of the angel Metatron (*qv*).

Galearii: The lowest ranking of all the angels. The name Galearii is of Hebrew origin and means 'Army Servants'.

Galgaliel: A chief angel of the sun alongside Raphael (*qv*). He also governs the wheel of the sun and is the leader of the order of Galgallim (*qv*).

Galgallim: A superior order of angels equal in rank to the Seraphim (*qv*). Known as 'the wheels of the Merkabah' they are equivalent to the order of the Ophanim (*qv*).

Galizur (Akrasiel, Gallizur, Raguel, Raziel): A great angel of Talmudic lore encountered by Moses in Heaven. As Raziel, Galizur gave Adam (*qv*) *The Book of the Angel Raziel* (*qv*). He is ruling prince of the Second Heaven. The name Galizur means 'revealer of the rock' in Hebrew.

Gallizur: *See* **Galizur**.

Galmon: An angelic guard of the Fourth Heaven.

Gamaliel: One of the great angels, an assistant to Gabriel (*qv*) who brings the souls of the Lord's elect to Heaven. He is described as an evil angel, however, by Eliphas Levi in his *Philosophies Occulte*, as an evil servant of Lilith (*qv*) who fights against the Cherubim (*qv*). Gamaliel means 'recompense of God' in Hebrew.

Gambiel: The ruler of the zodiac sign of Aquarius. In *The Sixth and Seventh Books of Moses* (*qv*) he is listed as a zodiacal angel.

Gambriel: A guardian angel of the Fifth Heaven.

Gamerin: An angel called in for special service in ceremonial magic ritual according to *The Book of Ceremonial Magic* (*qv*). Before beginning conjuration, his name should be engraved on the Sword of the Art.

Gamidoi: An angel of the first hour of the night.

Gamiel: The ruling angel of the first hour of the night.

Gamrial: One of the 64 angel guardians of the seven Heavens. *See* **Angel-Wardens of the Seven Celestial Halls** for complete list.

Gamsiel: An angel of the eighth hour of the night, under Narcoriel (*qv*).

Ganael: A planetary angel, or Elector (*qv*), serving under the joint command of the angels Apudiel (*qv*) and Camael (*qv*).

Gardon: An angel invoked in the blessing of the salt.

Garfial: A guard of the Fifth Heaven.

Gargatel: An angel of summer, the others being Tariel (*qv*) and Gaviel (*qv*).

Gariel: An angel who is a member of the order of Shinanim (*qv*) and is an angelic guard of the Fifth Heaven.

Garshanel: Name of an angel inscribed on a kamea.

Garthiel: Angelic servant to Gamiel (*qv*), ruler of the first hour of the night.

Garzanal: Name of an angel inscribed on a kamea.

Gaspard: A spirit invoked in magical rites when the invocant wants to obtain a lady's garter, according to *Grimorium Verum* (*qv*).

Gastrion: Serving under Narcoriel (*qv*), an angel of the eighth hour of the night.

Gat(h)tiel: An angelic guard of the Fifth Heaven.

Gauriil Ishliha: Talmudic angel ruling over the East whose job is to make sure that the sun rises on time. He corresponds to the Zoroastrian Sraosha (*qv*) or the Hebrew Gabriel (*qv*) and also appears in Mandaean legend.

Gaviel: An angel of summer, with Tariel (*qv*) and Gargatel (*qv*).

Gavreel (Gavriel): A version of Gabriel's name that is used by the Ethiopian Hebrew Rabbinical College of Black Jews of Harlem in New York. This group believes that there are four cardinal angels (Gavreel; Micharel, for Michael; Owreel, for Uriel; and Rafarel, for Raphael) that can be invoked to cure disease, restore sight, make friends of enemies and keep the invocate 'from going crazy in the night'. Gavreel is a guard at the gates of the East Wind and in Hechaloth lore is a guard of either the Second or Fourth Heaven.

Gavriel: *See* Gavreel.

Gazardiel (Gazardiya, Gezardia): A chief angel of the East, one of the angels responsible for ensuring that the sun rises and sets on time.

Gazardiya: *See* **Gazardiel**.

Gazarniel: An angel of 'flame and fire' who fought Moses (*qv*) when he visited Heaven, although Moses defeated him by pronouncing the 12 letters of the secret name of God. The only mention of this angel is in Saul Raskin's 1952 book, *Kabbalah, Book of Creation, Zohar*, and it is suspected that Raskin actually meant Hadraniel (*qv*) and not Gazarniel. It is also worth noting that all other sources point to God's secret name having 72 letters and not 12.

Gazriel: One of the 70 amulet angels (*qv*).

Gdiel: *See* **Gediel**.

Geal: An angel guard of the Fifth Heaven.

Gebiel: An angel of the fourth altitude.

ABOVE: *Archangel Gabriel of the Annunciation*
by Lucrina Fetta, *c*.17th century

Gabriel: One of the two highest-ranking angels – with Michael (*qv*) – in both Islamic and Judaeo-Christian lore. He is the angel of annunciation (*qv*), as well as mercy, resurrection, vengeance, death, revelation, and the month of January. He presides over Paradise and is ruler of the First Heaven, even though he is said to sit on the left-hand side of God who resides in the Seventh Heaven. His primary function is to carry messages from God to man and he also helps us to interpret dreams and visions. He also guides the spirits of the newly dead to a suitable place of rest. He is responsible for ripening all the fruits on Earth and Mohammed claimed that it was Gabriel who dictated the Koran to him. In Islam, he is known as Jibril (*qv*) and is considered the angel of truth and a great archangel stationed in the West where the sun sets. In Jewish lore, he dealt with death and the destruction of the sinful cities of Sodom and Gomorrah.

Gebril: An angel summoned in conjuring rites.

Geburael (Geburah): Seraphim associated with the fifth Sephira of the Tree of Life. He is equated with Gamaliel (*qv*) and descends from Heaven through the sphere of the planet Mars. He often features in Kabbalistic magic ritual and is said to hold God's left hand, the one used to dispense justice and severity.

Geburah: *See* **Geburael**.

Geburathiel (Geburatiel): Guardian angel of the fourth hall of the Seventh Heaven and an angel of Geburah (*qv*), the fifth Sephira (*qv*) of the Tree of Life.

Geburatiel: *See* **Geburathiel**.

Gedael: An angel of one of the seasons according to *1 Enoch* (See *The Book of Enoch*).

Gedariah: A regent of the Third Heaven who three times a day crowns prayers and sends them onwards and upwards.

Gedemel: A spirit of Venus, under Hagiel (*qv*).

Gediel (Gdiel): An angel of the zodiac and a regent of the Fourth Heaven and the fourth altitude. One of the 70 amulet angels (*qv*).

Gedobonai: An angel of the third chora or altitude invoked in magical prayer.

Gedudiel: An angel guarding the seventh heavenly hall.

Gedudim: An order of angels of the Song-Uttering Choirs under Tagas (*qv*).

Gedulael: A Sefiroth (*qv*) invoked in Kabbalistic magic ritual.

Gehatsita: An angel guarding the fifth heavenly hall.

Gehegiel: An angel guarding the Sixth Heaven.

Gehirael: An angel that guards the seventh heavenly hall.

Gehoriel: An angel guard of the first heavenly hall.

Gehuel: An angel guard of the sixth heavenly hall.

Geliel: One of the angels who govern the mansions of the moon (*qv*).

Gelomiros: An angel of the third chora or altitude who is invoked in magical rites.

Geminiel: A regent of the zodiac according to Cornelius Agrippa (*qv*).

Gemmut: A Gnostic archon (*qv*).

Genaritzod: An angel of the seventh hour of the night, under Mendrion (*qv*).

Geniel: One of the angels who govern the mansions of the moon (*qv*).

Genius: The singular form of 'genii'. It is an alternative name for angel, spirit or intelligence.

Genius of the Contretemps: *See* **Angel of the Odd**.

Geno: An angelic member of the order of Powers (*qv*).

Genon: An angel of the second chora or altitude invoked in magical ritual.

Gereimon: An angel of the second chora.

Gergot: An angel guarding the sixth heavenly hall.

Germael: The angel sent by God to create Adam (*qv*) from the dust.

Geron: An angel of the second chora or altitude, used in invocations.

Geroskesufael: An angel guarding the seventh heavenly hall.

Gerviel (Cerviel): In Jewish Kabbalah, the guardian angel of King David. As Cerviel (*qv*), he is chief of the order of Principalities (*qv*), along with Haniiel (*qv*), Nisroc (*qv*) and others.

Gethel (Ingethel): An angel set over hidden things. Assisted by the angel Zeruch (*qv*), he rendered the Amorites blind in their battle with Cenez.

Geviririon: Angelic personification of the fifth Sephira (*qv*) of the Tree of Life.

Geviriyah: One of the names of Metatron (*qv*).

Gezardia: *See* **Gazardiel**.

Gezuriya: An angel of the order of Powers (*qv*) who is a guard of one of the celestial halls as well as ruler over six other angels, amongst whom is the angel of the sun, Gazatdiya.

Gheoriah: An angel of the order of Powers (*qv*).

Giant Angels: The great demons of John Milton's *Paradise Lost*.

Giatiyah: One of the names of Metatron (*qv*).

Gibborim: An order of angels who sing the holy Trisagion, praising God, under Tagas's (*qv*) leadership.

Gidaijal: An angel of the seasons and the leader of 'the heads of thousands.'

Giel: An angel who governs the zodiac sign Gemini, in ceremonial magic.

Gippuyel: One of the names of Metatron (*qv*), mentioned in *3 Enoch* (See *The Book of Enoch*).

Glaras: An angel of the first hour of the night, under Gamiel (*qv*).

Glauron or Glaura: A benign spirit of the air who must be invoked from the North.

Glmarij: An angel of the third hour of the day.

Glorious Ones: Another name for the highest order of archangels.

Glory of God: The 11th- and 12th-century Jewish poet Judah ha-Levi describes this term as denoting 'the whole class of angels, together with their spiritual instruments – the Hashmallim, Chariots, Firmament, Ophanim, and the Spheres (Galgalim)'.

Gmial: One of the 64 guardians of the seven

Goap (Gaap, Tap): A fallen angel, formerly of the order of Powers (*qv*). Now one of the Underworld's 11 rulers.

Gog and Magog: Names of God that are used to command spirits, according to the grimoires of Honoriud III. In the Koran, they are spirits who have laid waste to the land.

Golab: Fallen angels who are perpetually at war with their sworn enemies, the Seraphim (*qv*) and are ruled by Usiel (*qv*), a spirit of wrath and sedition whose ruler is 'Sammael the Black'.

Golandes: An angel invoked in the exorcism of wax, mentioned in *The Greater Key of Solomon* (*qv*).

Gonael: An angelic guard at the gates of the North Wind.

Gonfalons: An order of angels, according to Milton's *Paradise Lost*.

Good Daimon: Also a name applied to the Egyptian deity Thoth (*qv*).

Gorfiniel: An angelic guard of the Seventh Heaven.

Gorson or Gorsou: *See* **Gurson**.

Governments: An order of angels.

Gradhiel: *See* **Gradiel**.

Gradiel (Gradhiel): An angel of the planet Mars when it is in the signs of the Ram and Scorpio.

Graniel: An angel of the second hour.

Granozin: An angel of the second hour of the night, under Farris (*qv*).

Graphathas: The *Gospel of Bartholomew* describes him as one of nine angels 'that run together throughout the heavenly and earthly places'.

Graphiel: A spirit in Kabbalistic conjuration.

Grasgbarben: An angel governing the sign of Libra with Hadakiel (*qv*).

Greater Key of Solomon, The: A grimoire from the Renaissance era attributed to King Solomon. This book contains curses and invocations to summon demons and wake the dead. It also includes instructions on how to perform exorcisms and what tools are needed for this.

Grial (Griel): Angelic guard of the Fifth Heaven. He is also one of the 70 amulet angels (*qv*) in Hebrew lore.

Griel: *See* **Grial**.

Grigori (Egoroi, Egregori): An exalted angelic order residing in both the Second and Fifth Heavens, depending on whether or not they are fallen angels. Those who fell are imprisoned in a wing of the Fifth where they mourn their eternal fate in silence. Salamiel (*qv*), an angel who rejected the Lord, is ruler. They resemble men, but are taller than giants. *See* **Watchers** for complete list.

Grimorium Verum (True Grimoire): This notorious black magic handbook is believed to have been written in 1517, although some sources place it later.

Guabarel: An angel of autumn. In Occult lore, Tarquam (*qv*) is also named as the angel of autumn.

Guael: *See* **Guel**.

Guardian Angels: *See* page 111.

Guardian Angels of Adam and Eve: Adam (*qv*) and Eve (*qv*) had two guardian angels of the order of Virtues (*qv*).

Guardian Angel of Barcelona: An unnamed angel who appeared to St Vincent Ferrer.

ABOVE: *The Guardian Angel*
by Bernardo Strozzi, *c*.1630

Guardian Angels: The Kabbalah lists four ruling princes of this order of ministering angels – Uriel (*qv*), Raphael (*qv*), Gabriel (*qv*) and Michael (*qv*). There are also 70 guardian angels of nations, one for each country. (Only four are named – Dobiel (*qv*) for Persia; Sammael (*qv*) for Rome (Edom); Rahab (*qv*), Uzza (*qv*), Duma (*qv*) and/or Semyaza (*qv*) for Egypt; and Michael (*qv*) for Israel.) They became corrupt, with the exception of Michael, and are now demons. Every human is assigned one or more guardian angels at birth. The liturgical feast day of guardian angels is 2 October.

Guardian Angel of France: *See* **Hakamiah**.

Guardian Angel of Heaven and Earth: An unnamed angel residing in the sixth of the Seven Heavens in the Islamic scheme of the Heavens. He is said to be composed of snow and fire.

Guards: An order of angels mentioned by Milton in *Paradise Lost*. They are equated with Cherubim (*qv*) and Powers (*qv*) and are commanded by Michael (*qv*).

Guel (Guael): An angel of the Fifth Heaven who rules on Tuesday and must be invoked from the East.

Gulacoc: An angel of the seal (*qv*), used in conjuring rituals, according to *The Sixth and Seventh Books of Moses* (*qv*).

Gurid: An angel of the summer equinox who may be invoked as an amulet against the evil eye, in Hebrew lore.

Guriel: An angel ruling the zodiac sign of Leo.

Gurson (Gorson or Gorsoyu): In occultism, Gurson is a fallen angel, serving in the Underworld as king of the South.

Guth: An angelic ruler of the planet Jupiter.

Gutrix: In Occultism, Gutrix is an angel serving Suth, ruler of the angels of the air on Thursday. He is also a guard at the gates of the South Wind.

Guziel: An evil angel invoked to defeat an enemy, mentioned in *The Sword of Moses* (*qv*).

Gvurtial: An angelic guard of the Fourth Heaven, in Hebrew lore.

Gzrel: An angel invoked to countermand evil decrees. The word Gzrel is part of a 42-letter name of God.

Haael: One of the 72 angels of the zodiac.

Haaiah: One of the 72 angels that carry the name of God Shemhamphorae. He is an angel of the order of the Dominations (*qv*) and regent of ambassadors and diplomats.

Haamiah: An angel of the Powers (*qv*) who rules religious cults and 'protects all those who seek the truth.' He is also one of the 72 angels bearing the name of God Shemhamphorae.

Haarez: *The Sixth and Seventh Books of Moses* (*qv*) describes him as an angel of the seal (*qv*).

Haatan: An angel who hides treasures.

Habiel: See **Habbiel**.

Habbiel (Habiel): A Monday angel of the First Heaven who is invoked in matters of love and romance, according to the *Sword of Moses* (*qv*).

Habriel: An angel of the order of Powers (*qv*), invoked in conjurations.

Habuhiah: An angel who holds dominion over agriculture and fecundity. One of the 72 angels bearing the name of God Shemhamphorae.

Habudiel: In Occultism, Habudiel is an angel of the Lord's Day. He resides in the Fourth Heaven and can be invoked from the South.

Hachashel: One of the 72 angels of the zodiac.

Hadakiel (Chadakiel): An angel governing the zodiac sign of Libra, along with Grasgarben.

Hadar: One of the Sephira (*qv*) of the Tree of Life.

Hadariel: *See* **Hadraniel**.

Hadariron: An archon (*qv*).

Hadarmiel: A holy angel used in Solomonic ritual.

Hadarniel: *See* **Hadraniekl**.

Hadasdagedoy: An angel guarding the sixth heavenly hall.

Hadiririon: An angel who may be invoked in ritual magic, according to *The Sword of Moses* (*qv*).

Hadraniel (Hadarniel, Hadariel, Hadriel): An angel who bears one of the many names of the angel Metatron (*qv*) and with whom he is identified. He is a guard of the Second Heaven and when he proclaims God's will his voice is said to traverse 200,000 worlds. With each word he utters, 12,000 bolts of lightning fly from his mouth. He is said to be taller than Kemuel (*qv*) by 60 myriads of parasangs and a 500-year journey shorter than Sandalphon (*qv*). He is one of seven angels who serve the prince of fire, Jehuel (*qv*), and is one of the many angels who stand guard at the gates of the East Wind.

Hadriel: *See* **Hadraniel**.

Haduriel: An angel guarding the sixth heavenly hall.

Hafaza: A special class of four Islamic angels who protect mortals from evil spirits. They also have the duty of writing down the actions of humans.

Hafkiel: An angel invoked to exorcise demons.

Hagai: An angel guarding the fifth heavenly hall.

Hagedola: An angel of the seal (*qv*), invoked in ceremonial ritual.

Haggai Minor: Hebrew prophet known as God's messenger or angel.

Haggo: An angel of the seal (*qv*) who can be invoked in conjuring rites.

Hagiel: The intelligence (*qv*) of Venus when it is in Taurus and Libra. His corresponding angel is Gadamel (*qv*), the spirit ruler of Venus.

Hagios: A secret name of God as well as the name of a great angel.

Hagith: One of the seven Olympian spirits, one of the seven stewards of Heaven and ruler of Venus, this angel governs either 28 or 35 of the 196 Olympian Provinces. Cornelius Agrippa (*qv*) says that he commands 4,000 legions of spirits of light and can transmute metals.

Haglon: Angel of the third hour of the night, under Sarquamich (*qv*).

Hahael (Hahahel): An angel of the order of Virtues (*qv*) who is also one of the 72 angels that bear the name of God Shemhamphorae. It is his duty to protect Christian missionaries and all disciples of Christ. His corresponding angel is Chantare (*qv*).

Hahahel: *See* **Hahael**.

Hahaiah (Hahael): An angel of the order of Cherubim (*qv*) who reveals divine mysteries to mortals and can influence human thought, a power he uses to inspire positivity and love.

Hahayel (Chayyliel): Prince-angel of the divine judgement council.

Hahia: One of the 72 angels that bear the name of God Shemhamphorae.

Hahiniah: An angel of the order of Hashmallim (*qv*).

Hahowel: In Judaism, a ministering angel.

Hahuiah: One of the 72 angels that bear the name of God Shemhamphorae.

Haiaiel (Hahhahel): One of the 72 angels that bear the name of God Shemhamphorae as well as one of the 72 angels of the zodiac.

Hailael: Presiding angel of the order of Hayyoth or 'holy beasts'.

Haim: An angel holding dominion over the zodiac sign of Virgo according to *The Hierarchy of Blesséd Angels* (*qv*).

Hakael: Known as 'the seventh Satan'; one of the seven chiefs of the apostate angels (fallen angels), mentioned in *The Book of Enoch* (*qv*).

Hakamiah: An angel of the order of Cherubim (*qv*) who is invoked against traitors. He is also a guardian of France and one of the 72 angels bearing the name of God Shemhamphorae.

Hakem: An angel guarding the fourth heavenly hall.

Hakha: An angel of the seal (*qv*), as mentioned in *The Sixth and Seventh Books of Moses* (*qv*).

Hakham: One of the many names of the angel Metatron (*qv*).

Halacho: An angel of the 11th hour.

Halliza: An angel's name engraved on the outer ring of the pentagram of Solomon.

Haludiel: An intelligence (*qv*) of the sun residing in the Fourth Heaven. He may be invoked on the Lord's Day, Sunday, as long as the invocant is facing South.

Halwaya: One of the many names of the angel Metatron (*qv*).

Hamabiel: The angel holding dominion over the zodiac sign of Taurus. In ceremonial magic, however, Tual (*qv*) takes that role. Asmodel (*qv*) is another angel credited with power over Taurus.

Hamal: An angel holding dominion over water. He

is invoked in Arabic incantation rituals.

Hamaliel: An angelic member of the order of Virtues (*qv*) who is also a regent of August and the zodiac sign of Virgo.

Hamartyzod: An angel of the 11th hour, under Dardariel (*qv*).

Hamatiel: In Occultism, an angel governing the zodiac sign of Virgo.

Hamaya: A ministering angel in *The Sixth and Seventh Books of Moses* (*qv*).

Hamayzod: An angel who serves Jefischa, ruler of the fourth hour of the night.

Hameriel: An angel of the fifth hour of the night, under Abasdarhon.

Hamied (Miracles): The glorious angel of miracles.

Hamiel: *See* **Haniel**.

Hamneijs: An angel of the seal (*qv*).

Hamon: Another name for the angel Gabriel and one of the guards at the gates of the South Wind. Enoch describes him as a 'great prince, fearful and honoured, pleasant and terrible, who maketh all children to tremble when the time draweth nigh for the singing of the Thrice Holy.'

Hamshalim (Hashmallim): An angelic order.

Hamwak'il: Islamic guardian angel invoked in exorcism rituals.

Hanaeb: One of the 12 angels of the zodiac.

Hanael: *See* **Haniel**.

Hananiel: Archangel whose name is inscribed on a pentagram that is used as a kamea.

Hanhl: One of seven angles worshipped by Balaam. He is said to have ordered Balaam to build the first seven altars.

Haniel (Anael, Hamiel, Hanael): Chief angel of the orders of Principalities (*qv*) and Virtues (*qv*) and regent of December, Capricorn and Venus. The simple invocation of his name is sufficient to provide protection from the evil eye. He is one of the seven archangels as well as one of the ten Sephira (*qv*) of the Tree of Life and is reputed to have transported Enoch to Heaven. He is also one of the 72 angels bearing the name of God Shemhamphorae.

Hanniniel: Aramaic angel invoked in the creation of love charms.

Hannuel: An angel who has dominion over the sign of Capricorn.

Hanoziz: An angel of the eighth hour of the night, under Narcoriel (*qv*).

Hanozoz: Angel of the ninth hour of the night, under Narcoriel (*qv*).

Hantiel: An angel of the third hour of the day, under Veguaniel (*qv*).

Hanum: An angel of the First Heaven who rules Monday. He can be invoked in either the North or the South.

Haqemel: One of the 72 angels of the 72 quinaries of the degrees of the zodiac.

Harabael: An angel who holds dominion over the Earth.

Harahel: In Kabbalism, an angel with responsibilities for archives, libraries and places of learning as well as for students and scholars. He is one of the angels bearing the name of God Shemhamphorae.

Harariel: Name of an angel inscribed on a kamea.

Harbonah: An angel of confusion (*qv*) and annihilation (*qv*).

Harchiel: An angel invoked in black magic to command the demons who grant the gift of invisibility.

Harhazial: *See* **Harhaziel**.

Harhaziel: An angel guarding one of the halls of the Third Heaven.

Hariel (Behemial): Cherubim (*qv*) holding dominion over domesticated animals who is regent of arts and sciences and is invoked against impieties. He is also one of the 72 angels bearing the name of God Shemhamphorae.

Hariph: Alternative name for the angel Raphael (*qv*).

Hariton: Fictional archangel invented by Greek-Armenian mystic and writer, G.I. Gurdjieff.

Harmozei: *See* **Harmozey**.

Harmozey (Harmozei): One of the four Gnostic wise and benevolent angels who surround God.

Harshael: *See* **Harshiel**.

Harshiel: A spellbinding angel – along with Azrael (*qv*), Gabriel (*qv*), Michael (*qv*), Sarphiel (*qv*) and others – especially in the blinding of sorcerors. He was invoked in Syriac conjuring rituals.

Haroth: *See* **Harut**.

Harta'il: Islamic guardian angel used in exorcism rites.

Harudha: To the ancient Persians, a female angel who rules the element of water. To the Mandaeans, she is the equivalent of Haurvata, the female Amesha Spenta (*qv*) who is the spirit of health and vegetation as well as water.

Harut (Haroth): A Jewish angel, linked with Maroth (*qv*) who teaches mortals how to govern. These two Amesha Spentas (*qv*) told the secret name of God to a mortal woman with whom they had both fallen in love and when she rose up to Venus uttering the name, they became fallen angels. Their punishment was to be kept head down in a pit near Babylon where they were supposed to teach magic and sorcery.

Harviel: An angel guarding the Second Heaven.

Hasdiel: The angel of benevolence, with Zadkiel (*qv*), and the partner of Uriel (*qv*) and Samshiel (*qv*) in battle. He is also an angel of the planet Venus.

Haseha: One of the 15 angels of the throne (*qv*) listed in *The Sixth and Seventh Books of Moses* (*qv*).

Hashesiyah: One of the many names of the angel Metatron (*qv*).

Hashmal (Chasmal): Powerful regent of the Dominations (*qv*) who breathes fire from his mouth when he speaks.

Hashmallim: Exalted order of angels, equivalent to the Dominations (*qv*) and ranked alongside the Cherubim (*qv*) and Seraphim (*qv*). The chief is Hashmal (*qv*), Zadkiel (*qv*) or Zacharael (*qv*).

Hashul: One of the principals of the angelic order of the Hashmallim (*qv*).

Hasmed: One of the five angels of punishment (*qv*) encountered by Moses (*qv*) in Heaven and also an angel of annihilation.

Hasmiyah: One of the many names of the angel Metatron (*qv*).

Hasmodai: An angel of the moon, invoked in talismanic magic.

Hasriel: An angel's name inscribed on a kamea.

'Hastening Angel': Description of Michael (*qv*) in the poet Milton's *Paradise Lost*, referring to the expulsion of Adam (*qv*) and Eve (*qv*) from Eden. However, the poet John Dryden writes in his work, "State of Innocence", that it was Raphael (*qv*), not Michael (*qv*) who expelled them.

Hatach: An angel invoked in medieval Jewish incantations. The name is created from the initial letters of the words 'chanted'.

Hatiphas: An angel of finery, mentioned in *The Nuctemeron* (*qv*).

Hatspatsiel: One of the many names of the angel Metatron (*qv*).

Hauras (Flauros): Fallen angel who can tell the future and answer questions about the past. He is said to be one of the 72 angels that Solomon trapped inside a brass vessel and threw into the sea. He tells Solomon that he was once a powerful celestial being and talks about the creation of the world and the fall. In Hell he commands 36 legions of demons and he usually manifests as a leopard but can appear in human form during exorcisms.

Haurvatat: An Amesha Spenta (*qv*) in Zoroastrian lore. She is the female personification of salvation and rules over water. She equates to the Mandaean Harudha.

Haven: One of the 12 angels who preside over the 12 hours of the day and also the genius of dignity.

Havhaviyah, Haviyahu, Hayat: Three more names for Metatron (*qv*).

Hayya: The singular form of Hayyoth (*qv*).

Hayyael: *See* **Hayyel**.

Hayyel: Regent of the Hayyoth (*qv*) who protects wild animals.

Hayyliel: *See* **Hayyel**.

Hayyoth (Chayoh, Chayyliel H, Chiva): A class of Merkabah angels, also known as the Dominations (*qv*) who are ranked alongside the

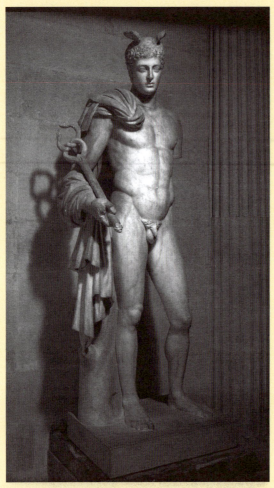

ABOVE: *Statue of Hermes,*
by an unknown artist (ancient Greek era)

Hermes: A Greek god with the talent of predicting the future who carries a golden wand and wears winged sandals. He is the agathodaemon (good spirit) and the creator of the musical instrument the lyre. He has the duty of escorting the ghosts of killed suitors to Hades and is also the daemon of reincarnation as well as the god of flocks and herds. He was the first angel to instruct man about the celestial realms. It has been suggested that he and Moses (*qv*) are one and the same, but Jews vehemently dispute this.

Cherubim (*qv*) and reside in the Seventh Heaven. They are angels of fire and support the Throne of Glory. Enoch reported them to have 'four faces, four wings, 2,000 Hashmallim and are placed next to the wheels of the Merkabah'. *The Zohar* (*qv*) numbers them as 36, but Enoch says there are only four. They constitute the whole of the Shekinah (*qv*).

Haziel: A Cherubim (*qv*) invoked in order to solicit God's compassion. He is one of the angels bearing the 72 names of God Shemhamphorae. He is, according to I Chronicles, a mortal, the progeny of the Gershonites.

Heavenly Academy: According to *The Zohar* (*qv*) the Heavenly Academy is a body of angels that meets to judge humans when they arrive in Heaven. The worthy mortal is 'crowned with many radiant crowns', while the unworthy human is 'thrust outside, and stands within the pillar until he is taken to his punishment.'

Heavenly Host: A term meaning all the angels of Heaven.

Hebdomad: A Gnostic term for the seven angelic rulers of the Seven Heavens.

Hechaloth (Hekhaloth): The seven female emanations of God from his right side, the opposite of the ten male Sephiroth (*qv*). In *The Zohar* (*qv*) the word is translated as 'beautiful virgins'. The term also denotes the heavenly halls and palaces guarded by the angels.

He'el: In *1 Enoch* (See *The Book of Enoch*), He'el is the ruler of one of the seasons.

Heiglot: An angel of snowstorms and ruler of the first hour.

Heikhali: An angel of the Seventh Heaven.

Hekaloth: *See* **Hechaloth**.

Hel: Another name for God or the name of an angel invoked during magic ritual.

Helayaseph: An angel ruling one of the seasons.

Helech: *See* **Abelech**.

Helel: A fallen angel, son of Sahar or Sharer and in Canaanite legend a winged deity. He was formerly chief of the Nephilim (*qv*).

Heleleth: A great Gnostic angel.

Helemmelek: An alternative name for Milkiel (*qv*). In *1 Enoch* (see *The Book of Enoch*) Helemmelek is an angel governing one of the seasons.

Helias the Prophet: *See* **John the Baptist**.

Helison: An angel of the first altitude alongside Alimiel (*qv*), Barakiel (*qv*) Gabriel (*qv*) and Lebes (*qv*). When invoked he manifests crowned with roses, carrying a banner adorned with a crimson cross.

Hemah: An angel of wrath (*qv*), death (*qv*) and destruction (*qv*) who rules over the death of all domestic animals. He is made up of chains of red and black fire and is 500 parasangs in height. *The Zohar* (*qv*) describes how he and another angel, Af (*qv*), almost swallowed Moses (*qv*) but were prevented from doing so by God. When freed, Moses slew Hemah – this was one of the few occasions in which a mortal has killed an angel.

Heman: Leader of one of the heavenly choirs that sings in the morning while those led by Jeduthun (*qv*) sing in the evening and those led by Asaph (*qv*) sing at night.

Herald Angel: *See* page 118.

Herald of Hell: The angel called Zophiel (*qv*).

Hermes: *See* page 116.

Hermesiel: A heavenly choir-leader who was created from the Greek god, Hermes.

Heroes of Heaven: A term for good angels.

Hetabor: An angel invoked in the exorcism of wax.

Heziel: One of the angels of the zodiac.

Hibel-Ziwa: *See* **Hiwel-Ziwa**.

Hiel: Name of an angel inscribed on an oriental charm (kamea) to ward off evil.

Hierarchy of Blesséd Angels, The: An instructive poem written by Thomas Heywood in 1635.

Hierimiel: *See* **Jeremiel**.

Hilofatei and Hilofei: Angels guarding the fourth heavenly hall.

Hiniel: A spellbinding angel invoked in Syriac ritual.

Hipeton (Anaphaxeton): An angel of the planet Jupiter, along with Jophiel (*qv*).

Hiphkadiel: Name of an angel inscribed on a kamea.

Hismael: In Occultism, Hismael is the spirit of the planet Jupiter.

Hivvah: One of the sons of the fallen angel Semyaza (*qv*).

Hiwel-Ziwa (Hibel-Ziwa): One of 360 divine beings, according to Mandaean lore, created by the Supreme Being known as Alaha.

Hiyyah: One of the sons of the fallen angel, Semyaza (*qv*).

Hizarbin: A spirit of the sea and an angel of the second hour.

Hizkiel: A guard at the gate of the North Wind.

Hngel: An angel of the summer equinox who can be invoked to ward off the evil eye.

Hochmal: *See* **Hochmel**.

Hochmel (Chochmael, Hochmal, Hocroel, Hokmael): One of the ten Sephiroth (*qv*) who are believed to have inspired the important grimoire of Pope Honorius III (1216–1227).

Hocroel: *See* **Hochmel**.

Hodiel: Kabbalistic angel of the Briatic world – the world of creation – who can be invoked when creating amulets.

Hodiriron: Ninth of the ten holy Sephiroth (*qv*).

Hodniel: An angel invoked to cure stupidity.

Hoesediel (Choesed): An angel of the Briatic world who is a member of either the order of Hashmallim (*qv*) or Dominations (*qv*). He is also one of the ten Sephira (*qv*) of the Tree of Life.

Hofniel: A ruling angel of the Kabbalistic order of Bene Elohim (*qv*).

Hokmael: *See* **Hochmel**.

Holy Beasts: The Cherubim (*qv*) in Talmudic lore.

Holy Ghost: An alternative name for the Comforter (*qv*), the third name in the Trinity and sometimes viewed as female.

Holy Ones: A term for archangels.

Homadiel: The 'Angel of the Lord'.

Horaios: A Gnostic archon (*qv*) and ruler of one of the seven Heavens.

Hormuz: A Zoroastrian angel in charge of the first day of the month.

ABOVE: *Nativity*
by Luca Signorelli, 1667

Herald Angel: Indicated to be either Raziel (*qv*), Akraziel (*qv*) or Michael (*qv*). This angel is said to have announced Jesus' resurrection after his death by crucifixion. This angel is celebrated in Charles Wesley's 1793 hymn 'Hark the Herald Angels Sing!', a song which quickly became a traditional Christmas carol. Depicted with the right hand raised in blessing and wings outspread, the herald angel becomes the symbol of the Nativity.

Horses: *See* opposite.

Hosts: Another name for angels.

Hosts of the Lord: The ministering angels led by Michael (*qv*).

Hout: An angel invoked in Arabic conjuration.

Hoveh Haya: One of the many names of the angel Metatron (*qv*).

Hshahshiel: A Syrian spellbinding angel, mentioned in *Amulets and Talismans* (*qv*).

Hubaiel: An angel of the First Heaven, referred to in *The Sith and Seventh Books of Moses* (*qv*).

Hubaril: An angel of the planet Saturn.

Hufaltiel (Huphaltiel): An angel of Friday serving in the Third Heaven who must be invoked from the East. Mentioned in *The Magus* (*qv*) and *The Sixth and Seventh Books of Moses* (*qv*).

Hugron Kunya: A great conjuring angel, described in *The Sword of Moses* (*qv*).

Huha: The name of an angel or a name for God mentioned by the Jewish religious group Essenes in the Dead Sea Scrolls.

Hukiel: An angel guarding the seventh heavenly hall.

Hula'il: Islamic guardian angel invoked in exorcism rituals.

Humastrav: An angel of the First Heaven who rules on Monday and is invoked in the North.

Humiel: An angel who rules Capricorn.

Huphaltiel: *See* Hufaltiel.

Huphatriel: In grimoire, Huphatriel is an angel of the planet Jupiter.

Huristar: *See* Barinian.

Hurmin: An alternative name for Satan (*qv*).

Hurmiz: A daughter of Lilith (*qv*).

Hurtapal: One of the three angels of the Lord's Day, Sunday, the others being Michael (*qv*) and Dardael (*qv*).

Husael: An angel of the Third Heaven.

Hushmael: Name of an angel inscribed on a kamea.

Hutriel: One of the angels of punishment (*qv*), residing in the fifth lodge of Hell.

Huzia: One of the 64 angelic guards of the heavenly halls.

Huznoth: An angel invoked to consecrate water,

ABOVE: *The Vision of Zechariah* by Ambroise Crozat, *c.*18th century

Horses: Another name for angels according to Hebrew prophet Zechariah.

according to *The Greater Key of Solomon* (qv).

Hyniel: An angel ruling on Tuesday who is subject to the East Wind and must be invoked from the North. Mentioned in *The Magus* (qv).

Hyperachii: Archangels who guide the universe, according to the Chaldeans.

Hypezokos: One of the 'effable, essential and elemental orders' in Chaldean cosmology.

Iabiel: Malevolent angel used in ceremonial magic for separating a husband and wife, mentioned in *The Sword of Moses* (*qv*).

Iachadiel: An angel whose name is inscribed on the fifth pentacle of the moon, according to *The Greater Key of Solomon* (*qv*).

Iacoajul: An angel of the 11th hour of the night.

Iadalbaoth (Ialdabaoth, Jaldabaoth): In the Kabbalah, he is the Demiurge, a being who ranks second only to God. The Phoenicians considered him to be one of the seven Elohim (*qv*) who created the universe. The Gnostics believe he created the seven Elohim in his own image – Iao (*qv*), Sabaoth (*qv*), Adonai (*qv*), Ouraios (*qv*), Eloi (*qv*), Astaphaios (*qv*) and, somewhat surprisingly, his own mother, Achamaoth (*qv*). They consider him to be the first archon (*qv*) of darkness, an evil being. Enoch equates him with Sammael (*qv*) as a fallen angel and also as the supreme ruler of the Hashmallim (*qv*).

Iadara: An angel who governs the zodiac sign of Virgo, with Schaltiel (*qv*).

Iaeo: An angel summoned to get rid of demons, according to *Testament of Solomon* (*qv*).

Iahhel: An Kabbalistic archangel holding domininion over philosophers and people wishing to withdraw from the world. Also one of the 72 angels bearing the name of God Shemhamphorae.

Iahmel: An angel of the air (*qv*), mentioned in *The Book of the Angel Raziel* (*qv*).

Iameth: The only good spirit who can overcome Kunospaston, demon of the sea, mentioned in *3 Enoch* (See *The Book of Enoch*) and *Testament of Solomon* (*qv*).

Iaho (Jehovah): Moses (*qv*) used the name of this divine spirit to kill the Egyptian Pharaoh Necho.

Ialcoajul: An angel of the 11th hour of the night, under Dardariel (*qv*), according to *The Lesser Key of Solomon* (*qv*).

Iamariel: An angel of the ninth hour of the night.

Ialdabaoth: *See* Iadalbaoth.

Iao the Great: The Demiurge, master of the seven Heavens. An archon (*qv*) that makes up the Gnostic Hebdomad of primordial Powers (*qv*).

Iaoth: An archangel invoked to deal with bowel pains caused by the demon Kurteel.

Iaqwiel: An angel of the moon.

Iax: An angel who, when invoked, has the power to conquer Roeled, the demon of envy who causes stomach problems.

Iboriel: An angel guarding the Seventh Heaven, in Hebrew lore.

Iciriel: One of the angels ruling the mansions of the moon (*qv*).

Icthion: An angel who can inflict paralysis on mortals.

Idedi: An Akkadian order of angels.

Idrael: An angel guarding the fifth heavenly hall.

Idris: Enoch's name in the Koran.

Iealo: An angel invoked to exorcize demons.

Iedidiel: An angel summoned in magic ritual.

Iehuiah: An angel of the order of the Hashmallim (*qv*) summoned up in ritual invocation. One of the 72 angels bearing the name of God Shemhamphorae.

Ieiaiel: An angel of the future, a position shared with Teiaiel (*qv*) and one of the 72 angels bearing the name of God Shemhamphorae.

Ieilael: One of the 72 angels bearing the name of God Shemhamphorae.

Ielahiah: Former member of the order of Virtues (*qv*). When invoked before a trial, he protects judges and magistrates and decides the outcome of legal cases. He is also one of the 72 angels bearing the name of God Shemhamphorae.

Ieliel One of the 72 angels bearing the name of God Shemhamphorae.

Ierahlem: An angel invoked in ceremonial magic ritual, mentioned in *The Greater Key of Solomon* (*qv*).

Ierathel: *See* **Terather**.

Iesaia: One of the many names of Metatron (*qv*).

Ietuqiel: An ancient name for Moses (*qv*) that is used in invocations during childbirth.

Ifafi: An angel who guards the seventh heavenly hall, in Hebrew lore.

Iggereth bath Mahalath: An alternative spelling of Agrat bat Mahlat, mentioned in *The Zohar* (*qv*).

Ihiazel: One of the 72 angels bearing the name of God Shemhamphorae.

Iibamiah: One of the 72 angels bearing the name of God Shemhamphorae.

Ijasusael (Iyasusael): A chief of the angels of the seasons, in Enoch lore.

Ikkar Sof: An angel who rules the Hebrew month of Shevat (January-February).

Ilaniel: In Jewish tradition, Ilaniel is an angel holding dominion over fruit trees.

Ili-Abrat (Ili-Abrat, Papukkal): Winged chief messenger of the Babylonian god Anu.

Im Akkadian: Name for the fallen archangel Rimmon (*qv*).

Images: An order of angels in Talmud and Targum, as claimed by French philosopher Voltaire in *Of Angels, Genii, and Devils*.

Imamiah: Cruel fallen angel, formerly of the order of Principalities (*qv*) and one of the angels bearing the name of God Shemhamphorae. In Hell he controls the fate of voyages at sea and is known to destroy and humiliate his enemies on a whim.

Immiel: An angel who assists Metatron (*qv*) in reciting the Shema.

Imriaf: The angel in charge of the month of Tammuz (June-July in the Hebrew calendar).

Imriel: The angel in charge of the month of Sivan (May-June in the Hebrew calendar).

Incubi: Fallen and evil angels.

Indri: A Vedic deity equivalent to Judaeo-Christian angels.

Informer: Satan, in *The Zohar* (*qv*).

Ingethel: *See* Gethel.

In Hii: One of the four Mandaean angels of the North Star.

Innon: An angel used in conjuration to make demons appear, mentioned in *The Greater Key of Solomon* (*qv*).

Intelligences: Usually ten in number, Neo-Platonic beings that are the same as angels or Sephiroth (*qv*).

Iobel: One of the 12 Gnostic Powers created by the god Iadalbaoth (*qv*).

Ioelet: An angel invoked in the exorcism of demons. He can, with other angels, overcome the demon Saphathoreal.

Iofiel (Iophiel, Jophiel): Guardian angel of Shem, a prince of the Torah; one of the seven archangels; chief of the order of Hashmallim (*qv*). With Zaphiel (*qv*), he rules over the planet Saturn and Paracelsus (*qv*) also names him as the intelligence (*qv*) of the planet Jupiter.

Iomuel: A fallen angel.

Ioniel: With Sefoniel (*qv*) is believed in Solomonic lore to be a ruler of the universe.

Iophiel: *See* Iofiel.

Irel: An Occult angel residing the Fifth Heaven and ruling Tuesday. He is invoked from the West.

Irin: Twins of the Supreme Celestial Council living in either the Sixth or Seventh Heaven. They are amongst the eight hierarchs senior to Metatron (*qv*). With the twin Qaddisin (*qv*) they constitute the supreme judgement council of the heavenly court. According to Daniel (*qv*), 'each of the Irin is equal to the rest of the angels and princes put together.'

Isaac: When he was born there was an ethereal glow surrounding him and because of that he is known as the 'angel of light'.

Isda: The angel of nourishment.

Isfandarmend: To the ancient Persians, the angel of February who also rules the fifth day of each month.

Ischim: *See* **Ishim**.

Ishim (Ischim, Izschim): Angels made of snow and fire who represent the ninth Sephira (*qv*) and reside in the Fifth Heaven. The Kabbalah describes them as 'the beautiful souls of just men (the saints)'. They are equivalent to Bene Elohim (*qv*) and were created to perpetually sing praises to God. Chief angel of the Ishim is Azazael (*qv*). They rank ninth in the hierarchy of angels produced by Renaissance philosopher Giovanni Pico della Mirandola, but do not appear in the Dionysian scheme.

Ishlia: An angel ruling the East.

Isiael: A Tuesday angel residing in the Fifth Heaven, according to *The Magus* (*qv*).

Isis: An Egyptian deity that the poet John Milton places amongst the fallen angels. The Phoenicians believed Isis to be the same as Ashteroth, a Seraphim (*qv*) of Gnostic lore who became a grand duke in Hell.

Isma'il: An Islamic guardian angel invoked in exorcism rituals. Can also be found in the First Heaven, leading a group of angels disguised as cows who worship Allah.

Ismoli: In Occultism, the ministering angel to Samaz (*qv*), ruler of the Monday angels of the air (*qv*).

Isphan Darmaz (Spendarmoz): A Zoroastrian angel who guards the Earth and virtuous women and is also a ruler of the month of February.

Israel: An angelic member of the Hayyoth (*qv*) who is ranked sixth of the 15 angels of the throne (*qv*), according to *The Sixth and Seventh Books of Moses* (*qv*). In one utterance he claims to be the angel Uriel (*qv*) and the philosopher Philo of Alexandria identifies him with the Logos (*qv*). His job is said to be to 'call the hosts of angels to chant God's praise.

Israfel (Izrafel, Sarafiel): *See* opposite.

Itatiyah: One of the many names for the angel Metatron (*qv*).

Ithoth: According to *Testament of Solomon* (*qv*), an angel who can work against the demon Saphathoreal.

Ithuriel: An angel who serves Sephuriron (*qv*) as a deputy sarim (prince) of the holy Sephiroth (*qv*). He is an angel of the first pentacle of Mars.

Itmon: One of the many names of the angel Metatron (*qv*).

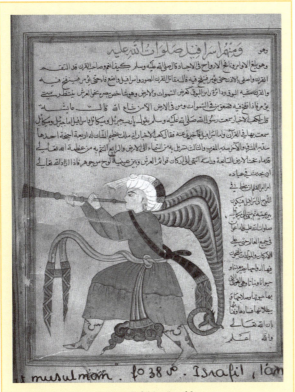

ABOVE: *Fol.38 v Israfel*
Islamic School, date unknown

Israfel (Izrafel, Sarafiel): In Islam, Israfel is the angel of song (*qv*) who will blow the trumpet on Judgement Day. An angel of music (*qv*), he provides mortals with musical inspiration. In Arabic lore, he is said to have four wings and that 'while his feet are under the seventh Earth, his head reaches to the pillars of the divine throne'. When he looks down into Hell, three times a day, he becomes consumed with grief and it is also said that he introduced Mohammed to the role of prophet during three years he spent with him before being replaced by Gabriel (*qv*). Another legend says that he was one of the angels sent to the corners of the Earth to collect seven handfuls of dirt that were used to create Adam (*qv*). With three other angels, he will be destroyed by fire at the third and fourth sounding of the trumpets at the end of the world but it is believed that Allah will resurrect them.

Itqal: An angel presiding over cooperation and affection who can be invoked to heal rifts or discord between friends.

Itra'il: Islamic guardian angel invoked in exorcism rituals.

Iurabatres (Eurabatres): An angel holding dominion over the planet Venus, according to *The Hierarchy of the Blesséd Angels* (*qv*). Others also given this role include Anael (*qv*), Hasdiel (*qv*), Raphael (*qv*), Hagiel (*qv*) and Noguel (*qv*).

Iuvart: A fallen angel.

Iyar: An angel of the Talmud with origins in Babylonian lore.

Iyasusael: *See* Ijasusael.

Izachel: An angel invoked in Solomonic ritual by the Master of the Art, according to *The Greater Key of Solomon* (*qv*).

Izads (Izeds): A Zoroastrian order of angels equivalent to the Cherubim, ranking second to the Amesha Spentas (*qv*). The order contains 27 or 28 angels who serve under Mithra (*qv*) as guardian angels of 'innocence, happiness and preservation of the world.'

Izeds: *See* **Izads**.

Iz'iel: An angel who guards the sixth heavenly hall.

Izrael: An angel who, like Israfel (*qv*), Michael (*qv*) and Gabriel (*qv*) will not be present during the first terrible trumpet blast at the end of the world. It is said in The Koran that there will be 3 blasts in a 40-year period and that after the final one 'the dry and rotten bones and dispersed parts of the bodies of all human creatures, even to the very hairs, will be called to judgement.'

Izrafel: *See* Israfel.

Izschim: *See* Ishim.

Jabril: *See* Jibril.

Jabriel: *See* Jibril.

Jael (Joel): One of the two Cherubim (*qv*), the other being Zarall (*qv*), who are carved into the Mercy Seat of the Ark of the Covenant. Jael is the angel of the zodiac sign of Libra.

Jahoel: *See* Jehoel.

Jaluha: The angel who carries a cup of oblivion to sinners who are about to be judged so that the soul may forget. In the Gnostic work *Texts of the Saviour*, it is written that Jaluha is 'receiver of Sabaoth Adamas', which is an evil power.

Janax: An angel residing in the First Heaven who rules Monday and must be invoked from the East.

Janiel: Angel residing in the Fifth Heaven, ruling on Tuesday and a guard at the gates of the East Wind.

Jareahel: *See* Jevanael.

Jareriael: *See* Jazeriel.

Jariel (Raziel, Sariel, Suriel): Angel of divine presence.

Javan: Guardian angel of Greece.

Jazar: An angel of the seventh hour who 'compels love', according to *The Nuctemeron* (*qv*).

Jazeriel (Jareriel): One of the angels of the mansions of the moon (*qv*).

Jeduthun or Jeduthum: Angelic lord of the evening choirs in Heaven. He is the master of howling, and leads myriads of angels in chanting hymns of praise of God at the close of each day. He was originally a mortal, a director of music at a temple, but in the early Middle Ages the Zoharists transformed him into an angel.

Jehoel (Jehuel, Metatron, Yahoel): A prince of elemental fire who, with Seraphiel (*qv*) a chief Seraphim (*qv*) reigns over seven angels. He is also the keeper of the unutterable name of God and a prince of the divine presence. Jewish lore has him as the angel with control over the demon Leviathan. The *Apocalypse of Abraham* describes him as the heavenly choirmaster who is the 'singer of the eternal' who accompanied Abraham on his visit to Heaven and showed him human history.

Jehudiam: According to *The Zohar* (*qv*), 'keeps the accounts of the righteousness and carries the 70 keys of all the treasures of the Lord.'

Jehudiel: Angelic ruler of the movement of the planetary spheres who is sometimes described as an archangel.

Jehuel: *See* Jehoel.

Jekusiel: An angel guarding one of the halls of the First Heaven.

Jekut(h)iel: One of the 70 amulet angels (*qv*).

Jeliel: Guardian angel of the nation of Turkey and a Seraphim (*qv*) who encourages faithfulness between married couples. He holds dominion over kings and provides victory to those who have been attacked or invaded.

Jeou: A great Gnostic power who chains the mighty god Ialdabaoth (*qv*) to a 'sphere of fate' and then after demoting him from his exalted position, puts his son, Ibraoth, on the throne.

Jeqon (Yeqon, Yikon): A leading fallen angel who incited others to follow his path and enjoy carnal relations with mortal women.

Jerazol: A powerful angel invoked in Kabbalistic magic ritual.

Jeremiel: Equated with both Uriel (*qv*) and Remiel (*qv*), one of the seven archangels. Described as 'the lord of souls awaiting resurrection.'

Jerescue: An angel of the Second or Third Heaven who rules Wednesday.

Jesodoth: An angel in the Jewish tradition who transmits God's wisdom and knowledge to mortals. Tenth in the hierarchy of the Elohim (*qv*).

Jesubilin (Serabilin): A Gnostic angel that can be invoked in magic rituals.

Jesus: Regarded by many sources as 'a leading angel'. He is identified as the Logos (*qv*) or Word who was one of the three angels who went to Abraham beneath the oak of Mamre.

Jetrel: A fallen angel.

Jeu: According to the Gnostics, a great angel who is said to sit on the right hand side of God while the angel Propator (*qv*) sits on the left.

Jevanael (Jareahel): One of the seven angelic princes who stand perpetually in front of God and to whom God has given the spirit-names for the planets.

Jibril (Abru-El, Jabriel, Jabril): The Islamic name for the archangel Gabriel (*qv*). In Koranic Scripture, he is regarded as a guardian angel.

Jinn: Created, according to Islamic theologians, around 2,000 years before Adam (*qv*), the Jinn were equal to angels in the Judaeo-Christian system, with their leader being Eblis (*qv*). When Adam was created, Eblis refused to worship him, being cast out by God along with the Jinn who became demons.

Jinniyeh: The feminine version of Jinn (*qv*).

Joel (Jael, Yahoel): Angel who told Adam (*qv*) to give names to everything and who allocated a seventh of the earthly paradise to him and Eve. Joel is the first of Metatron's (*qv*) many names.

Jofiel: *See* Iofiel.

Johiel: An angel of Paradise (*qv*). Although many others also bear that title.

John the Baptist: The 'forerunner angel' who is male when he procures blessings for the world, female when bringing chastisement. Jesus describes him in the Book of John the Baptist as 'Helias the prophet, an angel sent by Satan to baptize with water'. In the Eastern Church he is always depicted with wings, in his role as a messenger.

Jomiael: *See* Jomjael.

Jomjael (Jomiael): A fallen angel.

Jophiel: *See* Iofiel.

Jorkemo: *See* Yurkemi.

Josta: *See* Josata.

Josata (Josta): An angel used in the conjuration of Uriel (*qv*) and whose name is one of the four magical words uttered by God to Moses (*qv*). The others are Abla (*qv*), Ablati (*qv*) and Caila (*qv*).

Josephel: *See* Asfa'el.

Joustriel: An angel of the sixth hour of the day, under Samil (*qv*).

Jove: A fallen angel, according to the poet Milton in *Paradise Lost*. Milton borrowed him from the figure of Zeus in Greek mythology and Roman mythology where he is Jupiter or Jove.

Jukar: 'A prince over all the angels and all the Caesars,' noted in *The Greater Key of Solomon* (*qv*).

Jusguarin: Angel reigning over ten angelic chiefs and 100 lesser angels. He is also ruler of the tenth hour of the night.

Kabchiel: A Mandaean angel.

Kabiri: The seven angels of Phoenician mythology who created the world. Equivalent to the seven angels of the presence (*qv*) in Gnostic and rabbinic lore.

Kabniel: The angel invoked to cure stupidity.

Kabriel: *See* **Cabriel**.

Kabshiel: An angel of Jewish mysticism who may be invoked to bring grace and power to the invocant. His name is found inscribed on amulets.

Kadal: One of the 70 amulet angels (*qv*).

Kadashiel: An angelic guard of the gates of the South Wind.

Kadashim: *See* **Kadishim**.

Kadi(el): An angel of the Third Heaven ruling on Fridays and invoked from the West.

Kadir-rahman: An archangel in Yezidic devil-worship (*qv*).

Kadishim (Kadashim): Angels of the Sixth or Seventh Heaven who praise God unceasingly and are of a more exalted rank than the Merkabah angels (*qv*). They constitute the angelic Beth Din (seat of judgement) with the Irin (*qv*). The head of the order 'was made of hail and he was so tall, it would take 500 years to walk a distance to his height,' according to Jewish lore. Moses (*qv*) encountered them during his visit to Heaven.

Kadkadael: An angel who guards the Sixth Heaven.

Kadmiel: One of the 70 amulet angels (*qv*).

Kadosh: An angelic guard of the fourth heavenly hall.

Kadriel: One of three Kabbalistic angels of prophecy, called 'mouths', created by God on the eve of creation. Yahadriel (*qv*) is another of these 'mouths'.

Kafkefoni: A fallen angel who is one of the seven unholy Sephiroth (*qv*). King of the Mazzikin and husband of the 'little leprous one', as referenced in Bernard J. Bamberger's book *Fallen Angels*.

Kafziel: An angel governing the death of kings

and, to the Gnostics, one of seven archangels ruling Saturn. *The Zohar* (*qv*) describes him as a chief assistant to Gabriel (*qv*), along with Hizkiel (*qv*), in battle.

Kahaviel: *See* **Dahaviel**.

Kakabel (Kokabiel): Regent of the stars and the constellations, although according to Enoch he is a fallen angel. All sources agree that he is a powerful angel, in charge of 365,000 spiritual legions and that he teaches astrology.

Kale: Babylonian King Nebuchadnezzar's guardian angel.

Kalka'il: Islamic guardian angel invoked during exorcism rites. He is an angel of the Fifth Heaven who is regent of the Houris, black-eyed celestial nymphs that worship Allah.

Kalkelmiyah: One of the many names of the angel Metatron (*qv*).

Kalki Avatar: The lowest ranking of the ten Vedic avatars (*qv*).

Kalmiya: In Jewish mysticism, Kalmiya is one of seven powerful angelic princes of the Seventh Heaven who guard the veil, or curtain that hides God's throne from view. The other six are: Boel (*qv*), Asimor (*qv*), Psacher (*qv*), Gabriel (*qv*), Sandalphon (*qv*) and Uzziel (*qv*).

Kamuel: *See* **Camael**.

Kandile: One of the nine holy angels invoked by Kabbalists.

Kaniel: One of the 70 amulet angels (*qv*).

Kaphkaphiel: The name of an angel inscribed on a kamea.

Karkiel: One of the 70 amulet angels (*qv*).

Karmiel: A guard at the gates of the East Wind.

Karniel: A guard at the gates of the West Wind.

Karoz: 'Reporter angels' in Jewish lore.

Kartion: An angel of the Seventh Heaven.

Kasbak: A secret name of the angel Metatron (*qv*).

Kasbeel (Kaspiel, Kazbiel): A 'sinful angel' now 'chief of the oath in Hell', according to *1 Enoch* (See *The Book of Enoch*). His original name, Biqa (*qv*), means 'good person', but after his fall, he was re-named Kasbeel – 'he who lies to God'.

Kasdaye: A leading fallen angel whose teachings include 'a variety of demonic practices including abortion,' according to one source.

Kashriel: An angel of the First Heaven serving, or identified with Zevudiel (*qv*).

Kaspiel: *See* **Kasbeel**.

Katchiel: One of the 70 amulet angels (*qv*).

Katzfiel: An angelic prince who guards the Sixth Heaven with a sword that emits lightning.

Kautel: *See* **Ketuel**.

Kavod: The Cherub (*qv*) on the throne of God and also in Chasidic (Hasidic Judaism) legend a term meaning 'the glory of God', the aspect of God revealed to man.

Kazbiel *See* **Kasbeel**.

Kazviel: An angel guarding the Fourth Heaven.

Kedemal: The spirit of the planet Venus.

Keel: Angel of one of the seasons who, according to *1 Enoch* (See *The Book of Enoch*), is 'leader of the heads of thousands'.

Kelail: An Islamic angel who is regent of the Fifth Heaven.

Keliel: With Kelkheak (*qv*), one of two angels who have been told the secrets of creation.

Kelkheak: With Keliel (*qv*), one of two angels who have been told the secrets of creation.

Kemuel (Camael, Seraphiel, Shemuel): Chief angel of the Seraphim (*qv*) and one of the holy Sephiroth (*qv*), he is also the archon (*qv*) who stands at the windows of Heaven, where he receives the prayers of Israel and passes them to the princes of the Seventh Heaven. According to the *Revelation of Moses*, he leads 12,000 angels of destruction (*qv*), but was killed by Moses (*qv*) when he attempted to prevent him from receiving the Torah from God.

Kenunit: One of the 70 amulet angels (*qv*).

Kered: An angel of the seal (*qv*).

Kerubiel: Chief angel of the order of Cherubim (*qv*).

Ketheriel: An angel of the Sephiroth (*qv*) invoked in Kabbalistic magic ritual.

Ketuel (Kautel): In *The Sixth and Seventh Books of Moses* (*qv*), Ketuel is one of the three angels who

127

ABOVE: *Eighth Incarnation of Vishnu as Krishna: Playing to the Gopis*
Indian School, *c*.18th century

Krisn Avatar (Krishna): Eighth of the ten Vedic Avatars (*qv*). Krishna repeatedly shows himself in this world in various forms, each with their own special function. These avatars make themselves known by performing exceptional feats. They are referred to in the Vedas, which tells of several prominent incarnations from the beginning of creation.

make up the Triune God (Holy Trinity), the other two being Meachuel (*qv*) and Lebatei.

Keveqel: One of 72 angels of 72 quinaries of degrees of the zodiac.

Kezef: One of the angels of death (*qv*).

Kfial: One of the 64 angel guards of the seven celestial halls.

Khabiel: An angelic Head Supervisor of the First Heaven.

Khamael: *See* **Camael**.

Kharael: Solomonic magic gives this angel the power to be used to exorcise the demon Belbel when his name is pronounced.

Kharura'il: An Islamic guardian angel that is invoked in exorcism rites.

Khasdiel: An angel whose name is inscribed on kamea.

Khurdad: An Amesha Spenta (*qv*) and angel of May in Persian legend who is ruler of the sixth day of the month. He can be asked to intercede on God's behalf by prayer at the 56th gate of Paradise.

Kidumiel: One of the 70 amulet angels (*qv*) mentioned in *The Book of the Angel Raziel* (*qv*).

Kimos: A secret name of Michael (*qv*) or one of the many names of Metatron (*qv*).

Kinor: *See* **Kipod**.

Kipod (Kinor): One of three angels who guard the upper gates of Hell, the other two being Nagrasagiel (*qv*) and Nairyo Sangha (*qv*). Said to be the angel who led Rabbi Joshua ben Levi on his visit to Hell.

Kiramu 'l-katibin: One of two Islamic 'recording angels'.

Kirtabus: An angel of languages as well as of the ninth hour, according to *The Nuctemeron* (*qv*).

Kisael: An angel guarding the fifth heavenly hall.

Kmiel: An angel of the summer equinox in Jewish mysticism whose name is used on amulets to ward off the evil eye.

Kokabiel: *See* **Kakabel**.

Kokaviel: The name of an angel that is inscribed on the third pentacle of the planet Mercury.

Kolazonta: An angel of destruction (*qv*) who is considered the personification of destruction.

Korniel: A guard at the gates of the South Wind.

Korshid: A Mandaean archangel, equating to the Kabbalistic Metatron (*qv*).

Kotecha: An angel of the seal (*qv*) used in conjuration.

Koustiel: An angel whose name is inscribed on a carnelian (a semi-precious gemstone) in the British Museum.

Krisn Avatar: *See* page 128.

Kshathra Vairya: An Amesha Spenta (*qv*) in Zoroastrian lore.

Kshiel: *See* **Kushiel**.

Kso'ppghiel: Chief of the angels of fury.

Kunospaston: In Occultism, Kunospaston is the demon of the sea. In the form of a fish, he wrecks ships and steals gold from them.

Kuriel: *See* **Kyriel**.

Kurmavatar: One of the ten Vedic Avatars (*qv*).

Kurzi: *See* **Angel of the Footstool**.

Kushiel (Kshiel): A regent in Hell and one of the seven angels of punishment, using a whip of fire to punish the ten nations.

Kutiel: In Judaism, an angel invoked in spells that use divining rods.

Kyniel: An angel of the Third Heaven.

Kyriel (Kuriel): One of the angels governing the mansions of the moon (*qv*).

Kyriotates: An angelic order of the second of three celestial hierarchies in *Karmic Relationships* by Austrian philosopher Rudolph Steiner.

Kzuial: An angel guarding the Fourth Heaven.

Labarfiel: An angelic guard of the Seventh Heaven.

Labbiel: The great angel Raphael's (*qv*) original name. It was changed to Raphael when he accepted God's decision to create humanity. The angels of truth (*qv*) and the angels of peace (*qv*) who chose not to comply with God's decision were burned.

Labe Erin: The talismanic spirit of success who serves in the second hour of the day.

Labusi: One of the eight angels of omnipotence (*qv*).

Lad: One of the many names of Metatron (*qv*).

Lahabiel: An angelic assistant to Raphael (*qv*) as ruler of the first day. Also invoked to ward off evil spirits.

Lahariel: One of the 70 amulet angels (*qv*).

Lahash: A great angel who, with Zakun (*qv*), led 184 myriads of spirits in attempting to intercept Moses' (*qv*) prayer before it reached God. Their punishment was to be bound with chains of fire, given 70 lashes with a fiery whip and be cast out of Heaven by Samuel (*qv*).

Lahatiel: One of the seven angels of punishment (*qv*) and the angel presiding over the gates of death, the second of the seven lodges of Hell. A fallen angel who is involved in punishing the ten nations.

Lailah (Layla): An angel of conception (*qv*) who is, according to *The Zohar* (*qv*), 'appointed to guard the spirits at their birth.' It is disputed whether he is a good or bad angel, one Jewish legend describing him as a demon of the night, the prince of conception and equal to Lilith, the 'demoness of conception'. On the other hand, in Judaism, Lailah was a good angel, fighting on the side of Abraham in battle.

Lama: An angel of the air, ruling on Tuesday and residing in the Fifth Heaven. Invoked from the West.

Lamach: An angel holding dominion over the planet Mars.

Lamas: *See* **Nirgal**.

Lamassu: One of the four Chaldean classes of

angels of protection. They possess the body of a lion and the head of a man and are comparable in function to the Cherubim (*qv*).

Lamechalal (Lamechiel): A ruler of the planets and the only angel who had the power to overcome the demon named Deceit.

Lamechiel: *See* **Lamechalal**.

Lameck (Lamideck): An angel invoked in black magic ritual, especially in conjuring the sword.

Lamediel: An angel of the fourth hour of the night, under Jefischa (*qv*).

Lamedk: An angel invoked in the conjuration of the sword – not to be confused with Lameck (*qv*).

Lamideck: *See* **Lameck**.

Larzod: A 'glorious and benevolent' angel conjured in Solomonic ritual in order to give the invocant the secret wisdom of God.

Lauday: An angel invoked in the blessing of the salt, mentioned in the *Grimorium Verum* (*qv*).

Lauiah: One of the 72 angels bearing the name of God Shemhamphorae.

Lauviah: A fallen angel formerly belonging to the order of Hashmallim (*qv*) and the order of the Cherubim (*qv*). He has influence over geniuses and important people.

Láwidh: The Islamic angel-prince who offered the Sufi Abu Yazid 'a kingdom such as no tongue can describe' during the Sufi's mir'aj – ascent – to the Seven Heavens. The bribe was rejected, however, as Abu Yazid realized it was no more than a test of his devotion to God.

Layla: *See* **Lailah**.

Lazai (Lazay): An angel invoked in the exorcism of fire, referred to in *The Greater Key of Solomon* (*qv*) and the *Grimorium Verum* (*qv*).

Lazay: *See* **Lazai**.

Lebes: One of the five chief angels of the first chora or altitude, the other four being Alimiel (*qv*), Barachiel (*qv*), Gabriel (*qv*) and Helison (*qv*). When invoked, he manifests bearing a banner with a red cross on it.

Lecabel: An angel with dominion over vegetation and agriculture, according to *The Magus* (*qv*). He

is one of the 72 angels bearing the name of God Shemhamphorae.

Ledrion: An angel invoked to exorcize spirits using incense and fumigations, as mentioned in the *Grimorium Verum* (*qv*).

Lehachel: One of 72 angels of 72 quinaries of degrees of the zodiac.

Lehahiah: A fallen angel who was formerly one of the Shemhamphorae.

Lehavah: An angel guarding the halls of the Seventh Heaven, in Hebrew lore.

Lelahel: An angel of the zodiac who rules the arts, the sciences, love and good fortune. He equates to the Kabbalistic angel Asentacer (*qv*). He is one of the 72 angels bearing the name of God Shemhamphorae.

Lemanael: A Kabbalistic angel of the moon who corresponds with Elimiel (*qv*).

Lepha: An angel of the seal (*qv*) invoked in special conjurations, mentioned in *The Sixth and Seventh Books of Moses* (*qv*).

Lesser Key of Solomon, The: This book is also known as *The Lemegton*, and is believed to have been inspired by Jewish Kabbalists, Muslim mystics and *The Greater Key of Solomon*. The author of this 17th-century grimoire is unknown. It has become a very popular book on demonology; teaching the reader conjurations, rituals and spells.

Leuuiah (Leviah): One of the 72 angels that carry the name of god Shemhamphorae.

Levanael: A spirit of the moon according to Cornelius Agrippa (*qv*).

Leviah: *See* **Leuuiah**.

Leviathan: Created with Behemoth (*qv*) on the fifth day of creation, Leviathan is in Enoch's description an evil and monstrous sea dragon commanded in rabbinical texts by Rahab. She is described as a great whale in Job in the Bible while Psalm 74:14 says that she is a hippopotamus or crocodile. Isiah calls her 'that crooked serpent'. In the system of Justinus she is considered an evil spirit and the Mandaeans say

LEFT: *Lilith,* by John Collier, 1887

Lilith: The first wife of Adam (*qv*) and Cain's true mother, now the wife, concubine or grandmother of Sammael (*qv*). Associated with Friday, she manifests as a being with the torso of a naked woman and the lower body of a snake. She is a winged female demon of the night that is a danger to children and seduces men in order to give birth to demon sons. Originating in Jewish legend, she derives from the Lili of Mesopotamian demonology where she is known as Ardat Lili. When she was Adam's wife she gave birth to 100 children a day. Most demons are mortal, but Lilith – with the other wives of Sammael, Naamah (*qv*) and Agrat bat Mahlat (*qv*) – will, according to *The Zohar* (*qv*), 'continue to exist and plague man until the Messianic day when God will finally extirpate uncleanliness and evil from the face of the Earth.' She is said to have emanated from beneath God's throne when she was an angelic assistant to Sammael. Now, as a demon in Hell, she is known by many names, which she uses as her disguises when working her evil deeds amongst mortals.

that she will swallow up all but the purified souls.

Librabis: An angel who helps find hidden gold and is a spirit of the seventh hour, mentioned in *The Nuctemeron* (*qv*).

Lilith: *See* page 132.

Lifton: An angel guarding the seventh heavenly hall.

Lights: Another word for angels.

Lithargoel: A great angel.

Little Iao: One of the many names of the angel Metatron (*qv*).

Liwet: A Mandaean angel holding dominion over inventions and love, who also looks after humans who show originality of thought. Also one of the seven planetary spirits.

Lobkir: An angel guarding the gates of the West Wind.

Lobquin: An angelic ruler of Tuesday in the West, residing in the Fifth Heaven. One of the guards at the gates of the West Wind.

Loel: A guard at the gates of the South Wind.

Logos: A secret name for God but also known as Michael (*qv*), Metatron (*qv*), the Holy Spirit or the Messiah. Logos is, according to the philosopher Philo of Alexandria, 'the angel that appeared to Hagar, the cloud at the Red Sea, one of the three angels that appeared to Abraham at Mamre [and] the divine form that changed the name of Jacob to Israel at Peniel.' He is known as 'the Oldest Angel'.

Loquel: An angel of the First Heaven, according to *The Sixth and Seventh Books of Moses* (*qv*).

Lord of Hosts: Otherwise known as Sabaoth (*qv*), Akatriel (*qv*) or God.

Lords (or lordships): A celestial order of angels that appears in the *Apocalypse of the Holy Mother of God*. Sometimes Lords are given in place of Dominations (*qv*), they can also be equated with Principalities (*qv*) and Virtues (*qv*).

Lords of Shouting: 1,550 myriads of angels also known as masters of howling. They are led by the angel Jeduthun (*qv*) and it is said that because of the chanting of these beings, 'judgement is lightened and the world is blessed.'

Lords of the Sword: Fourteen angels used in conjuring the sword listed in *The Sword of Moses* (*qv*) as:

> Aziel, Arel, Ta'aniel, Tafel, Yofiel, Mittron (Metatron), Yadiel, Raziel, Haniel (Anael), Asrael*, Yisrael, A'shael, Amuhael, Asrael.
> * = repeated names

Lord Zebaot: The lord of hosts in Jewish lore; the name that God used when battling sinners.

Los: Possibly another name for Lucifer.

Lucifer: He is erroneously identified with Satan because of a passage in the *Book of Isiah* where he is described as 'son of morning', a reference to King Nebuchadnezzar. The name Lucifer actually refers to the morning or evening star of Venus. He is still an evil angel, however, even if he is not Satan.

Luel: In Jewish magic, Luel is an angel invoked in connection with the use of diving rods.

Luma'il: An Islamic guardian angel invoked in exorcism rituals.

Lumazi: The Assyrians believed that there were seven Lumazi who created the universe. They equate to the seven angels of the presence in rabbinic tradition, the seven Prajapati of the Hindus and the Middoth in Talmudic writings, although there were only two of these.

Maadim: An angel pointed out to Moses (*qv*) by Metatron (*qv*) in the Fourth Heaven during the latter's visit. The *Revelation of Moses* says that Maadim 'stands near the moon in order to warm the world from the cold.'

Maccathiel: An angel of hell (*qv*).

Mach: An angel summoned in Solomonic magic rites to render the invocant invisible.

Machal: An angel invoked during the exorcism of the bat, mentioned in *The Greater Key of Solomon* (*qv*).

Machasiel: An angel invoked from the South who resides in the Fourth Heaven and rules on the Lord's Day (Sunday).

Machatan (Macoton): An angel of the air (*qv*) who rules on a Saturday with Uriel (*qv*), Cassiel (*qv*) and Seraquiel (*qv*).

Machidiel (Melkajel): An angel of the tenth Sephira (*qv*) and of Earth and regent of the month of March as well as ruler of the zodiac sign of Aries. In grimoire, he may be invoked by a man trying to secure the love of a woman.

Machkiel: An angelic guard of the Sixth Heaven.

Machmay: An angel of the seventh hour of the night, under Mendrion (*qv*).

Machnia: One of the 70 amulet angels (*qv*), also a guard at the gates of the South Wind.

Macoton: *See* **Machatan**.

Macroprosopus: A Kabbalistic angel of the first Sephira (*qv*) known as the 'God of concealed form'.

Madagabiel: An angel guarding the gates of the North Wind.

Madan: An angel with dominion over the planet Mercury, mentioned in *The Hierarchy of the Blesséd Angels* (*qv*).

Madiel: An angel residing in the First Heaven, invoked from the East. Ruling archangel of the three water signs of the zodiac.

Madimiel: Name of one of four angels inscribed on the first pentacle of the planet Mars. The others are Ithuriel (*qv*), Barzachia (*qv*) and Eschol (*qv*). In Mosaic legend he is one of the angelic princes who stand perpetually in front of God and to which are allocated the spirit-names of the planets.

Mador: An angel guarding the fourth heavenly hall.

Madriel: An angel of the ninth hour of the day, under Vadriel (*qv*).

Mael: An archangel who rules the water signs of the zodiac and is an intelligence (*qv*) of the planet Saturn. He is a Monday angel residing in the First Heaven and must be invoked from the North.

Midiron: One of the many names for the angel Metatron (*qv*).

Magog: *See* **Gog and Magog**.

Magus, The: English Occultist Francis Barrett wrote this handbook on ceremonial magic, the Occult, alchemy, astrology and the Kabbalah in 1801.

Maguth: An angel serving in the South as a Thursday ruler of the air. He is one of the many angels who stand guard at the gates of the South Wind.

Mah: In Persian lore, the angel who governs the phases of the moon.

Mahadeo: One of the 11 Vedic angels who 'with matted locks and three eyes' symbolizes the sun, the moon and fire.

Mahalel: The name of an angel inscribed on a kamea.

Mahalkiel: The name of an angel inscribed on a kamea.

Mahanaim: As recounted in Genesis, when Jacob left Haran, he was escorted by a double host, or Mahanaim of angels, each host numbering 600,000.

Mahananel: An angelic guard at the gates of the North Wind.

Mahariel: An angelic guard at the gates of the First Heaven who guides the souls of the Elect to God and once they are purified, provides new souls for them.

Mahash: *See* **Mahish**.

Mahashel: One of 72 angels of 72 quinaries of degrees of the zodiac.

Mahasiah: One of the 72 angels who bear the name of God Shemhamphorae.

Mahish: An angel mentioned in the sacred Hindu scripture, the Bhagavad-Gita, who, along with Brahma and Vishnu (*qv*), was created from one of the primary properties.

Mahka'il: An Islamic guardian angel invoked during exorcism rituals.

Mahniel: Alternative name for 'Azriel the Ancient'.

Mahoninm: Name assumed by the devil during the exorcism of a noblewoman at Auch in 1618. He said he was 'of the third hierarchy and the second order of archangels' and that his enemy in Heaven was St Mark the Evangelist.

Mahzeil: A Mandaean angel.

Mahzian: An angel invoked in order to restore sight.

Maianiel: An angel residing in the Fifth Heaven.

Maion: An angel ruling over the planet Saturn.

Maiphiat: An angel invoked during the exorcism of the bat, written in *The Greater Key of Solomon* (*qv*).

Majesties: An order of angels, sometimes used instead of Hashmallim (*qv*).

Makatiel: One of the angels of punishment (*qv*).

Makiel: An angel invoked during Syriac spellbinding rituals.

Maktiel: An angel with dominion over trees and one of the angels charged with punishing the ten nations, in *The Sword of Moses* (*qv*). He resides in the fourth compartment of Hell.

Malach ha-Mavet: The Kabbalistic angel of death.

Malach ha-Sopher: Assistant to Dumah (*qv*), angel of the silence of death. With Malach Memune (*qv*) determines how long each mortal's life will be.

Malachi or Malachy: Named in 4 Esdras as 'angel of the Lord'.

Malach Memune: Assistant to Duma (*qv*), angel of the silence of death. With Malach ha-Sopher (*qv*) determines how long each mortal's life will be.

Malach Ra: An angel of evil, although he is possibly himself not evil. God sometimes orders good angels to perform wicked deeds.

Malakim: An order of angels equivalent to Virtues

(qv), ruled by Peliel (qv), Uriel (qv), Uzziel (qv) or Raphael (qv).

Malaku 'l-Maut: An Islamic angel of death who may be equated with Izrael (qv) or Azrael (qv).

Malashiel: Guardian angel of Elijah (qv).

Malchiel: *See* **Milkier**.

Malchira: *See* **Malkira**.

Malik: A fallen angel of Arabic lore who, along with 19 sbires (zabaniya) or guardians, serves as a guard in hell. When souls languishing in the Underworld appeal to him for help, he tells them that they are doomed to remain there forever because 'they abhorred the truth when the truth was brought to them.'

Milkier (Malchiel): A guard at the gates of the South Wind and one of three princes serving Aephuriron, the lowliest of the ten holy Sephira.

Malkira (Malchira): Samuel's surname as given in The Martyrdom of Isiah by G.H. Box.

Malkiyyah: An angel who governs blood and whose name is inscribed on amulets to stop haemorrhages.

Malkuth: The soul of the Messiah or Metatron (qv).

Malmeliyah One of the many names for the angel Metatron (qv).

Malthidrelis: An angelic ruler of the zodiac sign of Aries.

Maltiel: A Friday angel resident in the Third Heaven that must be invoked from the West. He is also one of the intelligences (qv) of the planet Jupiter. Maltiel is the preceptor angel of Elijah (qv) and serves as one of the numerous guards of the West Wind.

Maluzim: A holy angel invoked during magic rites, in grimoire.

Mambe'a: A powerful angel invoked during Babylonian ritual to guard against sorcery. Babhne'a (qv) is a companion angel, possibly assisting him.

Mameroijud: An angel serving Jusguarin (qv), ruler of the tenth hour of the night.

Mamiel: An angel of the seventh hour of the day, under Barginiel (qv).

Mamlaketi: An Egyptian angel otherwise known as Uzza (qv).

Mammon: Aramaic for 'riches'. A powerful arch-demon residing in Hell who governs wealth and incites greed and many other vices in mortals. He is Hell's ambassador to England according to *Dictionnaire Infernal* (qv), and is equated with some of the most evil of spirits – Lucifer (qv), Satan (qv) and Beelzebub (qv), as well as with Nebuchadnezzar.

Manah: An Islamic goddess-angel of fertility whose idol was destroyed on the orders of Mohammed.

Manakel (Menakel): An angel holding dominion over aquatic animals and also one of the 72 angels of the zodiac.

Man Clothed in Linen: Gabriel (qv) is described thus in *The Book of Ezekiel* (qv) and also in *The Book of Daniel* but is also applied to Enoch, Michael (qv) and Vretil (qv) in various sources.

Maneij: An angel of the fourth hour of the night, under Jefischa (qv).

Maniel: An angel invoked in Syriac spellbinding charms.

Man of Macedonia: An angel seen in a vision by St Paul.

Mansemat: Another name for Mastema (Satan).

Mantus: One of the nine Etruscan Novensiles, supreme spirits of worship resembling Greek muses. *See* **Novensiles** for complete list.

Manu: An angel known to the Babylonians as 'Manu the Great' who governs fate.

Manuel: An angel who rules over the zodiac sign of Cancer.

Many-Eyed Ones: Another name for the order of Ofanim, an exalted order equated to Hashmallim (qv). Patriarchs arriving in Heaven became members of this order of which Raphael (qv) is usually designated chief.

Mara: The Buddhist equivalent of Satan (qv).

Marax: *See* **Forfax**.

Marchosias: A great fallen angel formerly of the Dominations (qv). When invoked, he appears as either a wolf or an ox with the wings of a griffin and the tail of a snake, depicted in *Dictionnaire Infernal* (*qv*). He told Solomon that he aspires to be recalled to his heavenly position on the seventh Throne after 1,200 years.

Marfiel: An angel of the fourth hour of the day, under Vachmiel (*qv*).

Margash: One of the many names of the angel Metatron (*qv*).

Margesiel: One of the many names of the angel Metatron (*qv*).

Margiviel: An angel guarding the Fourth Heaven.

Mariel: An angel invoked in spellbinding charms.

Marifiel: An angel of the fourth hour of the day, under Vachmiel (*qv*). Mentioned in *The Lesser Key of Solomon* (*qv*).

Marioch: An angel who watched over the writings of Enoch and was tasked with being a guardian angel for Enoch's descendants as well as ensuring the preservation of his books, documented in *2 Enoch* (See *The Book of Enoch*).

Marmarao: An angel invoked to cure problems of the bladder caused by the demon Anoster, one of the 36 demons of disease.

Marmarath: One of the seven planetary angels and the only angel who can defeat the Islamic jinn of war, Klothod.

Marniel: Name of an angel inscribed on a kamea.

Marnuel: An angel whose name is found in the writings of Rabbi Akiba, a Judean sage who lived during the latter part of the 1st century and the beginning of the 2nd century.

Marnuthiel: An angel whose name is found in the writings of Rabbi Akiba.

Maroch: An angel of the fifth hour of the day, under Sazquiel (*qv*), according to *The Lesser Key of Solomon* (*qv*).

Maron: A holy name invoked to control demons conjured during Solomonic rites.

Maroth: The name Maroth is of Hebrew origin and means 'bitterness'. Maroth is an Angel originating in Persian mythology who, according to the Jews, was sent to Earth by God 'with full commission to exercise government over all mankind, and to tutor and instruct them.'

Marou: A fallen angel who is supposed to have possessed Elizabeth Blanchard, a nun, at Loudun in France in the 17th century.

Martyrs: The 11th and 12th orders of angels, with Gabriel (*qv*) at their head, according to *The Magus* (*qv*).

Mary The Virgin: Mary is often described as an angel sent by God to receive the Lord who enters her 'through the ear' and who 'comes forth by the ear'.

Masgabriel: An angelic ruler of Sunday, ruling in the Fourth Heaven and invoked from the North.

Mashhit: A fallen angel who is overseer of the deaths of children and with Af (*qv*) and Hemah (*qv*) punishes murderers and those guilty of incest and idolatry.

Masim: An angel guarding the gates of the East Wind.

Maskiel: An angel guarding the First Heaven.

Maskim: The seven great princes of Hell in the Akkadian religion who 'reside at will in the immensity of space.'

Masleh: In Occultism, an angel who 'actuated the chaos and produced the four elements.' He is the ruler of the zodiac.

Masniel: An angel who governs the zodiac according to Cornelius Agrippa (*qv*).

Maspiel: An angel guarding the Second Heaven.

Mass Massiah: In Judaism, Mass Massiah is an angel invoked for curing skin ailments.

Mastema: A fallen angel who is an angel of adversity and of hostility. Legend says that Mastema asked God to leave some of the demons alive so that they could be used to punish mortals and God agreed. Another legend names Mastema as the angel who helped the Egyptian sorcerers to perform their magic when Moses (*qv*) and Aaron confronted Pharaoh.

Master of Howling: The angel Jeduthun (*qv*).

Mastho: The 'genius of delusive appearances',

according to *Transcendental Magic* (*qv*). Also an angel of the tenth hour.

Mastinim: The accusing angels who are led by Sammael (*qv*).

Matafiel: One of the seven angels who guard the Second Heaven.

Matanbuchus: An evil spirit who is characterized as the angel of lawlessness.

Mataqiel: One of the seven angels who guard the First Heaven.

Matarel (Matariel): The angel of rain, but Riddia (*qv*) and Zalbesael (*qv*) are also thus named.

Matariel: *See* **Matarel**.

Mathiel: An angel of the Fifth Heaven, ruling Tuesday and invoked from the North.

Mathlai: An angel of the planet Mercury and a Wednesday angel residing in the Third Heaven. According to *The Magus* (*qv*) Mathlai is a resident of the Second Heaven and is invoked from the East.

Matmoniel: A 'holy minister of God', summoned during a Solomonic ritual designed to help obtain a magic carpet.

Matniel: *See* **Maktiel**.

Matrona: 'The angel of the Lord', according to *The Zohar* (*qv*).

Matsmetisiyah: One of the numerous names of the angel Metatron (*qv*).

Mavet: An angel of death.

Mavkiel: Name of an angel inscribed on a kamea.

Maymon: Regent of the spirits of the air and of Saturday.

Mbriel: A ruling angel of the winds.

McWilliams, Sandy: A fictional angel in Mark Twain's *Captain Stormfield's Visit to Heaven*.

Meachuel: One of three angels of the Holy Trinity, the Triune God, the others being Lebatei (*qv*) and Ketuel (*qv*). He is invoked in conjurations.

Mebabel: One of 72 angels of the 72 quinaries of degrees of the zodiac and a guardian angel of the innocent with the corresponding angel Thesogar. He is invoked in order to steal the good fortune enjoyed by others.

Mebahel: One of the 72 angels bearing the name of God Shemhamphorae.

Mebahiah: One of the 72 angels bearing the name of God Shemhamphorae who is invoked by those wanting to conceive a child. He governs morals and religion.

Mechiel: One of 72 angels of the 72 quinaries of degrees of the zodiac.

Mediat (Modiat): An angel of Mercury who is the chief angel of the rulers of Wednesday.

Medorin: An angel residing in Paradise, according to *The Zohar* (*qv*).

Medussusiel: An angel of the sixth hour of the day, under Samil (*qv*).

Meetatron: *See* **Metatron**.

Mefathiel: An angel invoked in order to gain entrance to locked places; he is favoured by criminals.

Megiddon: A Seraph in Klopstock's epic German poem *The Messiah*.

Mehahel: A Cherubim (*qv*).

Mehaiah: An angel who is a member of the order of Principalities (*qv*).

Mehalalel: One of the 72 angels bearing the name of God Shemhamphorae.

Mehekiel: One of the 72 angels bearing the name of God Shemhamphorae.

Meher: Mandaean yazata or angel who governs light and justice.

Mehiel: Guardian angel of authors, orators, and college professors. His corresponding angel is Astiro (*qv*).

Mehriel: A Kabbalistic archangel.

Mehuman: An angel of confusion (*qv*).

Meil: An angel of Wednesday invoked in ceremonial magic rituals, documented in *The Magus* (*qv*).

Meimiririon: Fourth of the ten holy Sephiroth (*qv*).

Mekhapperyah: One of the many names of the angel Metatron (*qv*).

Melahel: One of the 72 angels bearing the name of God Shemhamphorae.

Melchidael: In *Grimorium Verum* (*qv*) an angelic

prince conjured up in black magic ritual in order to obtain a woman desired by the invocant.

Melchisedec: An angel of the order of Virtues (*qv*) who is the king of righteousness and described as 'a celestial Virtue of great grace who does for heavenly angels and Virtues what Christ does for man', as mentioned in Francis Legge's book *Forerunners and Rivals of Christianity II*. The Phoenicians called him Sydik, father of the seven Elohim (*qv*) while the Gnostics knew him as Zorokothera. In the Bible he was the legendary king of Jerusalem when it was still called Salem. Some have considered him to be the Holy Ghost. Mormons know him as 'the prince of peace.' His symbols are the chalice and the loaf of bread and in the Midrash Tehillim (*qv*), as Noah's son, he helped to feed the animals on board the ark. Enoch describes him as the supernatural child of Nir, the brother of Noah who is kept in infancy by Michael (*qv*) until the Flood abates and he can become a great high priest with 'power to work great and glorious marvels that have never been.'

Melech: An angel of the order of Powers (*qv*), invoked in conjurations.

Melek-I-Taus: *See* **Taus-Melek**.

Meleyal or Melejal: An angel of autumn.

Melha: The Buddhist equivalent of the Seraphim (*qv*) and head of the angelic order of Flames (*qv*).

Melioth: One of nine angels 'that run together throughout heavenly and earthly places.'

Melkejal: *See* **Machidiel**.

Melkharadonin: One of the 12 angels created by Ialdabaoth (*qv*) in his own image.

Melki: A class of Maldaean angels who are semi-divine and are responsible for carrying out the Will of the Great Life. They can be invoked to aid in baptismal rites.

Melkiel: An angel of the seasons, the others being Helemmelek, Melejal and Narel.

Membra: The name of God, according to the Kabbalah, or an angel who is thought to be the very essence of God and an intermediary for Him.

Memeon: An angel invoked in the blessing of the salt, referenced in *The Greater Key of Solomon* (*qv*).

Memsiel: An angel serving Mendrion (*qv*), ruler of the seventh hour of the night.

Memuneh: A class of angels through whom it is said the universe operates, from Heaven they defend their mortal charges.

Memunim: The plural form of Memuneh (*qv*), a class of angels.

Menadel: One of the 72 angels of the zodiac and a member of the order of Powers (*qv*). He ensures that exiles remain loyal to their homeland. His Kabbalistic corresponding angel is Aphut.

Menafiel: An angel of the 11th hour of the day, under Bariel (*qv*).

Menakel: *See* **Manakel**.

Menaqel: *See* **Manakel**.

Mendrion: Chief angel of the seventh hour of the night.

Menerva (Menvra): A member of the Novensiles (*qv*), the nine supreme Etruscan gods.

Meniel: One of the 72 angels bearing the name of God Shemhamphorae.

Menor: An angel invoked in the exorcism of wax referenced in *The Greater Key of Solomon* (*qv*).

Menvra: *See* **Menerva**.

Mephistopheles: This mighty fallen archangel's name is made up of two Hebrew words – mephiz for 'destroyer' and tophel for 'liar'. He is one of the seven great princes of Hell where he sometimes stands in for Satan himself. He is said to stand 'under the planet Jupiter, his regent is named Zadkiel, who is an enthroned angel of the holy Jehovah.' In Goethe's *Faust*, he famously stands in for his overlord, Satan when sealing a pact with the eponymous hero. The philosopher Hegel saw in Mephistopheles the symbol of 'the negative principle.'

Merasin: *See* **Meresin**.

Mersin: *See* **Meresin**.

Merattron: *See* **Metatron**.

Mercury: The angel of progress (*qv*), an epithet also enjoyed by Raphael (*qv*). Mercury is also equated with the Greek god Hermes (*qv*).

Meresijm: An angel of the first hour of the day, under Sammael (*qv*).

Meriarijim: An angel serving under Sarquamish (*qv*), ruler of the night.

Meresin (Merasin, Mersin, Metris): A fallen angel who controls the power of the air and is also lord of thunder and lightning in Hell. Another source (Camfield's *A Theological Discourse of Angels*) says that as Mererim he is one of the four holy angels of revelation.

Meririm: Called by Paul in Ephesians 'the prince of the power of the air,' another name for Satan. An evil power who presides over the angels discussed in the Book of Revelation, 'to whom is given to hurt the Earth and the sea'. And Barret says in *The Magus* (*qv*), 'he is the meridian devil, a boiling spirit, a devil ranging in the south.'

Merkabah: An angel of the chariot, another name for Cherubim (*qv*).

Merkabah Angels: The six orders of angels who are closest to the Throne of Glory and act as its guardians. They included the Galgallim (*qv*), the Hayyoth (*qv*), the Ofanim (*qv*) and the Seraphim (*qv*).

Merkaboth: There are seven merkaboth, one for each of the seven heavens. They can be compared to the Sephiroth (*qv*).

Merloy: A lesser spirit summoned in magic rituals.

Mermeoth: One of nine angels 'that run together throughout heavenly and earthly places', according to the *Gospel of Bartholomew*.

Merod: 'A most holy angel' invoked in magic ritual, mentioned in *The Greater Key of Solomon* (*qv*).

Merof: An angel of the seal (*qv*).

Meros: An angel of the ninth hour of the day, under Vadriel (*qv*).

Merroe: 'A most pure angel' invoked in magic ritual, especially during the conjuration of the sword, recorded in the *Grimorium Verum* (*qv*).

Mesarepim (Mesharethim): A class of angels of the Song-Uttering Choirs, under the leadership of Tagas.

Meserach: *See* **Nisroc**.

Meshabber: The angel responsible for the death of animals.

Mesharethim: *See* **Mesarepim**.

Mesharim: An angel after whom the 5th-century Galilean Kabbalist, Joseph Caro, titled his book *Maggid Mesharim*, which details visions given to him by the angel.

Meshulhiel: Tenth of the unholy Sephiroth (*qv*).

Mesriel: An angel of the tenth hour of the day, under Oriel (*qv*).

Messiach: An angel summoned in connection with the rite of 'the water and the hyssop'. Passages from Psalms 6, 64, 67 and 102 must be recited.

Messiah: A Cherub (*qv*) and a guardian angel of Eden who carries a flaming sword. He is also a Sephira (*qv*) of one of the four worlds of creation, the Briatic, an angel of the Lord and an angel of the Great Council. Enoch describes him as 'head of days'.

Metathiax: One of the 36 decimi, the spirits of the zodiac who are demons of disease. He is responsible for causing problems and the only holy angel who can defeat him is Adnael (*qv*).

Metatron (Meetatron, Meratton, Miton): An angel known by many names. Sometimes identified with Michael (*qv*), in rabbinic lore, he is the greatest of all the angels, sitting next to God on his Throne of Glory. He sustains the physical world, and is the link between the human and the divine. As an angel of prayers, he transports prayers up through all the 900 heavens to God and, as the angel of the Lord, he stands on top of the Tree of Life. As angel of death, he is responsible for telling Gabriel (*qv*) and Samael (*qv*) which human souls they should take and when. He was once human – living as Enoch. After arriving in Heaven, he was transformed into a spirit of fire and given 36 pairs of wings and many eyes. He is the heavenly scribe, responsible for recording all the actions of man in the Book of Life. He is chancellor of Heaven and prince of the ministering angels. He resides in the Seventh Heaven, manifesting as a pillar of fire more dazzling than the sun and he is the teacher of prematurely dead children in Paradise. There are numerous alternative names for Metatron and *3 Enoch* lists 105. The 76 below are taken from the 1865 Hebrew tract, *Sefer ha-Heshek*:

ALTERNATIVE NAMES FOR METATRON

1. Tsahtsehiyah	39. Saktas
2. Zerahyahu	40. Mivon
3. Taftefiah	41. Asasiah
4. Hayat	42. Avtsangosh
5. Hashesiyah	43. Margash
6. Duvdeviyah	44. Atropatos
7. Yahsiyah	45. Tsaftsefiyah
8. Palpeltiyah	46. Zerahiyah
9. Havhaviyah	47. Tamtemiyah
10. Haviyahu	48. Adadiyah
11. Veruah	49. Alaliayh
12. Magirkon	50. Tahsasiyah
13. Itmon	51. Rasesiyah
14. Batsran	52. Amisiyah
15. Tishbash	53. Hakham
16. Tishgash	54. Bibiyah
17. Mitspad	55. Tsavtsiyah
18. Midrash	56. Tsaltseliyah
19. Matsmetsiyah	57. Kalkelmiyah
20. Patspetsiyah	58. Hoveh Hayah
21. Zevtiyahu	59. Yehovah Vehayah
22. Miton	60. Tetrasiyah
23. Adrigon	61. Uvayah
24. Metatron	62. Shosriyah
25. Ruah Piskonit	63. Vehofnehu
26. Itatiyah	64. Yeshayah
27. Tavtavel	65. Malmeliyah
28. Hadraniel	66. Gale Raziya
29. Tatriel	67. Atatiyah
30. Ozah	68. Emekmiyahu
31. Eved	69. Tsalselim
32. Galiel	70. Tsavniyah
33. Tsaftsefiel	71. Giatiyah
34. Hatspatsiel	72. Parshiyah
35. Sagmagigrin	73. Shaftiyah
36. Yefefiah	74. Hasmiyah
37. Estes	75. Sharshiyah
38. Safkas	76. Gevriyah

Metris: *See* **Meresin**.

Miahel: One of the 72 angels of the 72 quinaries of the degrees of the zodiac.

Mibi: A ministering angel who is invoked during magic rituals, mentioned in *The Sixth and Seventh Books of Moses* (*qv*).

Michael: *See* pages 142–143.

Michar: *See* **Mikhar**.

Micheu: A power over the waters of life.

Middoth: Similar to the Sephiroth (*qv*), the seven personifications of the divine emanations, two of whom, the angels of mercy and of justice, are said to have served as creator angels. The other five represent wisdom, right, love, truth and peace.

Midrash: One of the many names of the angel Metatron (*qv*).

Midrash Tehillim: A book of Hebrew lore known since the 11th century. It tells stories, myths, legends, fables and proverbs.

Miel: An angel of Mercury and of Wednesday.

Mights: An alternative name for the order of Virtues (*qv*).

Migon: One of the many names of the angel Metatron (*qv*), mentioned in *3 Enoch* (See *The Book of Enoch*).

Miha'il: An Islamic angel of the Second Heaven holding dominion over conjugal fidelity and fertility.

Mihael: A Kabbalistic angel holding dominion over conjugal fidelity and fertility who belongs to the order of Virtues (*qv*) and is one of the 72 angels bearing the name of God Shemhamphorae.

Mihr: To the ancient Persians, the angel ruling over September and over the 16th day of that month. He is the angel of Platonic love, friendship and companionship and is one of the two angels – the other being Sorush (*qv*) – who will, on Judgment Day, stand on the bridge called al Sirat – finer than a hair and sharper than the edge of a sword – examining every person who passes, weighing each individual's actions during his or her life. Those found

LEFT: *The Archangel Michael*
by Hans Memling (*c.*1433–94)

Michael: Possibly the greatest of all angels in Christian, Jewish and Islamic lore – a warrior, protector, healer and guardian, sometimes described as the Holy Ghost, Logos and even God. He was originally a Chaldean deity and is sometimes identified with Metatron (*qv*). In Islam he is called Mikail (*qv*) and is described as having emerald green wings and being covered with saffron hairs, each of which has a million faces and mouths that ask Allah in a million dialects to pardon the sins of the faithful. Michael's titles are many and amongst them are ruling Prince of the Fourth Heaven, Chief of the order of Virtues, Chief of the Archangels, Prince-regent of the Seraphim, Prince of the Divine Presence, Angel of Repentance, Mercy, Righteousness and Sanctification. The sacred Zoroastrian text, the Avesta, calls him Saosyhant, the Redeemer of the Faithful. He is the angel of rectitude and compassion and guardian angel of Israel and Germany. He is Prince of Light, Guardian of Peace, Commander-in-Chief of the Heavenly Hosts, Guardian Angel of the Catholic Church, Angel of the Earth and Prince of God. He protects Heaven from evil and acts as a benevolent angel of death through whose auspices it is possible to receive God's forgiveness and eternal life. He is the patron of firefighters, policemen, sailors, soldiers and shopkeepers. With others, he will weigh mortal souls on Judgement day and is the symbol of divine justice, holding all the keys to Heaven. He cannot be corrupted and is without blemish. It is said that the Cherubim (*qv*) were created out of the tears he shed over the sins of the faithful. He is the regent of the sun, Leo and Sunday, ruler of the eighth Sephira (*qv*) and the planet Mercury. He is said to have written Psalm 85, which is used to invoke him. He is associated with the element of fire, an angel who grants miracles and fosters many good virtues. To Christians he is St Michael, 'the benevolent angel of death'.

ABOVE: *The Archangel Michael defeating Satan*
by Guido Reni, 1636

worthy by Mihr will be allowed to continue to Paradise; those found unworthy by Sorush will be cast down into Hell.

Mijcol (Mijkol): An angel of the seal (*qv*), invoked in conjurations, mentioned in *The Sixth and Seventh Books of Moses* (*qv*).

Mijkol: *See* **Mijcol**.

Mikael: An angel who, with Arpien, influences the decisions of great statesmen – monarchs, nobles and governors. He can be invoked to help uncover conspiracies against states.

Mikail or Mikhael: An Islamic guardian angel invoked in exorcisms. *See* **Michael**.

Mikhar (Mikheus): One of the Gnostic celestial powers who holds dominion over the springs of the waters of life.

Mikheus: *See* **Mikhar**.

Mikiel: One of the 72 angels with responsibility for the zodiac.

Milkiel: An angel presiding over spring, according to *The Zohar* (*qv*), as well as an unspecified summer month.

Milliel: An angel of Wednesday residing in either the Second or Third Heaven and invoked from the South.

Miniel: In Occult lore, Miniel is a powerful spirit who can induce love in a woman where there was none, as long as the invocant is facing South, according to *The Magus* (*qv*). He can also be used in spells for magic carpets.

Ministering Angels: Malache Hashareth in Hebrew. A number of Talmudists consider this order of angels to be the highest in the celestial hierarchy, the 'Hosts of the Lord'. To others, however, they are of a lowlier rank and as there are so many of them they are expendable. Three of them served Adam (*qv*) while he and Eve were in Eden. The Talmud Hagiga says that 'the ministering angels are daily created out of the River Dinur...they sing a Hymn and thenceforth perish, as it is said, 'each morning they are new.'

Ministers: Another term for angels.

Mirael: An angel that can be invoked in Solomonic magic rites, according to *The Greater Key of Solomon* (*qv*).

Miri: An angel used by the poet H.D. (Hilda Doolittle) in her poem "Sagesse".

Miriael: An angel of the order of the Warriors (*qv*).

Misran: An angel of persecution and one of the angels of the 12th hour.

Missabu: Ministering angel to Arcan (*qv*), the ruler of the Monday angels of the air.

Missaln: An angel of the moon serving on Monday who can be invoked in magic ritual.

Mitatron: Possibly Metatron (*qv*), an angel of Wednesday residing in the Third Heaven who can be invoked from the West.

Mithghiiel: Prince of the Hosts of X, mentioned in *The Sword of Moses* (*qv*).

Mithra (Izads, Mitra): A Vedic shining god equivalent to the angels of Judaeo-Christianity. He equates to Metatron and is one of the 28 spirits that surround the great god Ahura-Mazda. The Aryans believe him to be the god of light. He allocates places in Heaven to the souls of the just.

Mitmon: An angel found in grimoire.

Miton: One of the many names of the angel Metatron (*qv*).

Mitox(t): A demon who serves Ahriman (*qv*) and a Zoroastrian daeva of the 'falsely spoken word.'

Mitra: *See* **Mithra**.

Mitzpad: One of the many names of the angel Metatron (*qv*).

Mitzrael (Mizrael): One of the angels bearing the name of the God Shemhamphorae and an archangel invoked to confer obedience upon those answering to superiors.

Mithraism: The Hebrew name for Egypt and the name of the guardian angel of Egypt.

Mivon: One of the many names of the angel Metatron (*qv*).

Mizan: An angel invoked in Arabic incantation rituals.

Mizgitari: An angel of the seventh hour who protects eagles.

Mizkun: An angel of the first hour of the day whose name is inscribed on amulets to ward off evil.

Mizrael: *See* **Mitzrael**.

Mizumah: To the ancient Persians the angel who 'attended the servants of God and promoted the better faith.'

Mnesinous: A great celestial power said to draw the Elect up to Heaven.

Moak(k)ibat: The Islamic recording angel, equivalent to Pravuil (*qv*) or Raduerie (*qv*) in Judaeo-Christian lore and Nabu (*qv*) in Babylonian legend.

Modiel: An angel who guards the gates of the East Wind.

Modiniel: An angel of the planet Mars.

Moloc(h) (Molech): A fallen angel, according to Milton in *Paradise Lost*. Also a Canaanite god of fire to whom children were sacrificed. Solomon erected a temple to him.

Monadel: One of the 72 angels bearing the name of the God Shemhamphorae.

Monker (Munkar): One of the two Arabic angels – the other being Nakir (*qv*) – with blue eyes and black skin. Monker examines the newly arrived souls and decides whether they are worthy of living in Paradise.

Morael: The angel of awe or fear ruling over the Hebrew month of Elul – August-September. He can make everything in the world invisible.

Morax: *See* **Forfax**.

Mordad: The angel of death to the ancient Persians.

Moroni: To the Mormons the angel of God, son of 'Mormon, the last great leader of the Nephites,' who gave Joseph Smith the Gospel of a New Revelation.

Moses: Often described as an angel or a patriarch-prophet who was ranked above angels. Three mortals ascended to Heaven – Moses, Enoch and Elijah (*qv*) – but unlike the other two, we do not have an angelic name for Moses.

Mtniel: An angel who, with Jehiel (*qv*) and Hayyel (*qv*), holds dominion over wild beasts.

Mufgar: An angel guarding the First Heaven.

Mufliel: An angel guarding the Seventh Heaven.

Mulciber: An angel mentioned in Milton's *Paradise Lost*.

Mumiah: An angel who can be invoked to bring good health and long life. He also rules physics and medicine, and has the corresponding angel Atembui (*qv*).

Mumol: An angel invoked along with Mutuol (*qv*) to bless the Pen and Ink, a device for the exorcism of evil spirits in Occult lore.

Munkar: *See* **Monker**.

Mupiel: An angel invoked in Mosaic rites in order to bring good memory and tolerance.

Murdad: Zoroastrian angel of the seventh day of July who is equivalent to the angel Azrael (*qv*) when he performs the task of separating the soul from the body at death.

Muriel: An angel of the month of June and the zodiac sign of Cancer and a regent of the order of Dominations (*qv*). He serves Veguaniel (*qv*), ruler of the third hour of the day and can be invoked from the South to help the invocant obtain a magic carpet.

Murmur (Murmus): A fallen angel, formerly of the order of Hashmallim (*qv*). In Hell, he commands 30 legions of demons and he manifests as a warrior wearing a crown and riding a griffin. He teaches mortals the art of prophecy and on his command the souls of the dead can be made to appear before him to answer questions.

Murmus: *See* **Murmur**.

Musanios: A Gnostic low-ranked aeon (*qv*) serving as a ruler of the realm of the invisible.

Mutuol: In Occult lore, an angel invoked in the blessing of the Pen and Ink.

Mzpopiasaiel: Chief of the angels of wrath (*qv*).

Naadame: 'A prince over all the angels and Caesars', according to *The Greater Key of Solomon* (*qv*).

Naamah: One of the four dark angels of prostitution (*qv*), all of whom are wives of Sammael. The other three are Lilith (*qv*), Eisheth Zenunim (*qv*) and Agrat bat Mahlat (*qv*). Naamah is mother to demons and Lilith is responsible for infecting children with leprosy. She corrupted Azael (*qv*) and Uzza (*qv*), the sons of the great biblical patriarch Isaac by seducing them; she is known as 'the great seducer of men, spirits and demons,' and is the mother of the devil Asmodeus, his father being the demon Shamdan. In Genesis Naamah can be found as a mortal, daughter of Lamech and sister of Tubal-cain.

Naar: One of the many names of the angel Metatron (*qv*).

Naaririel: The name Naaririel is Hebrew for 'lad'. An angel who guards the Seventh Heaven.

Nabu (Nebo): A Babylonian angelic prototype of the archangel of Judaeo-Christianity. Angel of the Lord in Sumerian theosophy and son and servant of the god Marduk. His symbol is the lamp and he is a recording angel, inscribing the deeds of man in the Book of Fate. The Akkadians considered him a deity ruling the planet Mercury, like Metatron (*qv*). One source claims that he gave Enoch to the Palestinian Jews, Metatron to the Jews of Babylon and it is for this reason that the two became one as Enoch-Metatron.

Nachiel (Nakhiel, Nakiel): The angel of the sun when it is in the sign of Leo, he has the Kabbalistic number 111 and his corresponding spirit is Sorath (*qv*).

Nachmiel: An angel guarding the gates of the South Wind.

Nacoriel: An angel of the ninth hour of the night.

Nadiel: The angel of migration (*qv*) and ruler of December.

Nafriel: An angel guarding the gates of the South Wind.

Nagrasagiel: A guardian at the gates of Hell and the prince who acted as Moses' (*qv*) guide during his visit to the Underworld.

Nahaliel: An angel who rules over streams, in Hebrew lore.

Nahoriel: *See* **Nahuriel**.

Nahuriel: One of the seven angels who guard the First Heaven.

Nairyo Sangha: One of three Persian angel princes guarding the three upper gates of Hell. He is also one of Ahura Mazda's messengers and is entrusted with the souls of the righteous.

Nahkiel: *See* **Nachiel**.

Nakiel: *See* **Nachiel**.

Nakir: One of two black angels in Islamic lore, the other being Monker (*qv*).

Nakriel: An angel guarding the gates of the South Wind.

Nanael: In Kabbalism, an angel presiding over the great sciences who can also influence philosophers and ecclesiastics. One of the 72 angels who bear the name of the God Shemhamphorae.

Naoutha: An angel of the Southwest who is described as holding in his hand a 'rod of snow' which he puts in his mouth in order to put out the fire that comes from it.

Narcoriel: An angel of the eighth hour of the night.

Narel: In Enoch lore, Narel is the angel of winter.

Nariel: An angel governing the South Wind who is also the ruler of the noonday winds.

Naromiel: An angel of the moon, ruler of Sunday and resident of the Fourth Heaven who must be invoked from the South.

Narsinha: The Vedic man-lion Avatar (*qv*). He is also lord of heroism.

Narudi: The Akkadian 'lord of the great gods'. His image was hung in houses to keep evil people at bay.

Nasarach: *See* **Nisroc**.

Nasargiel (Nasragiel): A powerful, lion-headed angel who, with Kipod (*qv*) and Nairyo Sangha (*qv*), is a guardian of the gates of Hell. He is the equivalent of the Sumerian-Chaldean angel Nergal (*qv*).

Nasharon: According *The Greater Key of Solomon* (*qv*), an angel who is a prince 'over all the angels and Caesars'.

Nashriel: One of three sarim – angel princes – serving Sephuriron who is tenth of the ten holy Sephiroth (*qv*). The other servants of Sephuriron (*qv*) are Ithuriel (*qv*) and Malkiel (*qv*).

Nasragiel: *See* **Nasargiel**.

Nasr-ed-Din: One of the seven archangels of the Kurdish Yazidic devil-worshipping religion. *See* **Yazidic Archangels**.

Nathanael (Xathanael): An angel of vengeance (*qv*) and ruling angel of the element of fire who was the sixth angel created by God, in order of appearance (all angels were created at the same time). Only six names of the angels of vengeance are known:

> Satanael (*qv*), Michael (*qv*), Gabriel (*qv*), Uriel (*qv*), Raphael (*qv*), Nathanael. He serves under Samil (*qv*) as an angel of the sixth hour and, with Ingethal (*qv*) and Zeruch (*qv*), is one of the three angels of hidden things.

Natiel: Name of an angel found inscribed on a kamea.

Nattig: One of the four principal Chaldean classes of protecting angels.

Natzhiriron: One of the ten holy Sephiroth (*qv*), the personification of the seventh Sephiroth, Netzach (*qv*), or in the Kabbalah, Anael (*qv*).

Nayá'il: An angel residing in the Fourth Heaven and encountered by Sufi Abu Yazid during his mir'aj, or ascension to the Seventh Heaven.

Nbat: A Mandaean angel.

Ndmh: In Judaism, an angel of the summer equinox invoked as protection against the evil eye.

Nebo: *See* **Nabu**.

Neciel: One of the angels ruling the mansions of the moon (*qv*).

Nectaire: A fictional flute-playing angel to be found in Anatole France's *Revolt of the Angels*.

Nefilim: *See* **Nephilim**.

Nefta: A fictional female angel loved by Asrael in Alberto Franchetti's opera 'Asrael'.

Negef: In Judaism, Negef is an angel of destruction invoked at the end of the Sabbath.

Nehinah: An angel invoked in necromantic ritual.

Neithel: One of the 72 angels governing the 72 quinaries of the degrees of the zodiac.

Nekir: An Islamic angel who assists Monker (*qv*) and Nakir (*qv*) in questioning the dead in order to ascertain which god they worshipped.

Nelapa: An angel of Wednesday residing in the Second Heaven and invoked from the South.

Nelchael: A fallen angel formerly of the Shemhamphorae and the Hashmallim (*qv*). In Hell he teaches astronomy, mathematics and geography to other demons and is closely associated with the angel Sith (*qv*).

Nemamiah: An archangel bearing the name of the God Shemhamphorae who is the guardian angel of those who fight for good causes, as well as admirals and generals.

Nememel: One of the 72 angels who rule the 72 quinaries of the degrees of the zodiac.

Nephilim (Nefilim): In Hebrew legend, these primeval giants are reputed to be the result of the mating of fallen angels with mortal females. They are closely related to the Emir ('terrors'), the Raphim ('weakeners'), the Gibborium ('giants'), the Zamzummim ('achievers') and others. Helel (*qv*) is their chief and, according to one source, they constructed the Tower of Babel.

Nephonos: One of the nine angels, that, according to the Gospel of Bartholomew, 'run together throughout the heavenly and earthly places.'

Neqael: A fallen angel formerly an archangel.

Nergal: A ruler of the planet Mars and probably a ruler of the zodiac sign Aries. Depicted as lion-headed with wings and clawed feet, he is one of the four main guardian angels of Chaldean lore. He is also known as the god Kutha and answers to the name of Baal (*qv*), a deity in Hell. To the Sumerians, Palestinians and Chaldeans, he is the ruler of the summer sun and in Gnosticism he is ruler of Hades. Occultists recognize him as the chief of the secret police in the Underworld, assisting Beelzebub by spying for him, and amongst his other titles are god of war, pestilence and fever. He is the angel of the planet Mars and one of the rulers of the signs of the zodiac.

Neriah: One of 70 amulet angels (*qv*).

Neriel: One of the angels who govern one of the mansions of the moon (*qv*).

Nesanel: An angel summoned, along with Meachuel (*qv*) and Gabril (*qv*), to free or purge the invocant of all sin.

Nestoriel: An angel of the first hour of the day.

Nestozoz: An angel serving Sarquamich (*qv*), ruler of the third hour of the day.

Nethahel: One of the 72 angels who rule the 72 quinaries of the degrees of the zodiac.

Netoniel: A black magic angel whose name is inscribed on the first pentacle of Jupiter.

Netzach (Netzael): The seventh Sephira (*qv*) of the Tree of Life of which the ruling angel is Haniel (*qv*).

Netzael: *See* **Netzach**.

Nibra Ha-Rishon: An emanation of God and one of the most exalted of all angelic beings. He may be compared with Logos (*qv*), Sophia (*qv*) and Metatron (*qv*).

Nichbadiel: An angel who guards the gates of the South Wind.

Nidbai: A Mandaean guardian angel, with Silmai (*qv*), of the River Jordan.

Nilaihah (Nith-Haiah, Nithaiah): An angel of the Occult sciences who reveals his prophecies in the form of rhymes, resulting in him being known as a poet-angel. He wields influence over wise men in pursuit of love, peace and solitude and can be invoked by pronouncing any of the divine names and the first verse of Psalm 9. He is one of the 72 angels bearing the name of God Shemhamphorae.

Ninip: Chief of the angels, to the Babylonians.

Ninth Heaven: The home of the 12 signs of the

zodiac, according to Enoch (qv). 'Kukhavim' is the Hebrew name for the ninth Heaven.

NINE ANGELS THAT RULE THE NINE HIERARCHIES IN HEAVEN

Metatron (over the Seraphim)
Ophaniel (over the Cherubim)
Zaphiel (over Hashmallim)
Zadkiel (over Dominations)
Camael (over Powers)
Raphael (over Virtues)
Haniel (over Principalities)
Michael (over Archangels)
Gabriel (over Angels)

Nirgal (Nirgali): To Chaldeans, one of the four classes of guardian angels, depicted generally as lions with men's heads.

Nisan: A Talmudic angel.

Nisroc (Nasarach): In Milton's *Paradise Lost*, a ruling angel of the order of Principalities (qv), although he was originally an Assyrian deity, worshipped by the ruler Sennacherib. To Occultists, he is a demon, serving in Hell as a chef. He can also be equated with Chemos, Baal-Peor, Meserach and Arasek (qv).

Nithael: A fallen angel formerly of the order of Principalities (qv) who, in spite of his fall, according to *The Magus* (qv), remains one of the 72 Shemhamphorae angels. In Hell he is ruler over kings, emperors and people of high rank.

Nithaiah: *See* **Nilaihah**.

Nitibus: An angel of the second hour who also governs the stars.

Nitika: An angel of the sixth hour of the day who is an angel of precious stones.

N'Mosnikttiel: Chief of the angels of rage.

Noaphiel: An angel's name inscribed on the fifth pentacle of the planet Saturn. To invoke, a passage must be read from Deuteronomy 10.

Nogah: Said to stand 'above the sun in summer to cool the Earth' and was one of two angels ('big stars') in the Fourth Heaven pointed out to Moses (qv) by Metatron (qv).

Nogahel One of the angel princes who stand perpetually before God and who receive the planets' spirit names.

Noguel: An angel of the planet Venus whose corresponding angel is Hagiel (qv).

Nohariel: An angel who guards the gates of the East Wind.

Noriel: An angel whose symbolic colour is the 'gold of brass lit with orange' and who is a guard at the gates of the East Wind.

Novensiles: The nine great Etruscan deities who control thunderbolts and oversee the renewal of things. They are:

Tina, Cupra, Menrva, Summanus
Vejovis, Sethlans, Mars, Mantus, Ercle.

Nuctemeron, The: Ancient Greek text by philosopher Apollonius of Tyana, believed by pagans in the 4th century to have been a contemporary of Jesus Christ.

Nudriel: An angel who guards the Third Heavenly Hall.

Nukha'il and Nura'il: Islamic guardian angels who are used in exorcisms.

Numiah: One of the 72 angels bearing the name of God Shemhamphorae

Nuriel: Jewish lore describes him as the angel of hailstorms (qv) and he is also associated with elemental fire. He is a ruler of the zodiac sign of Virgo and assists Michael (qv). Said to be 300 parasangs tall, he commands 50 myriads of angels all made of fire and water. Residing in the Second Heaven, he may be invoked during spellbinding rituals. He is powerful enough to be included among Michael (qv), Shamshiel (qv) and Seraphiel (qv) and is one of the seven angels ruled by Jehuel (qv), the prince of fire. His name can be used on a kamea to protect against evil.

N'zuriel Yhwh: One of the eight angel princes of the Merkabah who rank higher than all other angels, including Metatron (qv).

Obizuth: The winged female dragon put to flight by the great archangel Bazazath (*qv*).

Och: In ritual magic, Och is a ruler of 28 of the 196 Olympic provinces into which Heaven is divided and the angel who rules the sun. He has the power to give an invocant 600 years of good health and commands 36,536 legions of solar spirits. Also said to govern morals and to be a 'prince of alchemy'.

Octinomon (Octinomos): 'A most holy angel' of God invoked in the conjuration of the reed.

Octinomos: *See* **Octinomon**.

Oertha: An angel of the North and of the Fifth Heaven who, according to the *Gospel of Bartholomew*, has 'a torch of fire and putteth it to his sides, and they warm the great coldness of him [so] that he freeze not the world.'

Oethra: One of the nine angels that 'run together throughout heavenly and earthly places' according to the *Gospel of Bartholomew*.

Ofael: An angel of Tuesday residing in the Fifth Heaven who may be invoked from the South.

Ofaniel (Aufniel, Ofniel, Ophaniel): Chief of the Ofanim (*qv*) who also holds dominion over the moon and, as such, is sometimes known as the angel of the wheel of the moon. According to Enoch, he has 16 faces, 100 pairs of wings and 8,466 eyes. He is one of the seven angels of the throne (*qv*) who carry out the commands of the powers. He is identified with Sandalphon (*qv*).

Ofanim (Auphanim): The Ofanim are equivalent to the order of Hashmallim (*qv*) and according to *The Zohar* (*qv*), rank higher than the Seraphim (*qv*). The scheme devised by Italian Renaissance philosopher, Giovanni Pico della Mirandola, places them sixth in the nine-choir celestial hierarchy. Ofaniel is the head of this order although Rikbiel (*qv*) and Raphael (*qv*) are sometimes also listed in this position.

Ofiel: One of the 70 amulet angels (*qv*).

Ofniel: *See* **Ofaniel**.

Og: A nephilim (*qv*), son of Ahijah, brother of

Sihon and grandson of the fallen angel, Semyaza. Jewish lore describes him as a giant who was killed by Moses with a blow to his ankle. In the Bible, he is the King of Bashan whom God sends to Israel. Another story tells how he survived the Flood by climbing onto the roof of the ark.

Ogdoas: A Gnostic order of angels of the highest rank. To the ancient Greeks, Ogdoas was the eighth Heaven, the dwelling place of divine wisdom.

Ohazia: An angel that guards at the gates of the Third Heaven.

OIrin: The angels who watch over the kingdoms of the Earth, according to Chaldean cosmology.

Ol: A regent of the zodiac sign of Leo and one of the fiery triplicities.

Olivier: A fallen angel, formerly a prince of the order of archangels.

Olympian Spirits: The 16th-century work of ritual magic, the *Arbatel of Magic*, says that there are seven great Olympic Spirits, also known as the Stewards of Heaven, who dwell in the air and space and that each of them governs a number of the 196 Olympic provinces that constitute Heaven. They are: Araton (*qv*), Bethor (*qv*), Phaleg (*qv*), Och (*qv*), Hagith (*qv*), Ophiel (*qv*) and Phul (*qv*).

Omael: One of the 72 angels bearing the name of the God Shemhamporae who is also a member of the order of Dominations (*qv*). He is the ruler of alchemy and helps creatures, including humans, to reproduce. He may be a fallen angel, but evidence of his status is inconclusive as he seems to function in both Heaven and Hell.

Omeliel: One of the four names of angels engraved on the third pentacle of the planet Saturn.

Omiel: A fallen angel.

Omophorus: To the Manicheans a 'world-supporting angel' who carries the Earth on his shoulders like the Greek Atlas.

On: In black magic, a demon who can be used to help contact Lucifer and in Solomonic ritual, an angel invoked in the conjuration of the reed.

Onafiel: A regent of the moon.

Onayepheton: An angel that God will call upon to resurrect the dead, according to *The Greater Key of Solomon* (*qv*).

Onomatath: One of the nine angels who 'run together throughout the heavenly and earthly places', according to the *Gospel of Bartholomew*.

Onzo: An angel invoked in the exorcism of wax.

Ophan: *See* **Sandalphon**.

Ophaniel: *See* **Ofaniel**.

Ophanim: Another name for the order of the Hashmallim (*qv*) and the Hebrew for Cherubim (*qv*).

Ophiel: In ritual magic, an Olympian Spirit and ruler of the planet Mercury with 100,000 legions of spirits under his command. His name can be found inscribed on the Necromantic Bell of Girardius, a bell that is rung to call the dead. He may be invoked in magic ritual and should not be confused with Ofiel.

Ophiomorphus: The Gnostic name for the Hebrew devil Sammael (*qv*).

Ophis: Often described as 'head of the rebellious angels', Ophis was also revered by Gnostics as a serpent, a symbol of divine wisdom. The same serpent is said to have been responsible for corrupting Adam (*qv*) and Eve. In *Magus II*, Francis Barrett describes him as a demon.

Opiel: An angel invoked in love charms.

Or: An angel invoked in exorcism rituals.

Orael: An angel of the planet Saturn.

Oraios (Oreus): One of the seven Gnostic archons (*qv*).

Oranir: Chief of the nine summer equinox angels. He is also effective as an amulet to protect from the evil eye.

Ore'a: An angel who guards the fourth heavenly hall.

Oreus: One of the seven Gnostic archons (*qv*).

Oriares (Narel): An angel presiding over winter.

Oribel: *See* **Uriel**.

Oriel (Auriel): One of the 70 amulet angels (*qv*). Also known as the angel of destiny.

Orifel: *See* **Orifiel**.

Orifiel (Orifel, Oriphiel, Orphiel): Cited by Pope Gregory 'the Great' as an archangel and elsewhere listed as a prince of the order of Hashmallim (*qv*) and an angel presiding over the planet Saturn as well as an angel who protects the wilderness. Another source lists him as one of the seven regents of the world and an angel of the second hour of the day, under Anael (*qv*). To Paracelsus (*qv*), he is a chief Talisman and also replaces one of the planetary spirits of Egypt. He is also listed as an angel of Saturday.

Oriockh (Ariukh): One of the two angels, the other being Marioch (*qv*), instructed by God to guard the writings of Enoch.

Orion: In Klopstock's *The Messiah*, the guardian angel of St Peter.

Oriphiel: *See* **Orifel**.

Ormael: An angel of the fourth hour of the night.

Ormary: An angel of the 11th hour of the day.

Ormas: An angel of the tenth hour of the day.

Ormazd (Ormuzd): The Zoroastrian God, the supreme power of good, prince of light and twin brother of Ahriman (*qv*) who is the prince of evil. The Zoroastrians believed that each was supreme in his own realm, but the Jews and Christians rejected this in favour of the concept of monotheism, where only God is supreme and evil exists only because God allows it to.

Ormijel: An angel of the fourth hour of the day.

Ormisiel: An angel of the second hour of the night.

Oroiael: One of the four great Gnostic angels of wisdom who are said to be equivalent to Uriel (*qv*) or Raguel (*qv*).

Oromasim: One of three princes of the world, along with Araminem and Mitrim, according to *The Sixth and Seventh Books of Moses* (*qv*).

Orphaniel: A great angel who is 'ruler of the first legion.' Ruler of the star, Luna, he may be invoked on Mondays.

Orphiel: *See* **Orifel**.

Orus (Horus): A fallen angel, according to Milton's *Paradise Lost*.

Osael: A Tuesday angel of the Fifth Heaven, invoked from the South.

Oseny: A Cherub (*qv*), or Seraph (*qv*), invoked in magic ritual.

Osgaebial: An angel ruling the eighth hour who is said to command 'a great cloud of attending spirits.'

Osiris: *See* opposite.

Otheos: An angel invoked for discovering treasure.

Othriel: An angel invoked in magic incantation.

Otmon: One of the many names for the angel Metatron (*qv*), this one used 'when he seals the guilty in Israel'.

Ou: *See* **Uriel**.

Ouestucati: Written in the poem 'Sagesse' by Hilda Doolittle as 'the lady of chaste hands', Ouestucati originates in the Hesperides and bringing the sea wind. Corresponding angel of Iehuiah (*qv*).

Oul: An assistant to the angel Dalquiel (*qv*) in the Third Heaven.

Oumriel: A ministering angel of the Fourth Heaven.

Ouraios: One of the seven Elohim (*qv*).

Ourpahil: A Mandaean angel.

Ouza (Uzza): A fallen angel.

Overseer of Light: *See* **Jeu**.

Overshadowing Cherub: King Nebuchadnezzar was referred to as the 'Overshadowing Cherub' in Ezekiel 28:16.

Ozah (Uzah): One of the many names of the angel Metatron (*qv*).

ABOVE: *Relief depicting Osiris*
Egyptian 18th Dynasty

Osiris: A fallen angel in *Paradise Lost*, borrowed by Milton from the great Egyptian god, Osiris.

Pa'aziel: Another name for the angel Metatron (*qv*).

Pabael: An angelic messenger of the moon.

Pabel: A Sunday angel who is a resident of the Fourth Heaven and is invoked while facing West.

Pachdiel: A chief guardian angel of the Fourth Heaven.

Pachriel: One of the powerful angels who each rules one of the seven Heavens and commands 496,000 myriads of angels.

Padael: *See* **Phadihel**.

Paffran: An angel serving Samax (*qv*) as ruler of the air on Tuesdays.

Pagiel: In grimoire, an angel invoked for the satisfaction of the invocant's desires.

Pahadiel: An angel guarding the Seventh Heaven.

Pahadron: An angel ruling the Hebrew month of Tishri (September-October). In Jewish mysticism, he is regarded as the angel of terror (*qv*).

Pahaliah: An angel who is invoked in order to help convert heretics to Christianity. He is one of the 72 angels bearing the name of God Shemhamphorae and governs morality and theology. Sothis (*qv*) is his corresponding angel.

Paimon: A fallen angel, formerly of the order of Dominations (*qv*). A great prince of Hell, obeying only Lucifer (*qv*), he commands 200 legions of demons and manifests as a young woman, wearing a crown, riding on a camel.

Palalael: An angel guarding the gates of the West Wind.

Palatinates: One of the orders of angels, used as another name for Powers (*qv*). Can be invoked to grant invisibility.

Palit: A name used in Jewish legend for Michael (*qv*) when he escaped from Satan (*qv*) while Satan was being cast out of Heaven.

Palpeltiyah: One of the many names for the angel Metatron (*qv*).

Paltellon: An angel invoked in the blessing of the salt, according to *The Greater Key of Solomon* (*qv*).

Paltriel: An angel guarding the Fifth Heaven.

Pammon: An angel of the sixth hour of the night, under Zaazonash (*qv*).

Panael: An angel guarding the North Wind, not to be confused with Paniel.

Panaion: Another of the many names for the angel Metatron (*qv*).

Pancia: An angel invoked in magic ritual.

Paniel (Penuel): Name of an angel inscribed on a kamea.

Papsukul: An angelic messenger of the greater Chaldean Gods.

Paracelsus: 16th-century Swiss botanist, alchemist, Occultist and astrologer. Paracelsus was not a magician but believed in the use of talismans during certain astrological phases.

Paraclete: *See* **Paraqlitos**.

Paradise: *See* below.

Paraqlitos (Paraclete): The guardian angel of the sorrows of death, according to the *Falasha Anthology*.

Parasiel: Name of an angel inscribed on the first pentacle of the planet Jupiter. He is lord and master of treasures.

Parasim (Parashim): A class of angels or angelic horsemen who serve Tagas (*qv*) as one of the Song-uttering Choirs.

Parashim: *See* **Parasim**.

Parasurama: The sixth of the ten Vedic Avatars (*qv*), also known as Chirangivah the Immortal.

Pariel: Name of an angel inscribed on a kamea.

Pariukh (Mariokh): Appointed with Ariukh and Oriockh (*qv*) to act as guardian to Enoch's writings.

Parmiel: An angel of the third hour of the day, under Veguaniel (*qv*).

Parshiyah: One of the angel Metatron's (*qv*) many names.

Paratshah: One of Lilith's (*qv*) many names.

Partsufim: The plural form of Partsuf. The essence of God residing in the Sephiroth (*qv*). The five ruling Partsufim are:

    Abba (the Partsuf of Hochma or Wisdom)

    Aruikh Anpin (long face or long-suffering) **or** Attika Kaddisha (holy ancient one)

    Imma (the Partsuf of Binah or Understanding – a feminine spirit)

ABOVE: *Central Panel from the Threshold of Paradise* by Victor Mikhailovich Vasnetsov, 1885–96

Paradise: Located by both Moses (*qv*) and Enoch as being in the Third Heaven, but according to the Gnostic Valentinians it lies in the Fourth.

Shekinah (the female equivalent of God)
Zeir Anpin (the impatient, the Holy One)

Parvardigar: To the ancient Persians, Parvardigar was the angel of light.

Parymel: One of 15 angels of the throne (*qv*) according to *The Sixth and Seventh Books of Moses* (*qv*).

Parziel: An angel who guards the Sixth Heaven, in Hebrew lore.

Paschar (Psachar): Paschar is responsible for carrying out the orders of the celestial powers and is one of the angels guarding the Seventh Heaven in Hevrew lore.

Pasiel: An angel holding dominion over the zodiac sign of Pisces. In the Kabbalah, he is an angel of Hell (*qv*), ruler over Abaddon (*qv*), the sixth of Hell's seven lodges.

ABOVE: *Statuette of Pazuzu*
*c.*8th century BC

Pazuzu: The king of demons of the wind in Assyrian and Babylonian mythology. In ancient stories, despite being an evil spirit, Pazuzu can be invoked using amulets to protect against his rival, Lamashtu, who strikes during childbirth.

Paisiel: An angel guarding the seventh heavenly hall.

Paspassim: An angel who serves as an assistant to the angel Metatron (*qv*).

Pastor: An angel invoked to ensure the fulfillment of the invocant's desires.

Pasuy: An angel who guards the fourth heavenly hall.

Patha (Pathicl): An angel who is summoned at the end of the Sabbath.

Pathatumon (Patheon): Another name for God in Solomonic conjurations, used in magic ritual to bind demons. He was invoked by Moses (*qv*) to bring darkness to Egypt.

Patheon: *See* **Pathatumon**.

Pathiel: *See* **Patha**.

Patriarchs: *The Zohar* (*qv*) states that all Jewish patriarchs are transformed into great angels on arriving in Paradise and that they are one of the three highest grades of the celestial order.

Patrozin: An angel of the fifth hour of the night, under Abasdarhon (*qv*).

Patspetsiyah: One of the angel Metatron's (*qv*) many names.

Patteny: A ministering angel who can be invoked in Kabbalistic ritual.

Pazriel: A great archangel of the First Heaven.

Pazuzu: *See* left.

Peacock Angel: *See* **Taus-Melek**.

Pedael: The angel of deliverance to Jewish mystics.

Pedenij: An angel of the seal (*qv*).

Peliel: Guardian angel to Jacob and chief of the order of Virtues (*qv*). He shares the position of second of the ten holy Sephiroth (*qv*) with Zekuniel (*qv*).

Penac: An angel of the Third Heaven.

Penael: A messenger of the planet Venus, residing in the Third Heaven, who rules Fridays and must be invoked from the North.

Penarys: An angel of the third hour of the night, under Sarquamich (*qv*).

Penat: An angel of Friday who resides in the Third Heaven and is an angel of Venus.

Penatiel: An angel of the 12th hour of the day, under Beratiel (*qv*).

Pendroz: An angel of the seventh hour of the night, under Mendrion (*qv*).

Peneal: An angel of the Third Heaven.

Peneme: *See* **Penemue**.

Penemue (Peneme): According to Enoch lore, Penemue was a fallen angel who instructed mortals in the art of writing, an activity that was condemned as corrupting. He also taught humans 'the bitter and the sweet and the secrets of wisdom.'

Peniel: Another name for the angel Jehovah. He is a ruler of Fridays residing in the Third Heaven and is invoked to cure stupidity.

Penitent Angel: *See* **Abbadona**.

Penpalabim: An angel invoked in order to find hidden treasure.

Penuel: *See* **Paniel**.

Peor: *See* **Chemos**.

Peri: A group of Islamic fallen angels who come under the rule of Eblis (*qv*). To the ancient Persians they were beautiful but evil spirits; the offspring of fallen angels and will be allowed into Paradise after they have served their penance.

Periel: One of the many names for the angel Metatron (*qv*).

Permaz: An angel of the second hour of the night, under Farris (*qv*).

Permiel: An angel of the fourth hour of the day, under Vachmiel (*qv*).

Perrier: A fallen angel, formerly of the order of Principalities (*qv*).

Pesagniyah: A ruling angel of the southern region of Heaven and the keeper of the keys to the ethereal places. He kisses the prayers of those who are in deep sorrow before transporting them to God.

Pesak: An angel who guards the fifth heavenly hall.

Peshtvogner: According to G.I. Gudjieff's *All and Everything, Beelzebub's Tales to His Grandchildren*, an arch-Cherub whose other name is 'All-Quarters-Maintainer'. He orders that horns grow on the head of Beelzebub (*qv*).

Petahel: An angel invoked at the close of the Sabbath.

Petahyah: In *The Zohar* (*qv*), Petahyah is the Chief of Heaven's northern region, appointed 'over that side to which prayers offered for deliverance from enemies ascend.'

Phadahel: *See* **Phadihel**.

Phadihel (Padael, Phadahel): The angel God sent to the wife of Manoah who conceived a child who was born as Samson. Also named as the angel that appeared to Abraham, Jacob and Gideon.

ABOVE: *Apotheosis of the Corsican Phoenix* by James Gillray (1757–1815)

Phoenixes: The Phoenixes and the Chalkydri (*qv*) are, according to the Chaldeans, angels of a high order, equivalent to the Seraphim (*qv*) and the Cherubim (*qv*). They dwelt in the Fourth or Sixth Heaven and had 12 sets of wings. Their song at dawn was renowned and their colour was purple.

Phaiar: An angel invoked in the Solomonic conjuring of the reed.

Phakiel: An angel who rules the zodiac sign of Cancer.

Phaldor: An angel of oracles (*qv*), documented in *The Nuctemeron* (*qv*).

Phalec: A ruler of the order of Angels, also a governing spirit of the planet Mars.

Phalgus: An angel of judgement and genius of the fourth hour of the day.

Phamael: *See* **Phanuel**.

Phanuel (Ramiel, Uriel): An angel of penance sometimes acknowledged as one of the four main archangels. He rules the repentance of those who aspire to eternal life and protects against Satan (*qv*). According to the Sybilline Oracles, he is 'one of the five angels who know all of the evils that men have wrought.' He is celebrated by the Ethiopians on a holy day as the archangel Fanuel (*qv*).

Pharmaros: *See* **Armaros**.

Pharniel: An angel of the 12th hour of the day, under Beratiel (*qv*).

Pharzuph: An angel of fornication and lust (*qv*) as well as one of the rulers of the fourth hour.

Phatiel: An angel of the fifth hour of the night.

Phenex: A fallen angel, formerly of the Hashmallim (*qv*), who aspires to return to the seventh throne in Heaven in 1,200 years. He commands 20 legions of infernal spirits.

Phinehas: According to Judges 2:1, 'the angel of the Lord [who] came up from Gilgal' and whose countenance 'when the holy Ghost rested upon it, glowed like a torch.'

Phoenixes: *See* page 157.

Phorlakh: An angel of the Earth whose name is inscribed on the seventh pentacle of the sun.

Phorsiel: An angel of the fourth hour of the night.

Phronesis: A Gnostic angel emanating from the divine will.

Pi-Hermes: Equated to the angel Raphael (*qv*) and, in Hermetics, the genius (*qv*) of the planet Mercury as well as head of the order of archangels.

Pihon: Another name for the angel Metatron (*qv*) when he is opening the doors of Heaven to let prayers in. When he is closing the doors, he is known as Sigron (*qv*).

Pi-Ioh: *See* **Pi-Joh**.

Pi-Joh (Pi-Ioh): Equivalent to the angel Gabriel (*qv*), the Hermetic angel of the moon and a ruler of the order of Angels.

Pilalel: One of the angels who guard the gates of the West Wind.

Pillared Angel: The angel 'clothed with a cloud' of Revelation 9. With one foot on the land, the other in the sea, he supports Heaven with his right hand, swearing 'time shall be no more.'

Pilot Angel: In Dante's *Purgatorio*, an unnamed angel ferries souls to Purgatory from the south bank of the Tiber. He is the angel who greets the poet and Virgil at the beginning of their journey.

Pi-Ré: An angel who is of the seven Hermetic planetary archangels as well as chief of the order of Virtues (*qv*). Identified with Michael (*qv*).

Pisqon: One of the names of Metatron (*qv*).

Pistis Sophia: The Gnostic text *Pistis Sophia* is believed to date back to the 2nd century. It relates the Gnostic teachings of Jesus to his disciples.

Pi-Zeus: Chief of the order of Dominations (*qv*) and an angel of Jupiter.

Plesithea: Depicted as a woman with four breasts, she is said to be the 'mother of angels', in Gnostic lore.

Pniel: An angel ruling over the months of the year.

Poiel: One of the 72 angels of the zodiac who is a member of the order of Principalities (*qv*) and the ruler of philosophy and good fortune. He is also one of the 72 angels bearing the name of God Shemhamphorae.

Porna: An angel of Friday residing in the Third Heaven who may be invoked from the South.

Poro: An angel of the order of Powers (*qv*), invoked for conjuration. Mentioned in *The Sixth and Seventh Books of Moses* (*qv*).

Porosa: An angel of Friday residing in the Third

Heaven who may be invoked from the South.

Posriel: A fallen angel who governs the sixth of Hell's lodges in which resides the prophet Micah.

Poteh: The angel of forgetfulness, invoked during necromantic ritual by Jews at the end of the Sabbath.

Potentates: Another name for the Powers (*qv*).

Powers: An order of angels; the term is first found in the Septaguint, the Koine Greek version of the Hebrew Bible translated between the 3rd and 1st centuries B.C.E. Equivalent to the Greek idea of the Lord's Hosts, Dionysius' system for the celestial hierarchy placed Powers third in the second triad, erroneously equating them with the Seraphim (*qv*). Sammael (*qv*) is sometimes named as chief of this order but Camael (*qv*) is also frequently named as leader. The chief in Hermetics is Ertosi. The raison d'être of this order is to establish order on the heavenly pathways, preventing demons from making progress. St Paul suggests in various places in his epistles that the Powers are, or could be, evil.

Prajapati: A class of spirits similar to the Vedic Rishis, the seven angels of the presence and to the Zoroastrian Amesha Spentas (*qv*).

Praklit: *See* Palit.

Pravuil (Vretil): The heavenly record-keeper.

Praxil: An angel of the second hour of the night, under Farris (*qv*).

Preceptor Angels: Angelic advisors and guides to each of the great patriarchs. They are:

Abraham – Zidikiel (Zadakiel)

Adam – Raziel

David – Cerviel (Gerviel, Gernaiul)

Elijah – Malashiel or Maltiel (Elijah became the angel Sandalphon)

Isaac – Raphael (also guardian angel of Toby the Younger)

Jacob – Peliel (Pehel)

Joseph, Joshua and Daniel – Gabriel

Moses – Metatron

Noah – Zaphkiel

Samson – Camael (Gamael)

Shem – Jophiel (Yophiel

Solomon – Michael

Preil: A Mandaean angel.

Prenostix: An angel of the sixth hour of the night.

Primeumaton: An angel invoked during the exorcism of water. Moses (*qv*) used his name to bring down hail on Egypt.

Prince of Alchemy: *See* **Och**.

Prince of Angels: Jesus Christ.

Prince of Cherubim: Cherubiel (*qv*). Originally a position held by Satan (*qv*).

Prince of Conception: *See* **Lailah**.

Prince of Darkness: Satan (*qv*).

Prince of Death: Satan (*qv*), but Euronymous has this role in the Underworld, according to Occult texts. He is also the bearer of the Grand Cross of the Order of the Fly.

Princedoms: Another name for the order of Principalities (*qv*).

Prince of Fire: Nathanael (*qv*), also known as 'lord of fire'. The title is also given to Jehuel (*qv*). In the Underworld, Pluto holds this position.

Prince of Hades (Prince of Hell): Raphael (*qv*) is named thus in *The Book of Enoch* (*qv*). Uriel (*qv*) may also be given this title as 'presider over Tartarus'.

Prince of Heavenly Hosts: *See* **Michael**.

Prince of Light: *See* **Michael**.

Prince of Peace: Usually Jesus (*qv*), but is a title that has also been given to Melchisedec (*qv*).

Prince of Persia: Dubbiel (*qv*), who was defeated by Michael (*qv*) in battle.

Prince of the Power of the Air: Satan (*qv*), although Wormwood (*qv*), Meririm (*qv*) and other angels have also been thus named.

Prince of the Presence: *See* **Angel of the Presence**.

Prince of the Time of Iniquity: Satan (*qv*).

Prince of the World: Metatron (*qv*).

Prince of this World: Satan (*qv*) is described thus by Jesus (*qv*) in John 12:31.

Principalities (Princedoms): An order of the celestial hierarchy, usually placed first in the third triad. The Principalities protect religion and watch over leaders. Chief angels include Requel (*qv*), Anael (*qv*), Cerviel (*qv*) and Nisroc (*qv*). Egyptian Hermetics allocate this role to Suroth (*qv*).

Principals: Light, Darkness and 'An intermediary Spirit' are listed by the Gnostics as the three principals or primordial Powers.

Prion: A 'high, holy angel of God' invoked in magic ritual, particularly in the conjuration of the reed. Prion is referred to in *The Book of Ceremonial Magic* (*qv*) and *The Greater Key of Solomon* (*qv*).

Propel: *See* **Crocel**.

Progenie of Light: A name for angels in Milton's *Paradise Lost*.

Pronoia: A great Gnostic archon (*qv*) or power that helped God make Adam (*qv*), providing the nerve tissue; a myth, it is said, borrowed from Chaldean lore.

Propator: An unmoving aeon (*qv*) who remains fixed on the constellation of the chariot (the Merkebah). He surrounds himself with many numbers of angels. He resides in Heaven's zenith with another aeon (*qv*), Sophia (*qv*) beside him.

Protoctist Angels: The angels who sent the Torah to men using angels. The first 'operating angels'.

Pruel: An angel who guards the gates of the South Wind.

Pruflas: A fallen angel, once of the order of the Hashmallim (*qv*) but also partly of the order of Angels (*qv*).

Prukiel: A Syrian spellbinding angel used for creating protective charms.

Psachar (Pascar): One of the seven angelic princes of power, the others being Kalmiya (*qv*), Boel (*qv*), Asimor (*qv*), Gabriel (*qv*), Sandalphon (*qv*) and Uzziel (*qv*).

Psdiel: A fallen angel invoked to use against enemies, documented in *The Sword of Moses* (*qv*).

Psisya: One of the 70 amulet angels (*qv*), according to *The Book of the Angel Raziel* (*qv*).

Psyche: *See* opposite.

ABOVE: *Cupid and Psyche* by Annie Louisa Swynnerton, 1891

Psyche: A Gnostic demiurge whose origin is in Greek mythology. In the ancient story, Psyche was the daughter of the king and queen of Sicily and was so beautiful that potential husbands travelled far and wide to ask for her hand in marriage. Psyche's ego grew so big that it caught the attention of Aphrodite (Venus) who was outraged to learn Psyche believed herself to be more beautiful than she. Aphrodite sent Eros (Cupid) to shoot her with an arrow of desire so that she would fall in love and stop being a nuisance. The plan backfired when Eros, too, fell in love with her. The pair married and Zeus made her a goddess. In ancient mosaics she is depicted with butterfly wings.

Psychopompoi: Angels who accompany souls after death toward their heavenly abode. Michael (*qv*) and Elijah (*qv*) are leaders amongst them.

Psychopomp(us): Singular form of psychopompoi.

Pthathil: Powerful angel ranked second only to God in Mandaean legend. He is a ruler of lesser angels and is said to have helped in Creation, having created Adam's body, although it fell to God to actually give it life. In other sources he is seen as a prince of evil.

Pucel: *See* **Crocel**.

Purah: An angel invoked at the close of the Sabbath. In Jewish legend, he is the lord of oblivion and the angel of forgetfulness.

Puriel: *See* **Puruel**.

Purson (Curson): A fallen angel, previously of the order of Virtues (*qv*) and also partly of the Hashmallim (*qv*). Now a prince of the Underworld with 22 legions of infernal spirits under his command. He is invoked as a revealer of the past, the future and of where to find hidden treasure. He manifests as a lion-faced man holding a snake and riding a bear. Purson is mentioned in *The Book of Ceremonial Magic* (*qv*).

Puruel (Puriel): A Greek version of Uriel (*qv*), the 'fiery and pitiless angel who probes the soul', according to the *Testament of Abraham* (*qv*).

Purusha: The cosmic spirit in Sanskrit legend, the First Cause, itself being uncaused. Also, in the Kabbalah, he is En Soph (*qv*), the 'unimaginable creator of the universe', the God of Christianity.

Pusiel (Puruel): An angel of punishment (*qv*), equated with Hadriel (*qv*) and residing in the sixth compartment of Hell.

Puziel: A fallen angel invoked against enemies, according to *The Sword of Moses* (*qv*).

ABOVE: *The Groves of Versailles. View of the Dragon Pool and the Pool of Neptune, with Apollo slaying Python* by Jean the Younger Cotelle (1642–1708)

Python: In the evil hierarchy, the second of the nine archangels or arch-demons. In Greek mythology, a huge serpent that is hatched from the mud of Deucalion's deluge, that lurked in a deep cleft of Parnassus, killed eventually by the sun god, Apollo.

Qaddis: Singular form of Qaddisin (*qv*).

Qaddisin: Two angels who with the two Irin (*qv*), make up the council of God. They are ranked, with the Irin, higher than the Seraphim (*qv*), 'greater than all the children of Heaven,' according to *The Book of Enoch* (*qv*).

Qafsiel (Qaphsiel, Quaphsiel): According to *3 Enoch* (See *The Book of Enoch*) Qafsiel guards the Seventh Heaven. In ancient Jewish magic he is invoked using kameas to ward off enemies. The words on the charm are written in the blood of a bird and it is then tied to the foot of a dove which is allowed to fly away, taking the enemy with it. In the event of the bird refusing to fly, it is a sign that the enemy will not go away.

Qalbam: An angel who guards the gates of the South Wind.

Qamiel: An angel who guards the gates of the South Wind.

Qaphsiel: *See* **Qafsiel**.

Qangiel Yah: Another of the names of the angel Metatron (*qv*).

Qaniel: An angel who guards the gates of the South Wind.

Qaus: An angel invoked in Arabic Occult rituals.

Queen of the Angels: *See opposite*.

Quelamia: One of the seven great archangels who resides in the First Heaven, carrying out the orders of the celestial powers. Mentioned in the *Book of the Angel Raziel* (*qv*).

Quaphsiel: *See* **Qafsiel**.

Quoriel: An angel of the fourth hour of the day, under Vachmiel (*qv*) who is invoked during the ceremonial rites, according to *The Book of Ceremonial Magic* (*qv*).

ABOVE: *Mary – Queen of Heaven, Master of the St. Lucy Legend*
Dutch school, *c.*15th century

Queen of the Angels: The Virgin Mary in Catholicism; in the Kabbalah, the Shekinah (*qv*); in Gnosticism, Sophia (*qv*).

Raahel: One of the 72 angels ruling the 72 quinaries of the degrees of the zodiac.

Raamiel: An angel of thunder (qv) who is, according to some, a fallen angel.

Ra'asiel X: An angel invoked in ritual magic, according to *The Sword of Moses* (qv).

Rabacyel: A regent of the Third Heaven.

Rabdos: An angel with the power to halt and change the paths of the stars. A fallen angel, he is now a demon who strangles people and only the angel Brieus (qv) has the power to stop him.

Rabia: One of the ten Mandaean uthri, or angels, who escort the sun in its daily course.

Rab-un-Naw: An Islamic angel of light, equated with the ancient Persian angel, Parvardigar (qv).

Rachab: *See* **Rahab**.

Rachel: According to the Kabbalah, she is the Shekinah (qv) when she is dressed as the Celestial Bride for her marriage to God. She is one of the four matriarchs, who also rule in a place in Heaven reserved for the daughters, wives and sisters of the great patriarchs.

Rachiel: An angel of the Ophanim (qv) who rules Friday and the sphere of the planet Venus. She is concerned with human sexuality.

Rachmiah: One of the 70 amulet angels (qv).

Rachmiel: *See* **Rahmiel**.

Rachsiel: One of the 70 amulet angels (qv).

Rad'adel: An angel who guards the sixth heavenly hall.

Radueriel (Dabariel): Identified with Daryoel (qv), Pravuil (qv) and Vretil (qv). In Enoch lore Radueriel is the keeper of the Books of Life and Death, as heavenly registrar and recording angel. He is also regent of poetry and chief among the Muses. He is senior to Metatron (qv), and Enoch tells us that from every word he speaks, a new song-uttering angel is formed.

Rael: In Occultism, Rael is an angel of Wednesday who resides in the Third Heaven. He is also an angel of the planet Venus who can be invoked from the North.

Raftma'il: An Islamic guardian angel invoked during exorcisms.

Ragat: An angel conjured in magic ritual, mentioned in *The Sixth and Seventh Books of Moses* (*qv*).

Ragiel: *See* **Raguel**.

Raguel (Ragiel, Raguhel, Rasuil, Rufael, Suryan): An archangel residing in the Second or Fourth Heaven who is responsible for punishing other angels for wrongdoing. He is equated by the Gnostics with Thelesis (*qv*) and is said to be the angel who transported Enoch to Heaven; Anafiel (*qv*) is also credited with this act.

Raguhel: *See* **Raguel**.

Rahab: *See* opposite.

Rahabiel: An angel invoked using a kamea.

Rahatiel: *See* **Rahtiel**.

Rahaviel: An angel who guards the second heavenly hall.

Rahdar: An angel who with his brother Phakiel (*qv*), guards the zodiac sign of Cancer.

Rahmiel (Rachmiel, Rhamiel): An angel of love, compassion and mercy who may be invoked to ward off the evil eye. He is the angelic version of St Francis of Assisi who, like Elijah (*qv*) and Enoch, was transformed into an angel when he arrived in paradise.

Rahtiel (Rahatiel): The Jewish angel of the constellations who positions the stars after Metatron (*qv*) has given them names.

Rahzeil: A Mandaean angel.

Rakhaniel: Name of an angel that appears on the fifth pentacle of the planet Saturn.

Ramael: *See* **Ramiel**.

Ramal: One of the 70 amulet angels (*qv*).

Ramamel: An angelic guard at the gates of the East Wind.

Ram Avatar: Seventh of the ten Vedic Avatars (*qv*).

Ramiel: An angel who leads souls to judgement and is often known as the angel of 'true visions'. According to Enoch, he is both a holy angel and a fallen angel.

Ram Izad: A Persian angel.

Ram Khastra: The Parsi equivalent of the

ABOVE: *The Angel of Death* by Evelyn De Morgan, 1890

Rahab: A fallen angel who according to legend was destroyed twice – once by God for refusing to separate the upper and lower waters at the time of the Creation and next for trying to prevent the Hebrews from crossing the Red Sea in their flight from Egypt. In the Talmud he is an angel of death and destruction and in the Bible, he is described as an angel of insolence and pride. He is said to have returned *The Book of the Angel Raziel* (*qv*) to Adam (*qv*) after it had been thrown into the sea by jealous angels. In the Babylonian Talmud, Rahab, Leviathan (*qv*), Behemoth (*qv*) and the angel of death are one and the same.

Mandaean angel, Ayar Ziva.

Rampel: An angel presiding over mountains and deep waters.

Raphael: *See* page 167.

Raquiel: An angel who guards the gates of the West Wind.

Rasamasa: Governs the zodiac sign of Pisces with Vacabiel (*qv*).

Rasesiyah: One of the many names of the angel Metatron (*qv*).

Rash (Rashin Rast, Resh): The angelic minister of justice, under Mithra.

Rashiel (Zavael): An angel who presides over whirlwinds and earthquakes.

Rashin Rast: *See* **Rash**.

Rasuil: *See* **Raguel**.

Rathanael: An angel of the Third Heaven who is the only angel with the power to prevent the evil deeds of the female demon Enepsigo, as documented in the *Testament of Solomon* (*qv*).

Ratsitsiel: An angel guarding the First Heaven, in Hebrew lore.

Ratziel: *See* **Raziel**.

Ratzuziel: An angel guarding the Third Heaven.

Raum: A fallen angel, previously of the order of Thrones (*qv*), who manifests in the form of a crow. He is responsible for the destruction of cities and the suppression of human dignity. In Hell he commands 30 legions of demons. *Dictionnaire Infernal* (*qv*) represents him as having three heads – those of a man, a cat and a viper.

Ravadlediel: An angel guarding the Fifth Heaven.

Raziel (Galizur, Ratziel): An angel guarding the secrets of the universe. In the Kabbalah the personification of divine wisdom and one of the nine archangels of the Briatic world, the second of the four worlds of creation. All celestial and earthly knowledge is said to be contained within *The Book of the Angel Raziel* (*qv*) upon which King Solomon is said to have based all his magic. Raziel is known as 'herald of the deity' chief of the Erelim (*qv*) and guardian angel to Adam.

Razvan: Arabic legend describes this angel as the 'treasurer of Paradise' and the 'porter of Heaven'.

Razziel: An angel of the seventh hour of the night, under Mendrion (*qv*).

Recabustira: An angel who can be prayed to in order to help obtain a magic carpet, according to *The Greater Key of Solomon* (*qv*).

Rectacon: An angel invoked in the blessing of the salt.

Rectores Mundorum: Divine Chaldean Powers that are in charge of the Underworld.

Red Angel: The angel in the painter Marc Chagall's work *Descent of the Red Angel*.

Regent: A fallen angel in Milton's *Paradise Lost* who is one of the great powers who fought in the Great Revolt.

Regents: A class of angels in Milton's *Paradise Regained*.

Region: An angel invoked in ceremonial magic.

Rehael: An angel of the order of Powers (*qv*) who rules over longevity and good health. He also inspires respect for parents and is one of the 72 angels bearing the name of God Shemhamphorae.

Rehauel: One of the 72 angels who govern the 72 quinaries of the degrees of the zodiac.

Reiiel: An angel of the order of the Dominations (*qv*) who is one of the 72 bearing the name of God Shemhamphorae.

Rekhodiah: One of the names of four angels that are inscribed on the second pentacle of the sun.

Relail: Governor of the Fifth Heaven in Arabic legend.

Remiel (Rumael): An archangel who is often confused with Uriel (*qv*) and who is said to oversee those who rise from the dead.

Rempha: To the Egyptians, ruler of the order of Hashmallim (*qv*) and an angel of time who is also said to be an archangel of the planet Saturn.

Requel: The chief of the order of Principalities (*qv*).

Requiel: One of the angels governing the mansions of the moon (*qv*).

ABOVE: *The Archangel Raphael and Tobias*
by Titian (*c*.1488–1576)

Raphael: One of the three great angels, with Michael (*qv*) and Gabriel (*qv*). Of Chaldean origin, he was originally called Labbiel. He is the angel of dawn, prince regent of the Second Heaven and of both the Cherubim (*qv*) and the Archangels (*qv*). He is also chief of the order of Virtues (*qv*) and a member of the Seraphim (*qv*), Dominions (*qv*) and Powers (*qv*). He rules the southern sector of Heaven, is a guardian angel of the West, a chief angel of the evening winds and an angel of prayer, love, joy, healing and light. He is the regent of the sun and stands in the middle of it. He is a guardian of the Tree of Life and is one of the six angels of repentance. His other angelic responsibilities include science, medicine and wisdom and he is ruler of elemental air. Enoch describes him as a Watcher (*qv*), a guide in Sheol which is the final destination of Jewish souls and an angel responsible for healing the ailments and wounds of human children.

Reschith Hajalalim: In Kabbalism, Reschith Hajalalim is the ministering angel through whom 'the essence of divinity flows'.

Resh: *See* **Rash**.

Retsutsiel: *See* **Rezoziel**.

Revealing Angel: The Revealing Angel is spoken of in the Koran as 'a plain warner from Him', but his identity remains unknown.

Rezoziel (Retsutsiel): An angel guarding the Third Heaven, in Hebrew lore.

Rhamiel: *See* **Rahmiel**.

Rhaumel: An angel ruling Friday and residing in the Fifth Heaven who is invoked from the North, according to *The Magus* (*qv*).

Ribbotaim: A group of angels who serve as God's Chariot, like the Cherubim (*qv*).

Richol: An angel of the order of Powers (*qv*), invoked in conjuration, according to *The Sixth and Seventh Books of Moses* (*qv*).

Riddia (Ridya): An angel of rain (*qv*) who presides over the element of water. He resides between two abysses and when he manifests, he appears as a three-year-old calf with cleft lips.

Rid Wan: Archangelic guardian of the Garden of Eden; an Islamic angel guarding the entrance to the earthly paradise.

Ridya: *See* **Riddia**.

Riehol: In Kabbalism, Riehol is one of the two angels who rule the zodiac sign of Scorpio, the other being Saissaiel (*qv*).

Rifion: An angel who guards the Fifth Heaven.

Rigal One of the 70 amulet angels (*qv*).

Rigziel: An angel who is eighth of the ten holy Sephiroth (*qv*).

Rikbiel: Chief of the divine chariot (Merkabah) and a prince of the Divine Council with more power than Metatron (*qv*). Also a chief of the Galgallim (*qv*).

Rimezin: An angel of the fourth hour of the night, mentioned in *The Lesser Key of Solomon* (*qv*).

Rimmon (Barku, Tessub): A fallen archangel, now the devil's ambassador to Russia. Prior to his fall, he was both an Aramaic god and a Syrian idol, as Barku, meaning 'lightning'. The Akkadians worshipped him as Im, god of storms and in Babylonian legend he is the god of thunder, depicted carrying a trident. The Kassites called him Tessub. His symbol is the pomegranate.

Rishis: Seven or ten Vedic angels from whom all of humankind is descended. They correspond to the Amesha Spentas (*qv*) of Zoroastrianism or the seven angels of the presence.

Risnuch: An angel of agriculture, named in *The Nuctemeron* (*qv*).

Riswan (Rusvon): The gatekeeper of Heaven.

Riyiel: In Kabbalism, Riyiel is one of the 72 angels of the 72 quinaries of the degrees of the zodiac.

Rochel: An angel who is invoked to find lost objects. He is one of the angels bearing the name of God Shemhamphorae and has Chontare as his corresponding angel.

Roelhaiphar: Name of an angel inscribed on the fifth pentacle of Saturn. To invoke, a passage from Deuteronomy must be recited, according to *The Greater Key of Solomon* (*qv*).

Rofael: *See* **Raphael**.

Rofocale (Lucifuge Rofocale): Prime minister of the Underworld and, as such, one of the most powerful infernal beings. He controls worldly wealth and treasures and commands angels such as Baal (*qv*), Agares (*qv*) and Marbas.

Rogziel: An angel of punishment (*qv*).

Rombomare: Lauviah's (*qv*) corresponding angel.

Romiel: In the Kabbalah, Romiel is an angelic ruler of one of the months of the year.

Rorex: In Solomonic magic, Rorex is an angel invoked to fight the power of Alath, a demon of disease. Referred to in the *Testament of Solomon* (*qv*).

Rosabis: A genius of metals and the 11th hour, mentioned in *The Nuctemeron* (*qv*).

Rosier: A fallen angel now a prince of Hell who was formerly a member of the order of Dominations (*qv*).

Roupa'il: A Mandaean angel.

Rsassiel: One of the 70 amulet angels (*qv*).

Ruah Piskonit: Another of the many names of the angel Metatron (*qv*).

Ruba'il: An Islamic angel of the Seventh Heaven who leads a group of angels whose job is to worship Allah disguised as mortals.

Rubiel An angel (with Uriel [*qv*] and Barachiel [*qv*]) who can be invoked in order to be successful in gambling, mentioned in *Dictionnaire Infernal* (*qv*).

Ruchiel: An angel of the wind, according to *3 Enoch* (See *The Book of Enoch*).

Rudiel: An angel guarding the third heavenly hall.

Rudosor: An angel of the sixth hour of the night, under Zaazonash, mentioned in *The Lesser Key of Solomon* (*qv*).

Rufael: *See* **Raphael**.

Rugziel (Dalkiel): An angel of the seventh compartment of Hell.

Ruhiel: An angel of the Jewish tradition ruling over the wind. One of Heaven's great angels but who still bows down before Metatron (*qv*).

Ruined Archangel: A description for Satan (*qv*), coined by Milton in *Paradise Lost*.

Rulers: According to the Septuagint, an order of the celestial hierarchy that is usually identified with the order of Dominations (*qv*) . One source places it first in the last triad of the nine divisions of the hierarchy.

Rumael: A fallen angel, according to Enoch's list.

Ruman: An Islamic angel residing in Hell who forces all new arrivals to record their misdeeds on Earth before passing them to Monker (*qv*) and Nakir (*qv*) who provide appropriate punishment.

Rumiel: An angel guarding the Sixth Heaven and one of the 70 amulet angels (*qv*), according to *The Book of the Angel Raziel* (*qv*) and *Amulets and Talismans* (*qv*).

Rumjal: A fallen angel, mentioned in *1 Enoch* (See *The Book of Enoch*).

Rusvon (Riswan): In Islam, an angel who holds the keys to the earthly Paradise.

Ruwano: A ministering angel who can be invoked in conjurations, according to *The Sixth and Seventh Books of Moses* (*qv*).

Ruya'il: An Islamic guardian angel invoked in exorcisms.

Sa'adiya'il: Islamic angel of the Third Heaven commanding a group of angels disguised as vultures that are engaged in worshipping Allah.

Saaphiel: An angel of hurricanes, according to the *Sefer Yetzirah*.

Saaqael: An angel of the presence.

Sabaoth: An angel of the presence and a divine name in Gnostic and Kabbalistic lore. To the Gnostics, one of the seven archons (*qv*) who created the universe.

Sabathiel (Sabbathi): A secret name for Michael (*qv*). An angel of the planet Saturn who passes on the divine light to those living in his kingdom.

Sabbath: Lord of the Sabbath and an angel who is seated on the Throne of Glory in Heaven, an honour bestowed on him by the chiefs of the celestial orders.

Sabbathi: *See* **Sabathiel.**

Sabiel: An angel of the first Sephira (*qv*) who can be invoked in magic ritual.

Sablil: An angel who captures thieves and is a spirit of the ninth hour.

Sabrael (Sabriel): Archangel who, with Tarshiel (*qv*), is chief of the Tarshishim (*qv*), the 'brilliant ones' who equate to the order of Virtues (*qv*). He is the only angel with the power to defeat the demon Sphendonael and guards the hall of the First Heaven.

Sabriel: *See* **Sabrael.**

Sabtabiel: An angel invoked during black magic ritual in *Transcendental Magic* (*qv*).

Sachiel ('covering of God'): A Cherubim (*qv*) who resides in the First Heaven, although some sources claim the Sixth. He is an angel of Monday, Thursday or Friday who is invoked facing South or West. He is a ruler of the planet Jupiter and is described as a servant of the four sub-princes of Hell.

Sachiel-Melek: According to Kabbalistic lore, a king of the Underworld reigning over priesthoods and sacrifices.

Sachluph: An angel of plants and of the second hour, according to *The Nuctemeron* (*qv*).

Sacriel: An angel of the Fifth Heaven, ruling on Tuesday and summoned from the South.

Sadayel: The name of one of three archangels, the others being Raphael (*qv*) and Tiriel (*qv*), inscribed on a pentagram on a ring that is used to protect from evil.

Sadial (Sadiel): An angel who governs the Third Heaven.

Sadiel: *See* **Sadial**.

Saditel: An angel of the Third Heaven.

Sadqiel: An angel who rules the fifth day of the month.

Saelal: In Kabbalism, Saelal was one of the 72 angels of the 72 quinaries of the degrees of the zodiac.

Saeliah: In Kabbalism, Saeliah was one of the 72 angels of the 72 quinaries of the degrees of the zodiac.

Safkas: One of the many names for the angel Metatron (*qv*).

Safriel: An angel who guards the Fifth Heaven whose name is inscribed on a kamea to ward off the evil eye.

Sagansagel: *See* **Sagnessagigel**.

Sagdalon: Angel who, with Semakiel, rules the zodiac sign of Capricorn.

Sagham: A governing angel, with Seratiel (*qv*), of the zodiac sign of Leo.

Sagiel: An angel of the seventh hour of the day, under Barginiel.

Sagmagigrin: Another of the many names of the angel Metatron (*qv*).

Sagnessagigel (Sagansagel): One of the great angel Metatron's (*qv*) many names. He is a prince of wisdom and chief of the fourth hall of the Seventh Heaven. He showed the holy books containing the decrees for Israel to Rabbi Ishmael during his visit to Heaven.

Sagras: An angel who, with Saraiel (*qv*), governs the zodiac sign of Taurus.

Sagsagel: *See* **Zagzagel**.

Sahaqiel: An angel who rules the sky, mentioned in *3 Enoch* (See *The Book of Enoch*).

Sahariel (Asderel): Ruler of the zodiac sign of Aries, he can be invoked in Syriac spellbinding charms.

Sahiviel: An angel who guards the Third Heaven.

Sahon: An angel both of the seal (*qv*) and of the planets.

Sahriel: One of the 64 angels who act as guardians of the heavenly halls.

Sahtail: A Mandaean angel.

Saint Francis: Known both as the angel of mercy and the angel of the Apocalypse. As the latter he cautions the wind not to complete the destruction of the world 'until the elect should be gathered.'

Saints: A Talmudic order of angels, according to French philosopher Voltaire. Also a term for angels in general.

Saissaiel: An angel governor of the zodiac sign of Scorpio, with Riehol (*qv*).

Sakniel: An angel who guards the gates of the West Wind.

Sakriel (Samriel): A porter angel residing in the Second Heaven.

Saktas: Another of the many names of the angel Metatron (*qv*).

Salamiel: A fallen angel, a prince of the Grigori (*qv*).

Salatheel: An archangel who governs the movement of the planets.

Salbabiel: An Aramaic angel used in the creation of charms to protect against evil.

Salem: The guardian angel of St John, legendary king of Salem, the city later called Jerusalem.

Salemia: One of the five transcribing angels – the five 'men' – of the 204 books of Ezra.

Salilus: An angel who may be invoked to open locked doors. He is also a ruler of the seventh hour of the day.

Sallisim: An order of angels which belongs to the Song-Uttering Choirs, led by Tagas (*qv*).

Salmael: An angel said to be a chief of one of the orders of the celestial hierarchy.

Salmay: An angel invoked during the blessing of the salt, according to *The Book of Ceremonial Magic* (*qv*).

Salmia: An angel who can be prayed to for the satisfaction of the invocant's desires.

Salmon: An angel of the sixth hour of the night, under Zaazonash.

Salpsan: A demon who is a son of Satan.

Salun: An angel invoked in ritual prayer.

Samael: *See* **Sammael**.

Sammael (Samael, Zamael): Equatable with Satan (*qv*). He is a ruler of violence and destruction. He is one of the most evil of all the spirits in Heaven, on Earth and in Hell. Jews recognize him as ruler of the Seventh Heaven while others place him in the Fifth. He is one of the seven regents of Earth, commanding more than 2 million angels and in the Talmud, he is Esau's guardian angel, while in Sotah he is the prince who protects Edom (Rome). In Kabbalism he is described as 'the severity of God' and is named as the fifth of the archangels who govern the four worlds of creation. He is the angel of the Sephira (*qv*) Geburah and is the equivalent of the Greek god, Typhon. However, the *Secrets of Enoch* describes him as the chief of the demons and the angel of death while in the Book of Revelation he is 'that great serpent with twelve wings that draws after him, in his fall, the solar system.' He is also said to be the serpent that seduced Eve in the Garden of Eden, fathering Cain, who slew his brother or half-brother, Abel.

Samaey: *See* **Salmay**.

Samaha'il: Islamic angel of the Sixth Heaven and leader of a group of angels who, disguised as humans, engage in the worship of Allah.

Samandiriel (Smandriel): A Mandaean angel of fertility who receives prayers and hangs on to them until he believes it appropriate to act upon them.

Samangaluf (Sammangaloph, Semanglaf, Smnglf): One of three angels who is said to have brought Lilith (*qv*) back to Adam (*qv*) after they

had been long separated in the days before Eve . The other two are Sennoi (*qv*) and Sansanui (*qv*).

Samas: An angel of Chaldean and Babylonian lore who is the personification of one of the signs of the zodiac.

Samax: An angel ruling the air on a Tuesday, served by Carmax (*qv*), Ismoli (*qv*) and Paffran (*qv*).

Samax Rex: An evil spirit found in a book of Elizabethan black magic. The name of the grimoire is now unknown, but a reference to its existence was recorded in a book entitled *Ritual Magic* by E.M Butler, first published in 1949.

Sambula: An Arabic angel invoked in conjurations.

Samchia (Samchiel): An amulet angel (*qv*).

Sameon: An angel of the sixth hour of the day, under Samil (*qv*).

Sameron: An angel of the 12th hour of the day, under Beratiel.

Sameveel: A fallen angel.

Samhiel: An angel who can be invoked to cure stupidity.

Sam Hii (Shom Hii): One of the four Mandaean uthri (angels) of the North Star.

Samiaza: *See* **Semyaza**.

Samiel: In some sources, an angel grouped with Michael (*qv*), Gabriel (*qv*) and other spellbinding angels. Voltaire, in his *Of Angels, Genii and Devils*, names him as one of the leaders of the fallen angels and, therefore, evil, considering his name an alternative version of Sammael (*qv*).

Samil: An angel ruling the sixth hour, according to *The Lemegeton* (*qv*).

Samjaza: *See* **Semyaza**.

Samlo: One of the great Gnostic aeons (*qv*) who will transport the elect up to Heaven on Judgment Day.

Sammangaloph: *See* **Samangaluf**.

Samoel: An angel invoked by the Master of the Art in Solomonic magic.

Samohayl: A ministering angel who may be invoked in Kabbalistic conjurations.

Samoy: An angel conjured in black magic, according to the *Grimorium Verum* (*qv*).

Samriel: *See* **Sakriel**.

Samsapeel (Samsaveel): A fallen angel who was formerly an archangel.

Samsaveel: *See* **Samsapeel**.

Samuil (Semil): An angel with dominion over Earth.

Samyaza: *See* **Semyaza**.

Sanasiel: A Mandaean angel who stands at the gate of life praying for souls.

Sanctities: A name of a celestial order of angels in Milton's *Paradise Lost*.

Sandalphon (Sandolfon, Sandolphon): Originally the prophet Elias (*qv*), he is, in rabbinic legend, a great sarim or prince, twin brother of Metatron (*qv*) and master of heavenly song. He is ruler of the Tenth Sephira (*qv*) and one of the tallest of all the angels. His job is to allocate a gender to each child upon conception and he transmits the prayers of the faithful, woven into a garland, to God. He is a regent of either the Third (according to Moses [*qv*]) Fourth (according to Islamic legend), Sixth (according to Enoch) or Seventh (according to the Kabbalah) Heaven. He is engaged in a constant battle with Satan (*qv*), like Michael (*qv*).

Sandolfon: *See* **Sandalphon**.

Sandolphon: *See* **Sandalphon**.

Sangariah: An angel who rules over religious fasts, according to *The Zohar* (*qv*).

Sangariel: An angel who guards the heavenly portals.

Sanigron Kunya: One of the 14 great angels found in *The Greater Key of Solomon* (*qv*) who may be invoked in special ceremonial ritual.

Sanul: *See* **Sannul**.

Sannul (Sanul): An angel belonging to the order of Powers (*qv*) who is invoked in magic ritual.

Sansanui: One of three angels who is said to have brought Lilith (*qv*) back to Adam (*qv*) after they had been long separated in the days before Eve, the other two being Sennoi (*qv*) and Samangaluf (*qv*). A very powerful angel, he can be invoked to protect from Lilith and her infernal followers.

Santanael: An angel of Friday, residing in the Third Heaven, invoked from the South.

Saphar: One of the three Seraphim (*qv*) in the Sefer Yetzirah (Book of Foundation) through whom, it is said, the world was made, the others being Sepher and Sipur.

Saphiel: *See* **Sapiel**.

Sapiel (Saphiel): An angel residing in the Fourth Heaven who rules on the Lord's Day. A guardian angel invoked from the North.

Sar: Singular form of 'sarim'. A Hebrew word meaning 'angel prince' of whom there is one for each of the 70 nations. They are also known as the 70 Shepherds.

Sarafiel: *See* **Israfel**.

Sarafsion: An angel who guards the seventh heavenly hall.

Sarahiel: A guard of the Second Heaven.

Saraiel: Ruler, with Sagras (*qv*), of the zodiac sign of Taurus.

Sarakiel (Saraquael): A prince angel who officiates at judgement councils. One of the seven angels who oversee human children who have sinned; ruler, in partnership with the angel Sataaran (*qv*), of the planet Mars and the zodiac sign of Aries.

Sarakika'il: An Arabic guardian angel invoked in exorcisms.

Saranac: A fallen angel.

Saranana: A Solomonic angel of the third altitude.

Saraquael: *See* **Sarakiel**.

Sarasael (Sarea, Sarga): A Seraph (*qv*) who is one of the five angels who transcribed the 204 books of Ezra. He presides over the souls of sinners and was sent by God to Adam to advise him how to re-plant the Tree in the Garden of Eden.

Saratan: An angel in Islamic legend who is invoked in incantation ritual.

Sarfiel: An angel whose name appears with six others in a Palestinian mezuzah (a piece of parchment inscribed with specific Hebrew verses from the Torah) for the creation of amulets to ward off evil. He is an angel of the eighth hour of the day, under Osgaebial (*qv*) and is also a guard at the gates of the East Wind.

Sarga: *See* **Sarasael**.

Sargiel: An angel responsible for transporting the souls of sinners to Hell.

Sarhma'il: An Islamic guardian angel invoked in exorcisms.

Sariel: Equated with Suriel. An archangel who rules Aries, is one of the Occult's nine summer equinox angels and is effective in warding off the evil eye. He is described as both a holy angel and a fallen angel. He teaches man the course of the moon and oversees the Sixth Heaven. He is an angel of cleanliness, hygiene and healing. In the Dead Sea Scrolls, his name appears on the shields of the 'third Tower', a name for one of the fighting units in The War of the Sons of Light Against the Sons of Darkness.

Saritaiel (Saritiel): Ruler of the zodiac sign of Sagittarius, with Vhnori (*qv*).

Saritiel: *See* **Saritaiel**.

Sarmiel: An angel who is a servant of Jehoel (*qv*), prince of fire.

Sarospa: An angel under the command of the great god Ahura-Mazda.

Sarphiel: A spellbinding angel.

Sarquamich: An angel who rules the Third hour of the night.

Sar Shel Yam: The angel Rahab (*qv*).

Sartael (Satarel): Evil Talmudic angel who rules over hidden things.

Sartamiel: One of the zodiac-ruling angels.

Sartziel (Saissaiel): An angel who governs the zodiac sign of Scorpio.

Sarush: *See* **Sirushi, Sraosha**.

Sasa'il: An Islamic angel of the Fourth Heaven commanding a group of angels engaged in worshipping Allah in the form of horses.

Sasgabiel: An angel invoked in exorcism rites.

Sasniel: *See* **Sasnigiel**.

Sasnigiel (Sasniel): Prince of wisdom, prince of

the world and prince of the presence. Also a Seraphim (*qv*) ruling over peace and one of the many names of the angel Metatron (*qv*).

Sataaran: An angel who rules over the zodiac sign of Aries.

Satael: A Tuesday angel of the air (*qv*) and ruler of the planet Mars who can be invoked in magic ritual.

Satan (Beliar, Beliel, Sammael): *See* opposite.

Satanael: One of the 12 angels of vengeance.

Satarel: *See* **Sartael**.

Sathariel: Called Sheriel in *The Zohar* (*qv*), a fallen angel ruling the Qliphira of the Infernal Tree that 'casts shadows upon Chesed (mercy),' the Fourth Sephira (*qv*) of the Tree of Life.

Saturn: A Persian angel ruling the Seventh Heaven and to Kabbalists angel of the wilderness. In Chaldean lore, he is Adar, one of the gods of the five planets. Milton describes him as a fallen angel.

Saulasau: A Gnostic power of the upper world.

Savaliel: An angel who guards the Third Heaven.

Savaniah: Name of an angel inscribed on the third pentacle of the planet Mercury.

Savatri (Savitar, Savitri): One of the seven or 12 Vedic adityas or 'infinite ones'.

Savitar: *See* **Savatri**.

Savitri: *See* **Savatri**.

Savaliel: In Hechaloth lore, an angel guarding the Third Heaven.

Savsa: An angel guarding the sixth heavenly hall.

Savuriel: An angel guarding the Third Heaven.

Sawael: An angel of whirlwinds.

Sazquiel: An angel who rules the fifth hour, commanding ten chiefs and 100 other officer angels.

Scamijm: An angel of the First Heaven.

Schabtaiel: *See* **Schebtaiel**.

Schachlil: An angel governing the rays of the sun, according to *Transcendental Magic* (*qv*). Also ruler of the ninth hour.

Schachniel: One of the 70 amulet angels (*qv*), in *The Book of the Angel Raziel* (*qv*).

ABOVE: *The Angel Binding Satan*
by Philip James (Jacques) Loutherbourg, *c.*1797

Satan (Beliar, Beliel, Sammael): A name meaning 'adversary' in Hebrew. In the Old Testament, he is a glorious angel and only in the New Testament does he become the fallen angel who is the personification of everything evil and whose existence is dedicated to tempting humans to commit sin and condemn themselves to eternal Hell. He is called 'prince of this world', and 'prince of the power of the air', and is closely identified with the serpent that tempted Eve in the Garden of Eden. He is the Great Seducer and Father of Lies. He became known as Lucifer (*qv*) through an erroneous interpretation of Isiah 14:12 and in rabbinic lore he is known as 'the ugly one.' Prior to his fall he was regent of the Seraphim (*qv*), Cherubim (*qv*), Powers (*qv*) and Archangels (*qv*), as well as prince regent of the order of Virtues (*qv*). It is claimed by the Kabbalah and St Jerome that one day he will repent and return to his former exalted positions.

Schaddyl: One of the 15 angels of the throne (*qv*), according to *The Sixth and Seventh Books of Moses* (*qv*).

Schaltiel: An angel governing the zodiac sign of Virgo.

Scharial: An angel from Sodom who is invoked to cure boils.

Schawayt: One of the 15 angels of the throne (*qv*), according to *The Sixth and Seventh Books of Moses* (*qv*).

Schebtaiel (Schabtaiel): A regent of the planet Saturn.

Schekinah: *See* **Shekinah**.

Scheliel: One of the angels who rule the mansions of the moon (*qv*).

Schiekron: An angel of the fourth hour and of bestial love.

Schimuel: One of the 15 angels of the throne (*qv*), according to *The Sixth and Seventh Books of Moses* (*qv*).

Schioel: Name of an angel inscribed on the first pentacle of the moon.

Schrewneil: A Mosaic angel invoked in order to obtain a good memory and an open heart.

Scigin: An angel who can be invoked in magic ritual.

Scourging Angels: Malache Habbala in Hebrew. Merciless angels encountered by Abraham on his visit to Heaven.

Scribe of Righteousness: Enoch.

Scribes: An exalted order of angels according to *3 Enoch*, who records the deeds of humans and reads aloud from the books of judgement at judgement sessions in Heaven. *See* Book of Enoch.

Sealiah: A Kabbalistic angel governing vegetation who is also one of the 72 angels bearing the mystical name of God Shemhamphorae.

Sealtiel: An archangel, according to Gertrude Jobes' *Dictionary of Mythology, Folklore and Symbols*.

Seats: An order of angels cited in the 5th-century work, *City of God* by St Augustine of Hippo that can possibly be identified with the Hashmallim (*qv*).

Seba'im: An order of angels mentioned in *3 Enoch* (See *The Book of Enoch*).

Sebalim: An order of angels in the Song-Uttering Choirs, according to *3 Enoch* (See *The Book of Enoch*).

Sebhael (Sebhil): An Islamic recording angel.

Seclam: An angel who is a member of the order of Powers and can be invoked in magic ritual.

Second Angel: Name for Adam in *2 Enoch* (See *The Book of Enoch*).

Second Heaven: Where Jesus and John the Baptist reside, according to Muslims. The Jews believe that fallen angels are imprisoned there and that the planets are fastened to it. While visiting Heaven, Moses met Nuriel (*qv*) here.

Seconds: The fictional name of an angel in Charles Angoff's story *God Repents*.

Sedekiah: An angel who can be invoked to locate hidden treasure. His name is inscribed on the pentacle of the planet Jupiter.

Sedim: Talmudic guardian angels used in the exorcism of evil spirits.

Sedu: Singular form of Sedim (*qv*).

Seehiah: A member of the order of Dominions (*qv*) and one of the 72 angels bearing the name of God Shemhamphorae. He is invoked to prolong life and grant good health.

Seeliah: One of the 72 angels bearing the name of God Shemhamphorae and a Kabbalistic angel of vegetation who is a fallen angel, formerly a member of the order of Virtues (*qv*). He is invoked using a verse from Psalm 93.

Sefoniel: With Ioniel (*qv*), one of two princes who rule the universe.

Sefriel: An angel who guards the Fifth Heaven.

Sage: An angel of destruction invoked at the end of the Sabbath. It should be pointed out that angels of destruction are not inherently evil and did not fall.

Sehaltiel: An angel invoked to fend off the evil angel Moloch (*qv*).

Seheiah A Kabbalistic angel who protects against

fire and sickness. Also an angel of longevity.

Sehibiel An angelic guard of the Second Heaven.

Seimelkhe: A Gnostic aeon (*qv*).

Seket: A Kabbalistic female angel residing in Egypt.

Seldac: A Gnostic angel of the order of Powers (*qv*), responsible for heavenly baptisms.

Selemia: One of the five angels who transcribed the 204 books of Ezra.

Selith: One of two guardian angels of the Virgin Mary in Klopstock's epic poem 'The Messiah'.

Semakiel (Semaqiel): With Sagdalon (*qv*), rules over the zodiac sign of Capricorn.

Semalion: The Talmudic angel who announced the death of Moses (*qv*), proclaiming 'The great scribe is dead!'

Semanglaf: An angel invoked to help pregnant women and one of the three angels who brought Lilith (*qv*) back to her husband Adam (*qv*) after their long separation.

Semaqiel: *See* **Semakiel**.

Semeliel (Semeschiah, Semishial): One of the seven angels standing perpetually before God who are given the names of the planetary spirits. Cornelius Agrippa (*qv*) describes him as angel of the sun in his *Three Books of Occult Philosophy*.

Semeschiah: *See* **Semeliel**.

Semishia: *See* **Semeliel**.

Semyaza (Amezyarak, Samjaza, Semiaza, Shemhazi): A leader of the fallen angels who is said to hang upside-down between Heaven and Earth in the constellation of Orion. He is said to be the Seraph (*qv*) that the girl, Ishtahar, attempted to seduce into speaking the Explicit Name (of God).

Senacher: Elemiah's (*qv*) corresponding angel.

Senciner: A member of the order of Powers (*qv*) and Michael's corresponding angel.

Senegorin: 1,800 advocate angels who serve the great angel Metatron (*qv*).

Sennoi: One of the three angels who brought Lilith (*qv*) back to her husband Adam (*qv*), after their long separation. Lilith was evil even during their marriage but an amulet with Sennoi's name inscribed on it prevented her from doing any harm, especially to children. He can be used to protect pregnant women.

Sensenya: One of the 70 amulet angels (*qv*).

Sepharon: An angel of the first hour of the night.

Sepheriel: A powerful angel whose name, if spoken by God, will bring on the Final Judgment.

Sephira (Sefira): The singular form of Sephiroth or Sefiroth. A divine emanation through which God manifested His existence in the Creation of the universe. The Kabbalah lists Archangels of the ten holy and ten unholy Sephiroth:

THE HOLY SEPHIROTH

1. Methattron – Kether (Crown)
2. Ratziel (Raziel) – Chokmah (Wisdom)
3. Tzaphqiel – Binah (Understanding)
4. Tzadqiel – Chesed (Mercy)
5. Khamael – Geburah (Strength)
6. Mikhael – Tiphereth (Beauty)
7. Haniel – Netzach (Victory)
8. Raphael – Hod (Splendour)
9. Gabriel – Yesod (Foundation)
10. Methattron (or the Shekinah) – Malkuth (Kingdom)

THE UNHOLY SEPHIROTH

1. Thaumiel – Kether (Crown)
2. Chaigidiel – Chokmah (Wisdom)
3. Sathariel (Sheireil) – Binah (Understanding)
4. Gamchocoth (Gog Sheklah) – Chesed (Mercy)
5. Golab – Geburah (Strength)
6. Togarini – Tiphereth (Beauty)
7. Harab Serap – Netzach (Victory)
8. Sammael – Hod (Splendour)
9. Gamaliel – Yesod (Foundation)
10. Lilith – Malkuth (Kingdom)

Sephuriron: Tenth of the ten holy Sephiroth whose deputies are Malkiel (*qv*), Ithuriel (*qv*) and Nashriel (*qv*).

Serabilin: *See* **Jesubilin**.

Serael: An angel of the Fifth Heaven.

Serakel: An angel ruling over fruit trees.

Seraph: The singular form of Seraphim (*qv*). An angel who is a member of the order of Seraphim and rules over the element of fire.

Seraphiel: Archangel chief of the Seraphim and an angel of the throne (*qv*). He is the prince of peace and one of the highest ranked of all the Merkabah's angels (*qv*). He rules Mercury and is a regent of Tuesday invoked from the North. Enoch describes his body as being covered in stars and he emits the light of the firmament from his feet to his knees; the light of the morning star from his knees to his thighs; the light of the moon from his thighs to his waist; the light of the sun from his waist to his neck and from his neck to the top of his head, is emitted the Infinite Light.

Seraphim: *See* page 178.

Serapiel: An angel of the fifth hour of the day, under Sazquiel (*qv*).

Seraquiel: An angel who is invoked on Saturday.

Seratiel: Governing angel of the zodiac sign of Leo, with Sagham (*qv*).

Seref: An angel responsible for carrying the bodies of dead Egyptian kings to Heaven.

Serpanim (Nathanael, Seruf, Seruph): A Seraph (*qv*) who is a ruler of the element of fire.

Seruph: *See* **Serpanim**.

Servant of God: *See* **Abdiel**.

Serviel: An angel of the third hour of the day.

Sesengesn-Barpharanges: The Coptic name of a group of angels and also the name of a powerful demon in Jewish mysticism.

Setchiel: An angel served in magic conjurations by Turiel (*qv*).

Seth: One of the seven Gnostic archons (*qv*).

Setheus: A great celestial being who resides in the Sixth Heaven.

ABOVE: *The Six Winged Seraph* from Alexander Pushkin's *The Prophet*
by Mikhail Vrubel, 1905

Seraphim: The plural form of Seraph (*qv*). The most exalted order of angels in the pseudo-Dionysian scheme of the celestial hierarchy. These are angels of love, light and of fire, they surround the Throne of Glory, singing the Trisagion – 'holy, holy, holy'. Enoch describes them as having four faces and six wings. They do not appear in the New Testament, except by implication and the role of ruling prince of the order has been allocated to a number of angels – Seraphiel (*qv*), Jehoel (*qv*), Metatron (*qv*), Michael (*qv*) and Satan (*qv*), prior to his fall.

Sethlans: A member of the nine Novensiles (*qv*), the Etruscan gods.

Setphael: An angel who guards the first of the seven heavenly halls.

Seven Archangels: The seven holy ones who surround God's throne. Ezra and Enoch list them as:

> Uriel, Raphael, Raguel, Michael, Sariel or Seraqel, Gabriel, Remiel or Jeremiel.

In Horoscopy and Hermetics, they are named as: Rampha (angel of Saturn), Pi-Zeus (angel of Jupiter), Ertosi (angel of Mars), Pi-Re (angel of the Sun), Suroth (angel of Venus), Pi-Hermes (angel of Mercury), Pi-Joh (angel of the Moon).

In the 17th-century work, *A Theological Discourse of Angels*, also Benjamin Camfield lists the 'seven spirits who always stand in the presence of God' as planetary rulers:

> Zapkiel (over Saturn), Zadkiel (over Jupiter), Camuel (over Mars), Raphael (over the Sun), Haniel (over Venus), Michael (over Mercury), Gabriel (over the Moon).

The seven Akkadian elemental spirits or deities, possible prototypes for later groups of seven rulers or creators, are:

> An (Heaven), Gula (Earth), Ud (Sun), Im (Storm), Istar (Moon, Ea or Dara (Ocean), En-lil (Hell).

Seven Heavens: Hebrew legend lists the seven Heavens as follows (with their governing angels:

First Heaven – Shamain or Shamayim (Gabriel)

Second Heaven – Raquie or Raqia (Zachariel and Raphael)

Third Heaven – Sagun or Shehaqim (Anahel and three sarim or subordinate princes, Jagniel, Rabacyel and Dalquiel)

Fourth Heaven – Machonon or Machen (Michael)

Fifth Heaven – Mathey or Machon (Sandalphon or Sammael)

Sixth Heaven – Zebul (Zachiel, assisted by Zebul by day and Sabath by night)

Seventh Heaven – Araboth (Cassiel) According to *2 Enoch* (See *The Book of Enoch*), which says there are ten Heavens, the Tree of Life and the Garden of Eden are both located in the Third Heaven. However, *The Zohar* (*qv*) speaks of 390 Heavens and 70,000 worlds while the Gnostic Basildes reckoned on 365 Heavens and Jellinek in Beth Ha-Midrasch speaks of 955. The Koran, the ancient Persians and the Babylonians were familiar, however, with the concept of seven Heavens, the Persians placing God in the highest of them.

Seven Holy Ones: *See* **Archangels**, **Seven Archangels**.

Seven Supreme Angels: The rulers of the 196 provinces into which Heaven is divided, according to the Kabbalah.

Seventh Heaven: The dwelling place of human souls waiting to be born and also where God resides as well as Zagzagel (*qv*), prince of the Torah and the Seraphim (*qv*) and Hayyoth (*qv*), amongst others.

Seventh Satan: *See* **Hakael**.

Shabni (Shabti): An angel invoked in ceremonial magic ritual.

Shabti: *See* **Shabni**.

Shachaqiel: *See* **Shahakiel**.

Shachmiel: Name of an angel inscribed on a kamea (*qv*).

Shadfiel: An angel who guards the gates of the North Wind.

Shaftiel: An angel of Hell who rules over the shadow of death and resides in the third lodge of the Underworld.

Shaftyah: Another of the many names of the angel Metatron (*qv*).

Shahakiel (Shachaqiel): According to *3 Enoch* (See *The Book of Enoch*) Shahakiel is an archangel and chief of the order of Shahakim (*qv*) that is named after him. He resides in the Fourth Heaven.

Shahakim: An order of angels.

Shahariel: An angel guarding the Second Heaven.

Shahiel: Name of an angel inscribed on a kamea.

Shaitan: Islamic demon usually identified with Iblis (*qv*). In the Koran it is said that he fooled the Queen of Sheba and her people into worshipping the sun instead of Allah.

Shahitans: A group of evil male spirits who have the feet of roosters. The females are called Lilin.

Shakti: The bride of the great Vedic god Shiva. She is an earlier version of Shekinah (*qv*).

Shakziel: An angel ruling over water insects.

Shalgiel: An angel who holds dominion over snow.

Shalhevita: An angel who guards the seventh heavenly hall.

Shalkiel and Shalmiel: Names of angels inscribed on a kamea.

Shaltiel: Name of an angel inscribed – along with those of Michael (*qv*), Raphael (*qv*) and Uriel (*qv*) – on earthenware bowls uncovered in the Euphrates Valley.

Shamain: A name for the First Heaven.

Shamdan (Ashamdon): The angel who mated with Naamah (*qv*), the sister of Tubal-cain, who led the angels astray with her beauty. Their child is the demon Asmodeus (*qv*).

Shamlon: A Solomonic 'prince over all the angels and the Caesars.'

Shammiel: Heavenly master of song and divine herald. Invoked in Syriac spellbinding charms, along with Michael (*qv*), Harshiel (*qv*), Nuriel (*qv*) and others.

Shamriel: A guardian angel in Occultism who protects against the evil eye.

Shams-ed-Din: One of the seven Yezidic angels invoked during devil worship.

Shamsha: A Solomonic angel who is 'prince over all the angels and the Caesars'.

Shamshiel: A regent of the Fourth Heaven, a prince of Paradise and a guardian angel of the Garden of Eden, he is an angel who crowns the prayers of the faithful prior to sending to the Fifth Heaven. According to Enoch, however, he is a fallen angel who was responsible for teaching humans about the sun and to Kabbalists he helped Uriel (*qv*) in the wars of the angels. He commands 365 legions of angels and can be invoked during spellbinding rituals. He is the angel who guided Moses (*qv*) around Heaven and whom the scribe Hilkiah entrusted with the treasures of David and Solomon.

Shaphiel: With Baradiel (*qv*) a ruling prince of the Third Heaven.

Sharivari: The ancient Persian angel of August and governor of the fourth day of the month.

Shariel: *See* **Asderel**.

Sharka'il: An Arabic guardian angel invoked in exorcisms.

Sharlaii: A Hebrew angel invoked to cure skin ailments.

Sharshiyah: Another of the many names of the angel Metatron (*qv*).

Shastaniel: An angel guarding the gates of the South Wind.

Shathniel: Name of an angel inscribed on a kamea.

Shatqiel: One of the seven archangels – in *3 Enoch* (See *The Book of Enoch)* – who is also a guard of the Fifth Heaven. Another source lists him as a guard of the Fourth Heaven.

Shaviel: One of the seven angels who guard the First Heaven.

Shavzriel: An angel who guards the second heavenly hall.

Shebniel: One of the 70 amulet angels (*qv*).

Shedu: A Babylonian guardian angel of households who can be invoked in conjurations.

Sheik Bakra and Sheikh Ism: Two of the archangels in the Yezidic devil-worshipping religion.

Shereil: *See* **Sathariel**.

Shekinah (Schechinah): The female manifestation of God in man, the 'bride of the Lord' like Shakti is to Shiva; an intermediary between God and man. The New Testament treats the Shekinah as the glory emanating from God. The Shekinah is the liberating angel who manifests in her male version as Metatron (*qv*). The Kabbalah lists her as the tenth Sephira Malkuth, otherwise known as the Queen. *The Zohar* claims that the Shekinah created the world. She has been identified with the Holy Ghost and the Epinoia of the Gnostic Valentinus. She is said to hover over all conjugal unions and blesses such unions with her presence. She rules the conception of children and the sexuality and sanctity of marriage. She is currently in exile on Earth as a result of Adam's (*qv*) sin and all good acts will contribute to her speedy return to Heaven. She unites with her husband only at midnight on the eve of the Sabbath which makes this the perfect time for union between husband and wife.

Shekiniel: An angel who guards the Fourth Heaven.

Shelemial: An angel who guard the Third Heaven.

Shelviel: An angel of the Tarshishim, an order of angels in Jewish legend.

Shemael (Camael, Kemuel): An angel who stands at the gates of Heaven listening out for Jewish songs of praise.

Shemhazi: *See* **Semyaza**.

Shepherd: One of the six angels of repentance. He is equated with Phanuel (*qv*) and it was he who dictated the vision to Hermas in the 2nd century apocryphon, The Shepherd of Hermas.

Shepherd of Hermas: *See* **Phanuel**.

Shetel: One of the three angels – with Aebel (*qv*) and Anush (*qv*) – appointed by God to serve Adam (*qv*).

Sheviel: An angel who guards the First Heaven.

Sheziem: An angel who can be invoked in Kabbalistic magic ritual.

Shimshiel: An angel who is one of the many guards at the gates of the East Wind.

Shinanin: An order of angels – 'the shinanin of the fire' – referred to in *3 Enoch* (See *The Book of Enoch*). Either Zadkiel (*qv*) or Sidqiel (*qv*) is their chief and they represent the sixth Sephira (*qv*) – Tiphereth.

Shinial: One of the 64 guardians of the heavenly halls.

Shlomiel: An angel who guards the Third Heaven.

Shmuiel (Samael): One source describes this angel as 'chief of all the angels and all the ten classes

who spoke to Solomon and gave him the key to the mysteries.'

Shoel: One of the 64 guardians of the heavenly halls.

Shoftiel: An angel of punishment (*qv*).

Shokad: One of the 64 guardians of the heavenly halls.

Shomrom (Shunaron): Described as 'a prince over all the angels and Caesars', in *The Greater Key of Solomon* (*qv*).

Shosoriyah: Another of the many names of the angel Metatron (*qv*).

Shriniel: An angel guarding the Fourth Heaven.

Shtukial: One of the 64 guardians of the heavenly halls.

Shufiel: A spellbinding angel like Michael (*qv*), Gabriel (*qv*), Harshiel (*qv*) and others. Invoked in Syriac conjurations.

Shunaron: *See* **Shomrom**.

Sialul: An angel of the seventh hour and of prosperity.

Sidqiel: A prince of the order of Ophanim (*qv*) or Shinanin (*qv*) who is ruler of the planet Venus.

Sidriel: An archangel who resides in the First Heaven.

Sieme: A Kabbalistic angel of part of an hour – 3.20pm to be precise. A member of the order of Virtues (*qv*), his corresponding angel is Asaliah (*qv*).

Sigron: A name for Metatron (*qv*) when he closes the doors through which the prayers of humans enter Heaven. He is known as Pihon (*qv*) when he opens the doors.

Sihail: One source believes Sihail is just another form of Michael (*qv*). A 12th-century manuscript says 'God sent two angels, Sihail and Anas, and four Evangelists to take hold of the 12 fever demons [all female] and beat them with fiery rods.'

Sij-ed-Din: One of the seven Yezidic archangels, who can be invoked by prayer.

Sikiel: An angel of the sirocco, a hot wind from North Africa, and a guard at the gates of the West Wind.

Sila: A Kabbalistic angel of power who is ruler of an hour and can be invoked during magic ritual.

Silat (Feluth, Tilath): A female Islamic demon who can be invoked.

Silmai: One of two Mandaean guardian angels of the River Jordan, Nidbai (*qv*) being the other.

Simapesial: A fallen angel.

Simkiel: An angel of destruction (*qv*) that God sent to Earth to chastise and purify sinners.

Siona: A Seraph in Klopstock's epic German poem, 'The Messiah'.

Sipur: One of the three Seraphim (*qv*) through which God created the world.

Sirbiel: An angel who is a prince of the Merkabah (*qv*).

Sirushi (Ashu): The ancient Persian angel of Paradise who is also known as the 'master of announcements.'

Sisera: The angel of desire. Also an angel who can be invoked during the second hour, according to *The Nuctemeron* (*qv*).

Sislau: An angel of poisons and of the fourth hour, mentioned in *The Nuctemeron* (*qv*).

Sitael: A Seraph (*qv*) who is one of the 72 angels of the 72 quinaries of the degrees of the zodiac and also one of the 72 Shemhamphorae angels. He can be invoked to overcome adversity.

Sith: In Kabbalism, Sith is an angel of the hour from six until seven o'clock and also a planetary regent.

Sithacer: Seheiah's corresponding angel.

Sithriel: Another name for Metatron (*qv*) when he is protecting children.

Sitiel: *See* **Sitael**.

Sitriel: Third of the ten unholy Sephiroth (*qv*).

Sittacibor: An angel invoked during the exorcism of wax, mentioned in *The Greater Key of Solomon* (*qv*).

Sittiah: An angel invoked during the exorcism of wax, mentioned in *The Greater Key of Solomon* (*qv*).

Six Highest Angelic (or Philonic) Powers: Angelic Powers derived from the six Amesha Spentas (*qv*) surrounding God's throne. Baruch III lists them as:

1. Divine Logos
2. Creative Power
3. Sovereign Power
4. Mercy
5. Legislation
6. Punitive Power

Sixth Angel: In the Book of Revelation, an unnamed sixth member of the angels of wrath (*qv*).

Sixth Heaven: The Dwelling place of the unnamed Islamic guardian angel of Heaven and Earth.

Sixth and Seventh Books of Moses, The: A grimoire allegedly written by Moses. The books include seals and incantations, as well as instructions on how to recreate the miracles from the Christian bible.

Sizajasel: An angel governing the zodiac sign of Sagittarius, mentioned in *The Lesser Key of Solomon* (*qv*).

Sizouse: The ancient Persian angel presiding over prayers.

Skd Huzi: *See* **Soqed Hozi**.

Sktm: One of the 14 angels invoked in the conjuring of the sword.

Slattery: A fictional angel in Mark Twain's *Report from Paradise*.

Smal: An angel of poison and of death who is married to the angel of prostitution, Eisheth Zenunim (*qv*)

Smandriel: *See* **Samandriel**.

Smat: Mebehiah's corresponding angel with whom he shares dominion over morals and religion.

Smeliel: The angel of the sun, according to François Lenormant's 1877 work, *Chaldean Magic*. He is corresponding angel to Nagiel.

Smnglf: *See* **Samangaluf**.

Sniel: One of the 70 amulet angels (*qv*).

Sochiel: An archangel in charge of the earthly triplicities that govern the 360 degrees of the zodiac.

Sociable Spirit, The: Raphael (*qv*) is thus described by Milton in *Paradise Lost*.

Socodiah: Name of an angel inscribed on the first pentacle of the planet Venus.

Sodiel: A regent of the Third Heaven.

Sodyah: An angel who helps Metatron (*qv*) when he is reciting the Shema, Judaism's most important prayer.

Sofiel: An angel who looks after garden fruit and vegetables, mentioned in *The Sword of Moses* (*qv*).

Sofriel (Sopher, Sopheriel): Bookkeeping angel who keeps records of the living and the dead. Sofriel exists in two forms – Sofriel Memith and Sofriel Mehayye.

Sohemne: An angel of the seal (*qv*).

Sokath: An angel serving Nakhiel (*qv*), ruling angel of the sun.

Solmis: A powerful Gnostic angel.

Soluzen: Name of an angel inscribed on the pentagon of Solomon.

Somcham: An angel who guards the gates of the West Wind.

Soncas (Soneas): An angel of the Fifth Heaven, invoked from the West.

Song-Uttering Choirs: An order of singing angels who are led by Tagas (*qv*). When they neglected their duty to sing the trisagion at the appointed time, they were consumed by fire.

Sonitas: An angel of the Fifth Heaven.

Sonneillon: A fallen angel formerly a member of the order of the Hashmallim (*qv*). With another two demons, he is said to have taken part in the notorious 17th-century possession of the nun, Sister Louise Capeau at Aix-en-Provence in France.

Son of God: An epithet commonly applied to Jesus.

Sons of God: A term meaning angels. The Kabbalah takes the term to mean a distinctive order of celestial beings – the Bene Elohim (*qv*) and Milton takes them to be fallen angels.

Sons of Heaven: Angels who participate in meetings of the divine council.

Sons of Princes: An order of angels, according to

the French philosopher, Voltaire.

Sophar: A fictional fallen angel in Anatole France's *Revolt of the Angels*.

Sopher, Sopheriel: *See* **Sofriel**.

Sophia: The female divinity of Gnosticism, Sophia, is amongst the greatest Gnostic archons (*qv*) and is said to have been the mother of 'the superior angels.'

Sophiel: An angel of the moon's fourth pentacle and in the Kabbalah an angel of the planet Jupiter.

Soqed Hozi (Skd Huzi): A great prince, keeper of the divine balances who weighs the merits of mortal souls on a scale before God. Soqed Hozi is also one of the angels appointed by God to the sword, tasked with presiding over law and order in Heaven and on Earth.

Sorath: An evil spirit, the bearer of the mystical number 666.

Sorush: Gabriel (*qv*), in ancient Persian lore. One of two angels that will stand on the bridge called al Sirat, finer than a hair and sharper than the edge of a sword, assessing the worth of every person crossing. The other angel 'Mihr' will weigh the actions of each and Sorush is charged with casting the unworthy into eternal damnation.

Sother Ashiel: One of the greatest princes of the Seventh Heaven through whom all angels must pass in order to enter into or leave the divine presence. An angel prosecutor serving the throne of divine judgement, he is 70,000 myriads of parasangss tall. According to the Kabbalah, he is married to Sophia (*qv*) and the Gnostics believe his to be another name for God.

Sovereignty: One version of the New Testament names this in Corinthians as an order of angels. Paul speaks of Jesus doing away with 'all sovereignty, authority and power' while in the King James Version, 'sovereignty' is replaced by 'rule'.

Sparks: An order of angels, according to French philosopher Voltaire. They are sometimes identified with the Tarshishim (*qv*).

Spendarmoz: *See* **Ishpan Darmaz**.

Sphener: An angel who is invoked to combat Mardero, one of the demons of disease.

Spheres: *See* **Galgallim**.

ABOVE: *Vision of Ezekiel*
English School, 20th century

Sphinxes: Another name for the Cherubim (*qv*) of Ezekiel's vision.

Spirit: An angel or a demon is a 'spirit'. While they are pure, man is an impure spirit. God is the divine spirit.

Spirit of Ill-Will: An angelic messenger of God.

Spirit of Jealousy: An angelic messenger of God.

Spirit of Knowledge: A term for an angel.

Spirit of Lying: An angelic messenger of God.

Spirit of Perversion: *See* **Angel of Darkness**.

Spirit of Whoredom: *See* **Angel of Lust**.

Splenditenes: A Manichean world-supporting angel who supports the heavens on his back. He appears on Mithraic monuments and is probably the model for the Greek Atlas.

Splendors: An alternative name for the Tarshinim (*qv*).

Spugliguel: An angel who presides over the sign of spring.

Sraosha (Srosh): An angel of Persian lore who, it is claimed, set the world in motion. He is the seventh Amesha Spenta (*qv*) and in Zoroastrianism is the angel who carries the soul up to Heaven after death, the red chrysanthemum being his symbol. The Manicheans consider him to be the angel of obedience and the 'fiend-smiter' who judges the dead. He is sometimes known as Sirushi, under which name he is an angel of Paradise and master of announcements. He is the guardian angel of the world and ensures that the poor do not starve.

Ssakmakiel: This angel governs the zodiac sign of Aquarius, documented in *Transcendental Magic* (*qv*).

Ssnialiah: An angel used in conjuring ritual, mentioned in *The Sword of Moses* (*qv*).

Sstiel YHWH: One of the Merkabah's (*qv*) eight powerful princes. According to *3 Enoch (See The Book of Enoch)*, he is senior to Metatron (*qv*).

Standards: An order of angels named by Milton in *Paradise Lost*.

Stars: In Bible legend, stars and planets were regarded as messengers or angels.

Strempsuchos: *See* **Astrompsuchos**.

Striel: An angel who guards one of the seven heavenly halls.

Strophaeos: A mysterios Gnostic being to whom the secrets of Creation were revealed.

Sturbiel: An angel of the fourth hour of the day.

Sturi(el): One of the 70 amulet angels (*qv*).

Suceratos: An angel of the Fourth Heaven who rules on the Lord's Day and must be invoked from the West.

Sukalli (Sukallin): A Sumerian-Babylonian order of angels.

Sukallin: *See* **Sukalli**.

Sumiel: According to French philosopher Voltaire, a leader of the fallen angels, but although he names his source as Enoch, there is no name Sumiel in those texts, suggesting that he meant

Sammael (*qv*) or even Simapesiel (*qv*). The name is inscribed on a kamea.

Summanus: One of the nine Novensiles (*qv*) of Etruscan lore.

Sun: The sun is regarded as a planet by Kabbalists as well as an angel of light.

Suna: A Cherub (*qv*) or Seraph (*qv*) invoked in conjurations, mentioned in *The Sixth and Seventh Books of Moses* (*qv*).

Suphlatus: The angel of dust, documented in *The Nuctemeron* (*qv*).

Suria (Suriya): An angel of the throne (*qv*) or an angel of the presence who is a guard of the 1st hall of the First Heaven.

Suriel: Equated with Sariel (*qv*), Uriel (*qv*), Metatron (*qv*), Ariel (*qv*), and Saraqael (*qv*). He is a prince of the presence and an angel of healing. He is, however, also an angel of death (*qv*), in which role, he was sent to Mount Sinai to collect the soul of Moses (*qv*). Enoch names him as one of the four great archangels and his name appears on Gnostic amulets along with Raguel (*qv*), Peniel (*qv*), Uriel, and Raphael (*qv*). In *Contra Celsum VI*, Origen of Alexandria names him as one of the seven Ophitic Hebdomad primordial Powers. When invoked, he manifests as an ox.

Suriya: *See* **Suria**.

Suriyel: An angel who is reputed to have led Adam (*qv*) and Eve from the top of the mountain where they were tempted by Satan to the cave of treasures.

Suroth: An Egyptian and Occult angel of Venus (*qv*). In Hermetics – chief of the angelic order of Principalities (*qv*) and a regent over vegetation.

Surtaq: An angel who helps Metatron (*qv*).

Surulph: An angel who is mentioned in Thomas Hyde's 1700 work, *Historia Religionis Veterum Persarum*.

Surya: The singular form of 'Suryas'. One of the seven celestial deities or angels in the Vedic pantheon . In *3 Enoch* (See *The Book of Enoch*), 'Surya' is one of the many names of the angel Metatron (*qv*).

Suryan: Another name for Raphael (*qv*).

Susabo: An angel of voyages and also an angel of the sixth hour, mentioned in *The Nuctemeron* (*qv*).

Susniel: A spellbinding angel.

Sut: One of five sons of the fallen angel, Iblis (*qv*), as the demon of lies. The complete list of Iblis's sons is:

> Awar (demon of lubricity)
>
> Dasim (demon of discord)
>
> Sut (demon of lies)
>
> Tir (demon of fatal accidents)
>
> Zalamar (demon of dishonesty in business)

Sutuel (Suryal): The angel who, according to Falasha legend, carried Baruch to Jerusalem.

Sword of Moses, The: An apocryphal Hebrew book of magic edited by Moses Gaster in 1896. The manuscript is believed to be from the 13th or 14th century.

Symnay: An angel who is a member of the order of Powers (*qv*) and is invoked in Kabbalistic magic ritual. It is not clear whether he fell. Symnay is mentioned in *The Sixth and Seventh Books of Moses* (*qv*).

Synesis: A great Gnostic luminary emanating from the Divine Will.

Synoches: One of the three angels of the Chaldean Empyrean, the highest part of Heaven.

Syth: An angel of an hour with the corresponding angel Teiaiel (*qv*).

Sywaro: A ministering angel invoked in Kabbalistic magic ritual, mentioned in *The Sixth and Seventh Books of Moses* (*qv*).

Ta'aniel: An angel who may be invoked in magic ritual, according to *The Sword of Moses* (*qv*).

Tabkiel: Another of the many names of the angel Metatron (*qv*).

Tablibik: An angel of the fifth hour as well as of fascination, documented in *The Nuctemeron* (*qv*).

Tabris: An Occult angel of free will as well as an angel of the sixth hour, referred to in *The Nuctemeron* (*qv*).

T'achnu: An angel who is mentioned in *The Book of Raziel* (*qv*).

Tacouin: Islamic fairy-like creatures that are 'beautiful, winged, minor angels who secure man against the wiles of demons, and reveal the future', as mentioned in *Dictionnaire Infernal* (*qv*).

Tadhiel: An angel said to have prevented the sacrifice of Isaac (*qv*), although in Genesis, Metatron (*qv*), Zadkiel (*qv*) and the angel of the Lord (*qv*) are also credited with this act.

Tafel X: An angel who may be invoked in magic ritual, according to *The Sword of Moses* (*qv*).

Tafsarim: An order of Merkabah (*qv*) angels who, according to *3 Enoch* (See *The Book of Enoch*), are superior in rank to 'all the ministering angels who minister before the throne of glory.'

Taftefiah: Another of the many names of the angel Metatron (*qv*).

Taftian: A Kabbalistic miracle-working angel who is a servant of Alimon (*qv*).

Tagas: The great angel prince who conducts the Song-Uttering Choirs.

Tagriel (Thigra): Head of the angels who guard the Second or Seventh Heaven and one of the angels who rule the mansions of the moon (*qv*).

Taharial: An angel of purity who is also one of the 70 amulet angels (*qv*), documented in *The Book of the Angel Raziel* (*qv*).

Tahasiyah: One of the many names of the angel Metatron (*qv*).

Takifiel: A spellbinding angel invoked in magic ritual.

Taliahad: An angel of water whose name is

inscribed on the seventh pentacle of the Sun, mentioned in *The Greater Key of Solomon* (*qv*).

Tall Angel: The huge angel encountered by Moses (*qv*) during his tour of Heaven. He had 70,000 heads and is assumed to be Sandalphon (*qv*).

Talmai: A fallen angel summoned in the conjuring of the reed.

Tamael: A Friday angel of the Third Heaven who is invoked from the East.

Tamarid: An angel of the second hour of the night, under Farris (*qv*).

Tamiel (Tamuel, Temel): An angel of the deep, a fallen angel according to *1 Enoch* (See *The Book of Enoch*).

Tamtemiyah: Another of the many names of the angel Metatron (*qv*).

Tandal: One of the 64 guardians of the seven heavenly halls.

Tandariel: An angel whose name is mentioned by both English orientalist Hyde and French philosopher Voltaire.

Tankf'il: An Arabic guardian angel invoked in exorcisms.

Tap: *See* **Gaap**.

Taptharthareth: *See* **Tophtharthareth**.

Tar: One of the ten angels or uthri of Mandaean lore who accompany the sun on its daily course.

Tara: An angel featured in H.D.'s (Hilda Doolittle) poem 'Sagesse' and also mentioned in Robert Ambelain's 1951 work, *La Kabbala Pratique*.

Taranava: A chief angel of the third altitude.

Tarfaniel: An angel who guards the gates of the West Wind.

Tarfiel (Tarpiel): In Kabbalism, Tarfiel is one of the angels who can be invoked to cure stupidity.

Tarniel: An angel of Mercury and of Wednesday, residing in the Third Heaven and invoked from the East. Also said to be a guard of the gates of the East Wind.

Tarpiel: *See* **Tarfiel**.

Tarquam: In Occultism, Tarquam is one of the two angels who rule autumn, the other being Guabarel (*qv*).

Tarshish: According to *The Zohar* (*qv*), a chief of the angelic order of the Tarshishim, the other chiefs being Haniel (*qv*) and Sabrael (*qv*).

Tarshishim: According to Jewish legend, an angelic order, equatable to the Virtues (*qv*).

Tarsisim: *See* **Tarshishim**.

Tartaruch: An angel with responsibility for punishments.

Tartaruchian: Angels Seen in the Vision of Paul, angels who have in their hands 'iron rods with three hooks with which they pierce the bowels of sinners'. *See* **Tartaruch**.

Tartaruchus: Chief of the angels in charge of punishments in Hell.

Tartarus: The fallen angel presiding over Hell, although a term sometimes used to mean Hell itself.

Tarwan: According to Mandaean legend, one of the ten angels who accompany the sun on its daily course.

Tashriel: An angel who guards the halls of the First Heaven.

Tata'il: An Arabic angel who can be invoked during exorcisms.

Tatonon: A Solomonic angel invoked to bless the salt, noted in *The Greater Key of Solomon* (*qv*).

Tatriel: One of the many names of the angel Metatron (*qv*).

Tatrusia: One of the 70 amulet angels (*qv*).

Tau: An angel whose name God used to cause the Flood.

Tauriel: A Mandaean angel or uthra.

Taurine Angel: 'The taurine angel of the abyss' is mentioned in Louis Ginzberg's *The Legends of the Jews*. His roar is heard when he causes the water of the lower abyss to be poured into the upper one.

Tausig: *See* **Taus-Melek**.

Taus-Melek (Tausig): The Yezidic peacock angel worshipped as a devil-god and benefactor of mankind. Buddhists use Melek as a name for Satan (*qv*). A Kurdish Muslim sect in Upper Mesopotamia believes Taus-Melek to be a pardoned fallen archangel to whom God has given 'the government of the world and the management of the transmigration of souls.'

Tavtavel: One of the many names of the angel Metatron (*qv*).

Tazbun: An angel who rules over one of the months of the year, noted in *The Book of the Angel Raziel* (*qv*).

Teba'at: One of the seven angelic leaders of the rebellious angels.

Tebliel: One of the seven angels who hold dominion over the Earth.

Techial: Leader of the angels who guard the fifth Heaven.

Tehom: One of the 15 angels of the throne (*qv*) listed in *The Sixth and Seventh Books of Moses* (*qv*).

Tehoriel: A guard at the gates of the South Wind.

Teiaiel: In Kabbalism, an angel of the throne (*qv*) who can tell what is going to happen in the future. He governs voyages at sea and commerce. *See* **Ieiaiel**.

Teasel (Teiazel): An angel who is a member of the order of Powers (*qv*) and who reigns over writers, artists and librarians. His corresponding angel is Aterchinis (*qv*).

Telantes: An angel invoked during wax magic ritual, mentioned in *The Greater Key of Solomon* (*qv*).

Teletarchae: Chaldean angels.

Teletiel: An angel who rules the zodiac.

Temel: *See* **Tamiel**.

Temeluch (Temlakos, Temleyakos): An angel who protects babies and infants, although he is also an angel of Hell and the 'merciless angel of all fire' who torments the souls of sinners after death.

Temlakos: *See* **Temeluch**.

Temleyakos: *See* **Temeluch**.

Tempast: An angel of the first hour of the night, under Gamiel (*qv*).

Temperance: A Kabbalistic angel.

Tempha: An angel of Saturn invoked in talismanic magic.

Tenaciel: Invoked from the East, an angel of Friday and of the third hour, noted in *The Magus* (*qv*).

Tendac: An angel invoked in the exorcism of the bat.

Tephros: An evil spirit responsible for the onset of darkness and wildfires. He is a demon of ashes summoned by Beelzebub (*qv*) at the request of Solomon. However, he cures fever with Azael's (*qv*) help and can be invoked in the names of Bultala, Thallel and Melchal.

Tepiseuth: An angel of part of an hour.

Teraphim: Kabbalistic magic-practitioners or wizards of the Middle Ages who were venerated as both male and female idols.

Terathel (Ierathel): An angel who is a member of the order of the Dominations (*qv*). He is an angel of light who encourages freedom and progress.

Teriapel: An angel of the planet Venus.

Terly: In Occultism, a good spirit who can be invoked to win the garter of a lady to whom the invocant is attracted.

Tessub: *See* **Rimmon**.

Testament of Abraham: A Jewish text from the Old Testament, the author is unknown.

Testament of Solomon: A text from the Old Testament allegedly written by King Solomon.

Tetra: An angel who can be invoked for the satisfaction of one's desires.

Tetrasiyah: One of the many names of the angel Metatron (*qv*).

Teumiel: The seventh of ten unholy Sephiroth (*qv*).

Tezalel: In Kabbalism, an angel invoked to ensure fidelity in marriage.

Thagrinus: An angel of confusion (*qv*), and of the fourth hour, mentioned in *The Nuctemeron* (*qv*).

Thammuz: A fallen angel, according to Milton in *Paradise Lost*. The Phoenician equivalent of the Greek Adonis.

Thamy: An angel of the order of Powers (*qv*), invoked in Kabbalistic conjurations.

Thaphabaoth (Thautabaoth): Origen, in his Ophitic work, *Contra Celsum*, describes this angel, or demon, as hostile towards man, along with Michael (*qv*) and Gabriel (*qv*). The Gnostics consider him to be a demon, one of the seven rulers of Hell. He manifests in the form of a bear and is the Hebrew version of the Greek Tartars.

Thaq: A Mandaean angel.

Tharsis: An angel who governs the element of water, noted in *The Hierarchy of the Blesséd Angels* (*qv*).

Thaumiel: One of the unholy Sephira (*qv*), corresponding to Kether.

Thaur: An angel invoked in Arabic incantation ritual.

Thausael: A leading fallen angel, mentioned in *The Book of Enoch* (*qv*).

Thauthabaoth: *See* **Thaphabaoth**.

Thegri: An angel who holds dominion over beasts.

Thelesis: One of the four great Gnostic aeons (*qv*) emanating from the divine will. Sometimes identified with Raguel (*qv*).

Theliel: An angel who is the prince of love. Invoked to secure the love of another.

Theodonias: A secret name of God used at vesting ceremonies and during Solomonic conjurations.

Theophile: A fictional angel in Anatole France's *The Revolt of the Angels*.

Theoska: Ministering angel who can be invoked in magic ritual.

Thief of Paradise: A name for Satan (*qv*) in Milton's *Paradise Regained*.

Thiel: A ruling prince of Wednesday and of the planet Venus who is invoked from the North. He is an angel of the Second Heaven but is also believed to serve in the Third.

Thigra: *See* **Tagriel**.

Third Angel, The: One of the seven angels that sound trumpets. At the sound of the third angel's trumpet, the great star Wormwood (*qv*) – also considered an angel – falls from Heaven.

Third Heaven: Where manna (honey) is stored or produced by angels. Dwelling place of John the Baptist, although in Islamic lore, he dwells in the Second Heaven. Azrael (*qv*), angel of death is located by Muslims in the Third Heaven. *2 Enoch (See The Book of Enoch)* says that the Third Heaven holds both Paradise and Hell, with Hell situated 'on the northern side'.

Thirteen Angels: Angels envisioned by William Blake in his apocalyptic poem, 'America'.

Thomax: The angel under Narcoriel (*qv*) who is ruler of the eighth hour of the night.

Thopitus: Kabbalistic angel invoked during ritual incantations, corresponding to the angel Lehahiah (*qv*).

Thoth: The Egyptian god of wisdom and a great Gnostic aeon (*qv*) – the 'aeon of aeons' – who is characterized as the Good Daimon.

Three Angels of Abraham: Three angels that Abraham entertained unknowingly at Mamre. They are identified as a number of entities – God, Michael (*qv*) and Gabriel (*qv*); the Logos (*qv*), Michael and Raphael; the Holy Ghost, God and Jesus (*qv*). One of the angels made a promise to 90-year-old Sarah that she would have a son – later she gave birth to Isaac (*qv*).

Thrgar: An angel of an unspecified month, as mentioned in *The Book of the Angel Raziel* (*qv*).

Thrones: These angels form the last choir of the first hierarchy and are also known as the Ophanim. In Jewish lore the Thrones are described as the great 'wheels' of God's chariot, with their main characteristics being submission and peace. The Thrones are also responsible for conveying God's spirit to mankind and the inferior angels.

Throne Bearers: An Islamic order of angels, a class in which it is said there are now only four angels but on the day of resurrection that number will be doubled.

Tiel: An angel guarding the gates of the North Wind.

Tifereth: *See* **Tiphereth**.

Tiftheriel (Tiphtheriel): The sixth Sephira (*qv*) of the Tree of Life.

Tijmneik: An angel of the seal (*qv*).

Tikarathin: A secret name of God, invoked in magic ritual.

Tilath (Silat): An angel who must be invoked by the Master of the Art.

Tileion: An angel invoked in the consecration of the salt.

Time: An angel on Tarot card number 14, winged and with the sign of the sun on his forehead, the square and triangle of the septenary on his chest. He is seen pouring the essence of life from one chalice into another.

Time Spirit: A special rank for Michael (*qv*), senior to that of archangel, as told by Rudolph Steiner in *The Mission of the Archangel Gabriel*. Steiner claims that Michael descended to Earth in the mid-19th century to help man against evil spirits.

Tiphereth: The sixth Sephira (*qv*).

Tiphtheriel: *See* **Tiftheriel**.

Tir: The ancient Persian angel of June. And the angel of the 13th day of the month. Also regent of the planet Mercury and in Muslim legend the demon of fatal accidents and one of the five sons of Iblis (*qv*).

Tiriel: An archangel who is the angel of the planet Mercury.

Tiril: A fallen angel, according to French philosopher Voltaire.

Tirtael: A guard at the gates of the East Wind.

Tishbash: One of the many names of the angel Metatron (*qv*).

Tishgash: One of the many names of the angel Metatron (*qv*).

Titmon: One of the many names of the angel Metatron (*qv*).

Tixmion: An angel who is invoked for the consecration of the salt.

Tmsmael: An evil angel invoked to break up a marriage, mentioned in *The Sword of Moses* (*qv*).

Tobiel: Another name for Tubuel used by French author Victor Hugo in *The Toilers of the Sea*.

Todatamael: An angel who guards the gates of the East Wind.

Tomimiel: An angel ruling over the zodiac.

Tophiel: One of the seven angels guarding the First Heaven.

Tophnar (Tophrag): One of the seven angels guarding the First Heaven.

Tophrag: *See* **Tophnar**.

Tophtharthareth (Taptharthareth): A spirit of the planet Mercury, according to Paracelsus (*qv*). The ruling angel of Mercury is Tiriel (*qv*).

Torquaret: An angel of fall (*qv*).

Totraviel: An angel who serves with Zahaftirii (*qv*), guards the Fifth Heaven and holds the seal.

Totrisi: One of the angels appointed by God to the Sword, tasked with presiding over law and order in Heaven and on Earth.

Tractatu: An angel that Cornelius Agrippa (*qv*) says had a book named after him.

Transcendental Magic: Written by Eliphas Levi in 1896, this book explores the subjects of ceremonial magic, the Kabbalah, the Occult and elementary spirits.

Transin: A name used to control demons, written in *The Greater Key of Solomon* (*qv*).

Trgiaob: An angel that holds dominion over wild fowl and creeping things, according to *The Sword of Moses* (*qv*).

Trsiel: An angel presiding over rivers.

Tsadkiel (Tzadkiel): An angel of justice who is fourth of the ten archangels of the Briatic world. He is also one of the angels guarding the gates of the East Wind. Tsadkiel is also an angel of Jupiter and guardian angel of Joseph.

Tsaftsefiah, Tsaftsehel, Tsahtsehiyah, Tsaltselim, Tsaltseliyah: Names of the angel Metatron (*qv*).

Tsaphiel: In Occultism, an angel of the moon.

Tsavniyah, Tsavtsiyah: Variant names of the angel Metatron (*qv*).

Tse'an: An angel guarding the sixth heavenly hall.

Tsedeck: Identified with the angels Tsadkiel (*qv*) and Zadkiel (*qv*).

Tshndirnis: An angel presiding over one of the months of the year, recorded in the *Book of the Angel Raziel* (*qv*).

Tsirya: One of the 70 amulet angels (*qv*).

Tsuria: One of the 70 amulet angels (*qv*).

Tsuriel: Another form of Zuriel (*qv*) as the angel ruling over the zodiac sign of Libra.

Tual: An angel of the sign of the zodiac, Taurus. Asmodel (*qv*) is also allocated this role.

Tubatlu: One of the angels of omnipotence (*qv*).

Tubiel: An angel invoked so that small birds can be returned to their owners and also head of the sign of summer, noted in *The Magus* (*qv*).

Tubuel: *See* **Tubuas**.

Tubunas: An angel guarding the First Heaven.

Tufiel: An angel who guards the First Heaven.

Tufriel: An angel who guards the Sixth Heaven.

Tuiel: An angel whose name is mentioned in the *Book of the Angel Raziel* (*qv*).

Tulatu: One of the eight omnipotent angels in *The Sixth and Seventh Books of Moses* (*qv*).

Tumael: *See* **Tamiel**.

Turel: A fallen angel who is a messenger of the spirits of the planet Jupiter and for the angel Sachiel (*qv*) or Setchiel (*qv*).

Turlos: An angel who conjures the reed, mentioned in *The Greater Key of Solomon* (*qv*).

Turmiel: An angel who guards the gates of the West Wind.

Tusmas: An angel of the seventh hour of the day, under Barginiel (*qv*), referred to in *The Lesser Key of Solomon* (*qv*).

Tutiel: An angel invoked in conjurations, according to *The Lesser Key of Solomon* (*qv*).

Tutrebial: An angel who guards the Seventh Heaven.

Tutrbebial: An angel who is one of the guardians of the 64 celestial halls.

Tutresiel: Another name for the angel Metatron (*qv*).

Tutrachiel: An angel who guards the First Heaven.

Tuwahel: A ministering angel invoked in magic ritual, referred to in *The Sixth and Seventh Books of Moses* (*qv*).

Twelve Spirits of the Zodiacal Cycle:

TWELVE SPIRITS OF THE ZODIACAL CYCLE

ACCORDING TO FRENCH OCCULT WRITER AND MAGICIAN, ELIPHAS LEVI

Sarahiel – Aries	Azariel – Virgo
Saraiel – Gemini	Sarzeil – Scorpio
Seratiel – Leo	Saritiel – Sagittarius
Chadakiel – Libra	Semaqiel – Capricorn
Araziel – Taurus	Tzakmaqiel – Aquarius
Phakiel – Cancer	Vocatiel - Pisces

TWELVE SPIRITS OF THE ZODIACAL CYCLE

ACCORDING TO BENJAMIN CAMFIELD IN HIS 17TH-CENTURY WORK, *A THEOLOGICAL DISCOURSE OF ANGELS*:

Malchedael – Aries	Hamliel – Virgo
Asmodel – Taurus	Barbiel – Scorpio
Ambriel – Gemini	Adnachiel – Sagittarius
Muriel – Cancer	Haniel – Capricorn
Verchiel – Leo	Gambriel – Aquarius
Zuriel – Libra	Barchiel – Pisces

Tychagara: A great angel of the throne (*qv*).

Typhon: An angel who is identified with the Greek god of darkness, Set. Cornelius Agrippa (*qv*) identifies him with the Kabbalistic angel, Sammael (*qv*).

Tzadiqel: An angelic Thursday ruler of the planet Jupiter, mentioned in *The Greater Key of Solomon* (*qv*).

Tzadkiel: *See* **Tsadkiel**.

Tzakmaqiel: An angel presiding over Aquarius.

Tzaphniel: An angel invoked in order to acquire a magic carpet, mentioned in *The Magus* (*qv*) and *The Greater Key of Solomon* (*qv*).

Tzaphquiel: The third of the ten holy Sephira (*qv*) and third of the ten archangels, according to *The Zohar* (*qv*). He also rules Saturday and the planet Saturn.

Tzarmiel: An angel who guards the gates of the North Wind.

Tzartak (Tzortaq): One of the 70 amulet angels (*qv*), mentioned in *The Book of the Angel Raziel* (*qv*).

Tzedeqiah: Name of an angel inscribed on the first pentacle of the planet Jupiter, referred to in *The Greater Key of Solomon* (*qv*).

Tzortaq: *See* **Tzartak**.

Tzurel: An angel who guards the gates of the South Wind.

Ubaviel: An angel who holds dominion over the zodiac sign of Capricorn.

Ublisi: An Occult angel and one of the eight angels of omnipotence (*qv*) invoked in conjurations.

Ucimiel: *See* **Ucirmiel**.

Ucirmiel (Ucimiel): An angel of Wednesday residing in the Second or Third Heaven who must be invoked from the North.

Udrgazyia: One of the 70 amulet angels (*qv*), listed in *The Book of the Angel Raziel* (*qv*).

Udriel: One of the 70 amulet angels (*qv*).

Uini: A ministering angel who can be invoked in conjurations, mentioned in *The Sixth and Seventh Books of Moses* (*qv*).

Umabel: An angel holding dominion over physics and astronomy and one of the 72 angels who bear the name of God Shemhamphorae.

Umahel: An archangel, according to *La Kabbale Pratique* (The Practical Kabbalah) by Robert Amberlain.

Umeroz: An angel of the second hour of the night, under Farris (*qv*), according to *The Lesser Key of Solomon* (*qv*).

Umiel: A spellbinding angel.

Umikol: An angel of the seal (*qv*) in Jewish mysticism.

Unael: An angel of the First Heaven whose name is inscribed on a kamea, according to *The Sixth and Seventh Books of Moses* (*qv*).

Ur: Meaning 'fire, or 'light' in Hebrew, a Mandaean king of the Underworld.

Urfiel: Head of the angelic order of Malakim (*qv*).

Urian: *See* **Uriel**.

Uriel: *See* pages 194–195.

Uriron: In Jewish magic, Uriron is an angel invoked to protect against sorcery and sudden death.

Urizen: Alternating with Orc as the angel of England in William Blake's *Book of Urizen*. One of the four Zoas and the embodiment of the god of reason.

Urjan: *See* **Uriel**.

Urpaniel: Name of an angel inscribed on a kamea.

Uryan: *See* **Uriel**.

Urzla: An angel who is either fallen and of the fifth unholy Sephira (*qv*), as the Kabbalah says, or, as in *The Book of the Angel Raziel* (*qv*), one of the seven angels who stand before God's throne and one of the nine who rule the winds. He is also said to be angel of the East and may be invoked to teach the invocant the secret wisdom of God.

Usera: An angel of the First Heaven, mentioned in *The Sixth and Seventh Books of Moses* (*qv*).

Usiel (Uziel): A fallen angel and fifth of the ten unholy Sephira (*qv*). *The Book of the Angel Raziel* (*qv*) lists him as one of the seven angels who stand before God's throne and one of the nine who rule the winds. Milton describes him as a good angel of the order of Virtues (*qv*) who fought with Gabriel (*qv*) against Satan (*qv*).

Uslael: An angel of the Fourth Heaven, mentioned in *The Sixth and Seventh Books of Moses* (*qv*).

Ustael: An angel of the Fourth Heaven who is one of the three messengers of the moon, rules on the Lord's Day and is invoked from the West.

Ustur: One of the four main Chaldean orders of guardian angels, resembling humans in appearance.

Uthra: The singular form of uthri. A Mandaean angel or spirit, one of the ten that accompany the sun on its daily course. The ten uthri are:

> Zuhair, Zahrun, Buhair, Bahrun, Sar, Sarwan, Tar, Tarwan, Rabia, Talia.

Uthri: *See* **Uthra**.

Uvabriel: An angel of the third hour of the night, under Sarquamich (*qv*).

Uvael: An angel of the First Heaven, ruling Monday, who can be invoked from the North.

Uvall: A fallen angel, formerly a member of the order of Powers (*qv*) who commands 37 legions of demons in Hell. He may be invoked to make a woman fall in love with the invocant.

Uvayah: Another of the many names of the angel Metatron (*qv*).

Uvmiel: An angel guarding the gates of the second heavenly hall.

Uwula: A ministering angel who is invoked during a solar or lunar eclipse, according to *The Sixth and Seventh Books of Moses* (*qv*).

Uzah: Another of the many names of the angel Metatron (*qv*).

Uzbazbiel: An angel guarding the first of the seven heavenly halls.

Uziphiel: An angel guarding the first of the seven heavenly halls.

Uzoh: *See* **Uzza**.

Uzza (Uzoh): A tutelary angel of the Egyptians.

Uzziel: An archangel of the order of Virtues (*qv*) and Cherubim (*qv*) who is one of the seven angels that stand before the Throne of Glory and one of the nine who preside over winds. He is a prince of compassion associated with the Shekinah (*qv*) and ruled by Metatron (*qv*).

ABOVE: *The Good being led to Heaven*
by Rogier van der Weyden, *c.*1451

Uriel: (Nuriel, Uryan, Urian, Urjan, Jeremiel, Vretil, Suriel, Puruel, Phanuel, Jehoel, Israfel)
An angel of vengeance, punishing sinners in Hell and guarding the gate of the Garden of

ABOVE: *The Three Archangels and Tobias*
by Francesco Botticini, *c.*1470

Eden. He is a prince of the Seraphim (*qv*) and the Cherubim (*qv*), ruler of the Sun, prince of the Divine Presence, angel of salvation and he provides protection against terror, thunder, lightning, earthquakes, cataclysms and volcanic eruptions. He is also described as an angel of repentance and is called the 'prince of lights' in *The Manual of Discipline* by W.H. Brownlee. The Sibylline Oracles calls him one of the 'immortal angels of the undying god' and says that he will play a major part in the Day of Judgment, bringing judgement to all. He can be invoked to help with problems of the eyes and provides advice to patriarchs and prophets. He presides over money and prosperity. He is the spirit of ministration and peace, a patron angel of literature and music and can bestow the power of prophecy.

Vacabiel (Vacatiel): Angel who presides over the zodiac sign of Pisces, in partnership with Rasamasa (*qv*).

Vacatiel: *See* **Vacabiel.**

Vachmiel: An angel who rules the fourth hour of the day, served by ten chief officers and 100 lesser angels, according to *The Lesser Key of Solomon* (*qv*).

Vadriel: Angel who rules the ninth hour of the day, served by ten chief officers and 100 lesser angels.

Vahoel: One of the 72 angels who rule over the signs of the zodiac.

Vaij: An angel of the seal (*qv*), mentioned in *The Sixth and Seventh Books of Moses* (*qv*).

Valiants: A term for angels.

Valnum: A Monday angel who dwells in the First Heaven and must be invoked from the North. Also one of the three angels of the planet Saturn.

Vametel: One of the 72 angels who rule over the signs of the zodiac.

Vamona(h): The Vedic Dwarf Avatar (*qv*).

Vaol: An angel whose name is inscribed on the first pentacle of the moon, documented in *The Greater Key of Solomon* (*qv*).

Vaphoron: An angel mentioned in black magic texts who is invoked in the blessing of the salt.

Varcan: An angel holding dominion over the sun. He governs the angels of the air (*qv*), ruling on the Lord's Day.

Varchiel: An angel who rules over either Leo or Pisces.

Variel: One of the 70 amulet angels (*qv*).

Varuna: Chief of the seven Vedic gods (Suryas) who can be equated with the angels of Judaeo-Christianity.

Vasariah: An angel bearing the name of God Shemhamphorae and a member of the angelic order of Dominations (*qv*).

Vashyash: 'A prince over all the angels and Caesars', according to *The Greater Key of Solomon* (*qv*).

Vasiariah: A Kabbalistic angel ruling over justice, nobility, magistrates and lawyers.

Vassago: A benevolent angel invoked to discover a woman's deepest secret. He is a prince of the Underworld where he finds lost things and predicts the future.

Vatale: 'A prince over all the angels and Caesars', according to *The Greater Key of Solomon* (*qv*).

Veguaniel: An angel who rules the third hour of the day.

Vehiel: Name of an angel inscribed on the first pentacle of the moon.

Vehofnehu: One of the numerous names of the angel Metatron (*qv*).

Vehuel: An angel of the order of Principalities (*qv*) who is one of the 72 angels bearing the name of God Shemhamphorae and an angel of the signs of the zodiac.

Vehuiah: An angelic ruler of the rays of the sun who is one of the eight Seraphim (*qv*) who may be invoked to answer the prayers of the faithful. He is one of the 72 angels bearing the name of God Shemhamphorae

Veischax: An angel of the seal (*qv*).

Vel: A resident of the Third Heaven who is also a Wednesday angel invoked from the South.

Vel Aquiel: An angel of the Fourth Heaven, ruling Sunday and invoked from the North.

Velel: An angel of Wednesday who resides in the Second or Third Heaven and is invoked from the North. He is identified with Vel (*qv*).

Veloas: A most pure angel of God invoked in Solomonic black magic ritual for the conjuring of the sword.

Venahel: A Wednesday angel who resides in the Second or Third Heaven and must be invoked from the North.

Verchiel: An angel who rules the month of July and the zodiac sign of Leo. A member of the order of Powers (*qv*) - he is a governor of the Sun. Equated with Zerachiel (*qv*).

Vertues: Milton's spelling for the angelic order of Virtues (*qv*), in *Paradise Lost*.

Veruah: One of the names of the angel Metatron (*qv*).

Vetuel: An angel of the First Heaven who rules on Monday and is invoked from the South.

Veualiah: One of the nine Virtues (*qv*) who empowers kings and grants prosperity to their kingdoms.

Vevalel: One of the 72 angels of the zodiac.

Vevaliah: One of the 72 Shemhamphorae angels.

Vevaphel: Name of an angel inscribed on the third pentacle of the moon.

Veyothiel: The name of an angel discovered in a north Italian manuscript that also contains the Alphabet of Rabbi Akiba.

Vhnori: With Saritaiel (*qv*), an angelic ruler of the zodiac sign of Sagittarius.

Vianuel: An angel of the Fifth Heaven, ruling on Tuesday and invoked from the South.

Victor: In *A Literary History of Ireland* by Douglas Hyde, the angel Victor appears to St Patrick and asks him to go back to Ireland to convert the pagans to Christianity.

Victor Angels: A group of angels in Milton's *Paradise Lost*.

ABOVE: *The Virgin Mary with the Infant Christ* European School, *c.*1900

Virgin Mary: The queen of angels, to Roman Catholics.

Vionatraba: An angel of the Fourth Heaven who rules on the Lord's Day and is invoked from the East. Also one of the three angels of the Sun.

Virgin Mary: *See* page 197.

Virgin of Light: *See* opposite.

ABOVE: *Allegory of the Virtues*, by Antonio Allegri Correggio, *c.*1529–30

Virtues: An exalted angelic order, usually ranked in the second or third triad of the nine choirs in the pseudo-Dionysian celestial scheme. The Hebrews equate them with the Tarshishim (*qv*) or the Malakim (*qv*). Their duty is the working of miracles on Earth and they bestow grace and valour. Michael (*qv*), Raphael (*qv*), Barbiel (*qv*), Uzziel (*qv*), Peliel (*qv*) and, before his fall, Satan (*qv*), have been named as chiefs of the order. The Egyptians and Hermetics name Pi-Rhé (*qv*) (Pi-Ré) as chief.

Virgins: An angelic order that is probably another name for Virtues (*qv*).

Vishna: A powerful angel of the Bhagavd Gita, who was born, with Brahma and Mahish, from the primary properties.

Vishnu: The Hindu Scripture, the Bhagavad Gita, describes Vishnu as the first avatar (*qv*) who was given the responsibility of protecting everything that had been created by Brahma.

Virtues: *See* left.

Vngsursh: A summer equinox angel who can be invoked to protect against the evil eye.

Vocasiel (Vocatiel): With Rasamasa (*qv*), a ruler of the zodiac sign of Pisces.

Vocatiel: *See* **Vocasiel**.

Voel: An angel of the zodiac, governing the sign of Virgo.

Vohal: An angel of power invoked in conjurations, mentioned in *The Sixth and Seventh Books of Moses* (*qv*).

Vohu Manah: A Zoroastrian Amesha Spenta (*qv*) who is the embodiment of good thought. The Avesta names this angel as the first of the Amesha Spentas and he is said to receive the souls of the faithful at death.

Voices: The seven Gnostic angels who reside in the Treasury of Light.

Voizia: An angel who rules the 12th hour of the day (noon), under Beratiel (*qv*).

Voval: S*ee* **Uvall**.

Vraniel: An angel of the tenth hour of the night, under Jusguarin (*qv*).

Vretil (Pravuil, Radueriel): The angelic recorder who maintains the secret books and God's wisdom and is often described as the wisest of all angels. He is an Archangel (*qv*) and is believed by some sources to be 'the man clothed in linen' who put the mark of Passover on Jewish houses in Egypt.

Vrihaspati: A Vedic guardian angel of hymns and prayers and an 'instructor of the gods' who is 'first-born in the highest Heaven of supreme light.'

Vulamahi: An angel invoked in the exorcism of the bat, noted in *The Greater Key of Solomon* (*qv*).

ABOVE: *Angel of Light*
by Sandro Botticelli, *c.*1488–90

Virgin of Light: A great Manichean angel of the order of Virtues (*qv*), dwelling in the moon. In the *Pistis Sophia* (*qv*), she is judge of souls and distributor of seals instead of Sophia. Coptic texts name her as the one who 'chooses the bodies into which the souls of men shall be put at conception.'

Wall: A fallen angel, formerly of the order of Powers (*qv*) now commanding 36 demonic legions, who manifests in the shape of a camel.

Wallim: An angel of the First Heaven, mentioned in *The Sixth and Seventh Books of Moses* (*qv*).

Warrior Angels: *See* opposite page.

Watchers: An exalted angelic order also known as the Grigori (*qv*) who, like the Irin (*qv*), never sleep. They were originally dispatched by God to instruct men but they fell, according to *1 Enoch* (See *The Book of Enoch*). Some sources claim that there are good and evil Watchers, the good residing in the Fifth Heaven, the evil in the Third. These are:

THE WATCHERS

Armaros – Taught men how to resolve enchantments.

Araqiel (Arakiel) – Taught men the signs of the Earth.

THE WATCHERS *(continued)*

Azazel – Taught men how to make knives, swords and shields, as well as how to make ornaments and women's make-up.

Baraqijal – Taught men astrology.

Ezeqeel – Taught men about fortune-telling.

Gadreel – Introduced humans to weapons of war.

Kakabel – Taught men about the science of the constellations.

Penemue – Taught men how to write, which was a sin, according to *1 Enoch* (See *The Book of Enoch*). He also taught children 'the bitter and the sweet, and the secrets of wisdom'.

Sariel – Taught men the course of the moon.

Semjaza – Taught men enchantments, root-cuttings etc.

Shamshiel – Taught men the signs of the sun.

ABOVE: *Warrior Angel*
by Ridolfo di Arpo Guariento, *c.*1348–54

Warrior Angels: An angelic order described by Milton in *Paradise Lost*. They are part of a large order whose main task is to protect God's servants in times of turmoil. Saint Michael is considered to be a major warrior angel, first fighting Satan and his demons and then the enemies of God and his people.

Weatta: An angel of the seal (*qv*), as mentioned in *The Sixth and Seventh Books of Moses (qv)*.

Wezynna: A ministering angel who can be invoked in Kabbalistic magic ritual, according to *The Sixth and Seventh Books of Moses (qv)*

Wheels: The Ofanim (*qv*), or 'many-eyed ones' as -they are known. Grouped by Talmudic scholars with the Cherubim (*qv*) and the Seraphim (*qv*) as a high angelic order, they are led by Rikbiel (*qv*).

Winds: Another term for angels in Hebrews 1:7.

Wisdom: In *2 Enoch* (See *The Book of Enoch)*, on the sixth day of Creation, God orders Wisdom 'to make man of seven substances'. He is the divine agent by which everything was created.

Woman Clothed with the Sun: A passage in Revelation reads 'and there appeared a great wonder in Heaven; a woman clothed with the sun, and the moon under her feet, and upon her head a crown of stars. And she being with child cried, travailing in birth and pained to be delivered.' It is probably the only instance when a heavenly being is represented as being pregnant. She is the celestial model for the Virgin Mary and, according to one source, she derives from the Egyptian Isis (*qv*).

Wormwood: The name of a star that fell from Heaven on the sound of the blast from the third angel. St Paul considered him to be the equivalent of Satan (*qv*) and elsewhere he is noted as a mighty prince bringing judgement to sinners on Earth.

Xaphan: A fallen angel ranked second in Hell who was welcomed into the rebellion by Satan (*qv*) because of the inventiveness of his imagination. He suggested the rebels set fire to Heaven, but before they could do it, they were cast into the abyss where he will eternally be engaged in fanning the furnaces. Needless to say, his symbol is a pair of bellows, a likeness appears in the book *Dictionnaire Infernal* (*qv*).

Xathanael: *See* **Nathanael**.

Xexor: A benevolent angel invoked in conjurations, mentioned in *The Sixth and Seventh Books of Moses* (*qv*).

Xomoy: A benevolent angel invoked in conjurations, according to *The Sixth and Seventh Books of Moses* (*qv*).

Xonor: A benevolent angel invoked in conjurations, noted in *The Sixth and Seventh Books of Moses* (*qv*).

Yaasriel: An angel of Jewish lore who is in charge of the '70 holy pencils'. Using these implements, he is engaged in constantly writing the Ineffable Name of God.

Yabbashael: One of the seven angels who are regents of Earth.

Yadael: *See* **Yadiel**.

Yadiel (Yadael): An angel invoked to assist in ceremonial ritual, according to *The Sword of Moses* (*qv*).

Yael: An angel of the throne (*qv*) invoked during rites at the close of the Sabbath.

Yahadriel: One of the 'mouths' created the night before the first Sabbath, the others being Kadriel (*qv*) and 'the mouth of the lord'.

Yahala: An angel who guards the gates of the West Wind.

Yahanaq Rabba: An angel who guards the gates of the East Wind.

Yahel: Name of an angel that is inscribed on the fourth pentacle of the moon.

Yahoel (Jehoel, Joel): The very first of the angel Metatron's (*qv*) many names and an angel who taught the Torah to Abraham and guided him on Earth and in Heaven.

Yahrameel: A powerful Occult angel who is equated with Yahoel (*qv*).

Yahriel (Yarheil): An angel who presides over the moon as befits his name which means 'moon' in Hebrew.

Yahsiyah: One of the many names of the angel Metatron (*qv*).

Yakriel: An angel who guards the Seventh Heaven.

Yalda Bahut: One of the seven Gnostic archons (*qv*) who is also known as Ariel (*qv*).

Yamenton: A Kabbalistic angel invoked in the blessing of the salt.

Yaqroun: A Mandaean angel.

Yarashiel: An angel who guards the gates of the East Wind.

Yarhiel: *See* **Yahriel**.

Yaron: A Cherub (*qv*) or Seraph (*qv*) invoked in the consecration of the Salt, according to *The Greater Key of Solomon* (*qv*).

Yashiel: Name of an angel inscribed on the first pentacle of the moon.

Yazatas: Zoroastrian celestial beings and angels of the Persian hierarchy who act as guardian angels to mankind, under the Amesha Spentas (*qv*), with Mithra as head of the order.

Yazidic Archangels: The seven Yazidic archangels are:

YAZIDIC ARCHANGELS

Fakr-ed-din ('the poor one of the faith')
Kadir Rahman ('power of mercy')
Nasr-ed-din ('help of the faith')
Shams-ed-din ('sun of the faith)
Sheik Bakra ('power of mercy')
Sheik Ism ('power of mercy')
Sij-ed-din ('power of mercy')

Yazroun: A Mandaean angel.

Yebemel: One of the 72 angels who rule the signs of the zodiac.

Yechoel: A zodiac angel, associated with Yebemel (*qv*).

Yedidieron: The sixth of the ten holy Sephiroth (*qv*) of the Tree of Life.

Yefe(h)fiah: *See* page 204.

Yehadriel: *See* **Akatriel.**

Yehemiel: Name of an angel inscribed on a kamea.

Yehoel: Another name for the angel Metatron (*qv*).

Yehova Vehayah: Another of the many names for the angel Metatron (*qv*).

Yehudiah: A beneficent angel of death (*qv*) who is one of the chief angelic envoys, according to *The Zohar* (*qv*). He descends to Earth with myriads of angels to carry aloft the souls of the dead or those about to die.

Yehakel: A Kabbalistic spirit of the planet Mercury whose name is inscribed on its first pentacle.

Yeliel An angel who guards the gates of the South Wind.

Yephiel: Name of an angel inscribed on a kamea.

Yeqon: *See* **Jeqon.**

Yerachmiel: A regent of Libra and one of the seven Kabbalistic angels who rule the Earth who are:

SEVEN KABBALISTIC ANGELS

Uriel (*qv*)	Gabriel (*qv*)
Raphael (*qv*)	Yerachmiel
Raguel (*qv*)	
Michael (*qv*)	
Suriel	

Yeruel: One of the 70 amulet angels (*qv*).

Yeruiel: Third of the ten holy Sephiroth (*qv*).

Yeshamiel: An angel who rules the sign of Libra.

Yeshayah: One of the many names of the angel Metatron (*qv*).

Yesod: Ninth of the ten holy Sephiroth (*qv*).

Yetsirah: Jewish mystics believe this to be the chief domain of the angels. It is the world of formation – the world of angels created from the emanations of God.

ABOVE: *The Child Moses on the Nile*
by Gustave Doré (1832–83), engraved by H. Pisan, 1866

Yefe(h)fiah (Jefefiah, Iofiel, Yofiel, Dina): Angel who is prince of the Torah and who is credited with teaching Moses (*qv*) the Kabbalistic mysteries. In Aramaic texts, he is described as one of the great Archangels. He may be identified with Metatron (*qv*).

Yetzer Hara: Man's evil tendency or, as some rabbis believe, the spirit of evil itself – Satan (*qv*).

Yezriel: One of the 70 amulet angels (*qv*).

Ygal: One of the 70 amulet angels (*qv*).

Yikon: *See* **Jeqon**.

Yisrael: A variant form of Israel in *The Zohar* (*qv*).

Yizriel: An angel that can be invoked, mentioned in *The Sword of Moses* (*qv*).

Yofiel: *See* **Iofiel**.

Yofiel Mittron X: An angel mentioned in *The Sword of Moses* (*qv*).

Yofim: A Mandaean angel.

Yomael (Yomiel): An angel who is a prince of the Third Heaven, invoked in Syriac conjurations.

Yomiel: *See* **Yomael**.

Yonel: An angel who guards the gates of the North Wind.

Yourba: *See* **Yurba**.

Yrouel: An angel of fear whose name is inscribed on amulets worn by pregnant women.

Yura: A Mandaean angel of light and of rain.

Yurba (Yourba): A Mandaean chief of the powers of darkness but who also acts as servant to the powers of light.

Yurkemi: The angel of hail (*qv*).

Yushamin: A Mandaean spirit of fertility residing in the wellsprings of light. One of the three supreme uthri (angels).

Za'afiel: An angel of destruction (*qv*) appointed by God to deal with mortal sinners who holds dominion over hurricanes. Fifth of the unholy Sephiroth (*qv*), sometimes regarded as good and sometimes as evil.

Zaamael: Sixth of the unholy Sephiroth (*qv*) and with dominion over storms.

Zabaniyah: Name of lesser Arabic angels serving Malik (*qv*).

Zabdiel: An angel whose surname is Kunya; one of the 14 ineffable names of God, according to *The Sword of Moses* (*qv*).

Zabesael: An angel of the seasons.

Zabkiel: An angel who is a ruler of the order of the Hashmallim (*qv*).

Zacharael (Yahriel, Zachariel): One of the seven archangels, prince of the order of Dominations (*qv*) and ruler of the Second Heaven. The Kabbalah lists him as an angel of the order of Powers (*qv*) and a ruler of Jupiter. Paracelsus (*qv*) describes him as Pi-Zeus, a planetary

Egyptian spirit and a ruler of Thursday.

Zacharel: An angel of the seventh hour of the night, under Mendrion (*qv*).

Zachariel: *See* **Zacharael**.

Zachiel (Zadkiel): Ruler of the Sixth Heaven.

Zachriel: An angel who holds dominion over memory.

Zaciel Parmar: A leader of the fallen angels, according to French philosopher Voltaire.

Zacrath: An angel summoned during the exorcism of the bat, mentioned in *The Greater Key of Solomon* (*qv*).

Zada: A ministering angel used in conjurations, documented in *The Sixth and Seventh Books of Moses* (*qv*).

Zadakiel: *See* **Zadkiel**.

Zaday: An angel of the seven planets.

Zades: Occult angel invoked in the exorcism of wax, mentioned in *The Greater Key of Solomon* (*qv*).

Zadikiel: An angel invoked in Syriac conjurations.

Zadkiel (Zadakiel, Zedekiel): The angel of mercy,

memory, benevolence, joviality and compassion who is also a regent of Jupiter and Sagittarius as well as a prince of Dominations (*qv*). He is co-ruler, with Gabriel (*qv*), of the Shinanim (*qv*), one of the ten orders that make up the hierarchy in the Kabbalistic work, the *Masseket Azilut*. He is one of the nine regents of Heaven and an Archangel. In *The Zohar* (*qv*), he is described as one of the two chiefs who, along with Zophiel (*qv*), helps Michael (*qv*) in battle. He is the angel in the Bible who prevents Abraham from sacrificing his son, Isaac. He can be invoked to bring good memory to the invocant.

Zafiel: An angel who holds dominion over showers of rain.

Zafniel: An angel ruling an unspecified month of the year. Noted in *Jewish Magic and Superstition*, by Joshua Trachtenberg, a book that explores Jewish mysticism.

Zafrire: Angels of the morning.

Zagiel: A fallen angel.

Zagin: A ministering angel, mentioned in *The Sixth and Seventh Books of Moses* (*qv*).

Zagnzaqiel: *See* **Zagzagel.**

Zagveron: An angel summoned during the blessing of the Salt.

Zagzagel (Sagsagel, Zanzagiel): An angel of wisdom and an instructor of other angels who is said to speak 70 languages. Prince of the Torah, and the Divine Presence and a prince regent of the Fourth Heaven who, nonetheless, resides in the Seventh Heaven. He is said to have taught the Ineffable Name to Moses (*qv*) and to have assisted in burying Moses and taking his soul to Heaven.

Zahabriel: An angel guarding the First Heaven.

Zahaftirii: An angel of the face (presence) who shares seal-holding duties at the fifth gate in Heaven, with Totraviel (*qv*).

Zahariel: A great angel invoked to help resist temptation by the arch-demon, Moloch (*qv*).

Zahari'il: A benevolent Mandaean angel of procreation and childbirth.

Zahbuk: An evil fallen angel invoked to break up marriages.

Zahun: An angel of scandal and also an angel of the first hour.

Zahzahiel: An angel of the celestial order of Shinanim (*qv*).

Zainon: An Occult angel invoked in the conjuration of the reed.

Zakiel: An angel who is invoked during the creation of Syriac spellbinding charms.

Zakkiel: An angel of storms who helped change Enoch from a mortal man into the great angel Metatron (*qv*).

Zakun: An angel who, supported by Lahash, led 184 myriad angels in snatching Moses' (*qv*) prayer before it could reach God. Lahash (*qv*) was dealt 60 blows of fire and cast out of the inner chamber for his misdeed, but we do not know what Zakun's punishment consisted of.

Zakzakiel: The angelic prince selected to write the merits of Israel on the Throne of Glory.

Zalbesael: An angel who rules over the rainy season.

Zalburis: The angel of therapeutics and one of the angels of the eighth hour.

Zaliel: An angel of the Fifth Heaven who rules on Tuesday and must be invoked from the South.

Zamael: *See* **Sammael.**

Zamarchad: The name of an angel inscribed on a kamea.

Zamiyad: An angel into whose care the Persian Magi place the black-eyed Houri or nymphs of Paradise.

Zaniel: An angel who holds dominion over the zodiac sign of Libra.

Zanzagiel: *See* **Zagzagel.**

Zanziel: An angel who guards the gates of the West Wind.

Zaphiel (Iofiel): Archangel who is a regent of the angelic order of Hashmallim (*qv*). Also a regent of Saturn and an angel of the third Sephira (*qv*) of the Tree of Life. One of the nine angels ruling over Heaven and ruler of the Cherubim (*qv*).

Zaqen: Another of the many names of the angel Metatron (*qv*).

Zarall: One of the two Cherubim (*qv*) – the other being Jael (*qv*) – whose names are engraved on the Mercy Seat of the Ark of the Covenant.

Zaraph: A fictional angel in Thomas Moore's *Loves of the Angels*.

Zarazaz: An angel who is the guard of the veil of the celestial treasure house.

Zaren: An avenging angel.

Zarobi: An Occult angel of precipices and a ruler of the third hour.

Zaron: An angel invoked in the Solomonic rite of conjuring the reed, noted in *The Greater Key of Solomon* (*qv*).

Zaroteij: An angel of the seal (*qv*), as mentioned in *The Sixth and Seventh Books of Moses* (*qv*).

Zarzakiel: Appointed by God to write down the merits of Israel on the Throne of Glory. Identified with Sopheriel the Lifegiver.

Zatriel: An angel invoked in Syriac spellbinding rituals.

Zaurvan: A Zoroastrian Daeva known as the demon of decrepitude.

Zavael (Rashiel): An angel with dominion over whirlwinds, mentioned in *3 Enoch* (*The Book of Enoch*).

Zavebe: A fallen angel.

Zawar: One of the 15 angels of the throne (*qv*), as listed in *The Books of Moses* (*qv*).

Zazahiel: An angel who guards the Third Heaven.

Zazaii (Zazay): An angel who can be invoked to exorcize demons through the use of incense and fumigation, according to the *Grimorium Verum* (*qv*).

Zazay: *See* **Zazaii.**

Zazean: An angel invoked in the exorcism of the bat.

Zazel: A Solomonic angel invoked in love rituals and either the 45th or 49th spirit of the planet Saturn. His name appears with that of Asiel's (*qv*) on a talisman to guard the bearer against sudden death.

Zazriel: A powerful prince of the Divine Presence, representing 'divine strength, might and power.'

Zeba'marom: A term for angels, referred to in Isaiah 24:21.

Zeba'Shamaim: A term for angels, used in Deuteronomy 17:3.

Zebul: An angel who rules the Sixth Heaven during the day. *Visions of Ezekiel*, however, claims that he rules the Third Heaven, while Enoch says he is ruler of the Fourth.

Zebuleon: One of the angels who will sit in judgement at the end of the world.

Zebuliel: Prince of the western region of the First Heaven who accompanies prayers to the Second Heaven. He rules only when the moon is out and is ruler of numerous angel chiefs who guard the nine doors, mentioned in *The Zohar* (*qv*).

Zeburial: An angel who guards one of the halls of the Seventh Heaven, in Hechaloth lore.

Zedekiel: *See* **Zadkiel.**

Zedereza: A great angel whose name, when uttered by God, will 'cause the sun and the moon to be darkened', according to *The Greater Key of Solomon* (*qv*).

Zeffar: The angel of irrevocable choice and an angel of the ninth hour, mentioned in *The Nuctemeron* (*qv*).

Zehanpuryu: Heaven's advocate general who dispenses divine mercy and with Michael (*qv*) is weigher of balances that cannot be wrong. He ranks higher even than Metatron (*qv*) and is guardian of the Seventh Heaven.

Zeirna: An angel of infirmities and also a spirit of the fifth hour, according to *The Nuctemeron* (*qv*).

Zekuniel: Sometimes named instead of Peliel (*qv*) as second of the ten holy Sephiroth (*qv*).

Zelebsel: An angel of the rainy season..

Zephaniah (Zephaniel): Chief of the order of Ishim (*qv*), second of the ten Kabbalistic angelic orders. Also a name for the Witch of Endor, the woman who called up the ghost of the recently deceased prophet Samuel (*qv*), at the demand of King Saul of the Kingdom of Israel, according to the Old Testament.

Zephaniel: *See* **Zephaniah**.

Zephon (Cafon): An angel prince who guards Paradise and is a member of the Cherubim (*qv*).

Zerachiel: A Grigori (*qv*) who is named as one of the angels 'who keep watch' according to *1 Enoch* (See *The Book of Enoch*). Another source names him as angel of the sun. Equated with Verchiel (*qv*), he is the angel of July and rules the zodiac sign of Leo.

Zerahiyah: One of the many names of the angel Metatron (*qv*).

Zerahyyahu: One of the many names of the angel Metatron (*qv*).

Zeroel: *See* **Zeruch**.

Zeruch (Zeroel, Zeruel): An angel with dominion over strength.

Zeruel: *See* **Zeruch**.

Zethar: An angel of confusion (*qv*).

Zevanion: A Kabbalistic angel invoked in conjuring the reed.

Zevtiyahu: One of the many names of the angel Metatron (*qv*).

Zevudiel: An angel who guards the First Heaven.

Zhsmael: An evil fallen angel conjured to break up a marriage, mentioned in *The Sword of Moses* (*qv*).

Zideon: A Kabbalistic angel invoked in conjuring the reed.

Zi'iel: An angel of commotion, according to *3 Enoch* (See *The Book of Enoch*).

Zikekiel: One of Abraham's guardian angels.

Zikiel: An angel of comets and lightning, according to *3 Enoch* (See *The Book of Enoch*).

Zimimar: An Occult angel, named by Shakespeare as 'the lordly monarch of the North'.

Zobiachel: An angel of the planet Jupiter, according to Henry Wadsworth Longfellow in *The Golden Legend*. The name appears nowhere else.

Zogenethles: One of the great Gnostic archons.

Zohar, The: Kabbalism is an aspect of Judaism that focuses on all things mystical about the Jewish faith. The central text used in the study and practice of Kabbalism is *The Zohar*. It discusses God, the Universe and the nature of souls.

Zoharariel: One of the most exalted angels or possibly a secret name for God.

Zoimiel: An angel of the ninth hour of the day, under Vadriel (*qv*).

Zomen: An angel in Occultism, invoked in exorcizing the wax.

Zoniel: One of the three messenger angels of the planet Saturn.

Zonoei: Chaldean planetary deities or intelligences that rank third amongst the celestial beings responsible for the direction of the universe.

Zophas: An angel of pentacles and a spirit of the 11th hour.

Zophiel or Zaphiel: Invoked by the Master of the Art in Solomonic ritual. He assists Michael (*qv*) in battle.

Zoroel: An angel who can overcome Kumeatel, one of the demons of disease, the decani, according to the *Testament of Solomon* (*qv*).

Zortek: An angel who guards the First Heaven, in Hechaloth lore.

Zotiel: A Cherub (*qv*), sometimes equated with Johiel (*qv*), who guards Paradise.

Zouriel: In Jewish Gnosticism, Zouriel is an angel whose name is inscribed on magic amulets.

Zsneil: An evil angel who is, nonetheless, invoked to cure a number of ailments, noted in *The Sword of Moses* (*qv*).

Zuhair: A Mandaean angel that accompanies the sun on its daily journey through the heavens.

Zumech: An angel invoked in magic ritual, according to *The Greater Key of Solomon* (*qv*).

Zumiel: One of the 70 amulet angels (*qv*).

Zuphlas: An angel of forests and an angel of the 11th hour, according to *The Nuctemeron* (*qv*).

Zuriel: A ruler of the zodiac sign of Libra who may be invoked to cure stupidity. He is also prince regent of Principalities (*qv*) and one of the 70 amulet angels (*qv*). He is also an angel of September.